I0096422

PLANTS OF BIG BEND NATIONAL PARK

PLANTS

OF BIG BEND
NATIONAL PARK

by W. B. MCDOUGALL, OMER E. SPERRY
and STEVE W. CHADDE

➤ in the text indicates a species illustrated with a color photograph.

PLANTS OF BIG BEND NATIONAL PARK
A Guide to the Trees, Shrubs, Wildflowers, Cacti, and Ferns of the Big Bend Region of Texas

W. B. McDougall, Omer E. Sperry and Steve W. Chadde

Copyright © 2025 by Steve W. Chadde

ISBN 978-1951682903
Printed in the United States of America

A Pathfinder Field Guide
Published by Orchard Innovations, Mountain View, Arkansas
Author email: *steve@orchardinnovations.com*

VERSION 1.0 01/12/2025

CONTENTS

INTRODUCTION, 9
TYPES OF VEGETATION IN THE PARK, 10
PLANT STRUCTURES, 11
HOW TO USE THIS BOOK, 13
FAMILY CONSPECTUS, 19
PLANT FAMILIES, 45
    Acanthaceae (Acanthus Family), 45
    Amaranthaceae (Amaranth Family), 46
    Amaryllidaceae (Daffodil Family), 52
    Anacardiaceae (Cashew Family), 53
    Apiaceae (Carrot Family), 54
    Apocynaceae (Dogbane Family), 55
    Aristolochiaceae (Birthwort Family), 61
    Asparagaceae (Asparagus Family), 61
    Asteraceae (Aster Family), 65
    Berberidaceae (Barberry Family), 108
    Betulaceae (Birch Family), 109
    Bignoniaceae (Trumpet-Creeper Family), 110
    Boraginaceae (Borage Family), 111
    Brassicaceae (Mustard Family), 113
    Bromeliaceae (Pineapple Family), 120
    Cactaceae (Cactus Family), 121
    Cannabaceae (Hemp Family), 143
    Campanulaceae (Bluebell Family), 144
    Caprifoliaceae (Honeysuckle Family), 145
    Caryophyllaceae (Pink Family), 146
    Celastraceae (Bittersweet Family), 148
    Cistaceae (Rock-Rose Family), 149
    Cleomaceae (Spider-Flower Family), 150
    Commelinaceae (Spiderwort Family), 151
    Convolvulaceae (Morning-Glory Family), 152
    Crassulaceae (Stonecrop Family), 154
    Cucurbitaceae (Gourd Family), 156
    Cupressaceae (Cypress Family), 157
    Ebenaceae (Ebony Family), 159
    Ehretiaceae (Scorpion-Bush Family), 159

A Big Bend **Ocotillo** (*Fouquieria splendens*, p. 184) in leaf in early summer, towering above surrounding **Creosotebush** (*Larrea tridentata*, p. 275).

INTRODUCTION

T HIS WORK was originally published in 1951 as *Plants of Big Bend
National Park* by W. B. Mcdougall and Omer E. Sperry. This
new 2025 edition has been extensively revised and updated to
reflect current botanical nomenclature, reformatted in a new layout,
and illustrated with more than 400 color photographs (illustrated
species are noted with ❧). In all, over 600 of the more than 1,200 plant
species of the Park are described, including trees, shrubs, 'wildflowers',
cacti, and ferns. Excluded are grasses (as well as sedges and rushes),
which although an important part of the Park's flora, can be quite difficult to identify and are often of less interest to the majority of the Park's
visitors. Also excluded from this book are non-vascular plants such as
mosses and liverworts.

While keys to some large genera and species within a number of plant
families are provided, a lengthy key leading to each plant family is omit-
ted in favor of a **Family Conspectus** (page 19), which features a color
photograph of a typical family member. Within the body of the book,
plant families are presented in alphabetical order by their scientific
name, and within each family, genera and species likewise are in alphabetical order. Once family characteristics are known, plant identification becomes much easier. For further study, a number of additional
guides to the Park's flora are listed in **References**, page 294.

Big Bend National Park derives its name from its location in that portion of Texas where the Rio Grande forming the boundary between
the United States and Mexico makes a large U-shaped bend in its
course. The gross area of the Park is 801,163 acres, making it the fif-
teenth largest in the National Park system. It is a land of contrasts. Although it consists predominantly of semiarid plains characterized by
gravel-covered slopes, arroyos, and washes, this general landscape is interrupted by conspicuous mountain belts and by the winding Rio
Grande This river has carved spectacular canyons through some of the

rugged highlands. Romantic interest is added by the close proximity of the peoples of Old Mexico and by the colorful legends and stories of the country. Students of history, archaeology, geology, animals, and plants all will find much of interest here.

The original 1951 publication was a result of several years of study of the Park's flora by both authors. An effort has been made throughout the book to avoid technical language so far as possible and to make use of characters that are readily observed in the field even without the use of a lens. Botanical terms used in the book are defined in the **Glossary** (p. 291); also refer to **Plant Structures**, p 11.

TYPES OF VEGETATION IN THE PARK

The vegetation of Big Bend National Park may be grouped into five general types of plant communities:

■ Chihuahuan desert scrub—This is the most extensive type of vegetation in the Park, occupying nearly all the lower parts of the area. The most characteristic plant of the desert scrub is creosotebush, which in some areas almost completely dominates the landscape, but desert vegetation is by no means monotonous. It varies greatly from place to place, often with lechuguilla, sotol, various yucca species, ocotillo, and a variety of cacti common, and where rainfall is low (7 to 12 inches per year) and evaporation is high. Thorny shrubs, such as honey mesquite, and acacias may also be present. During rainy seasons the desert is often covered with wildflowers of varying hues.

■ Desert grassland—This type of community occupies all the lower slopes of the Chisos Mountains and the upper parts of other low mountains and high hills in the area; elevations range from about 3,500 to 5,000 feet. Deeper soils and rainfall of 10 to 18 inches per year support grasses such as blue grama (*Bouteloua gracilis*), chinograss (*Bouteloua ramosa*), tobosa grass (*Pleuraphis mutica*), threeawns (*Aristida*), needlegrass (former *Stipa* species), and bluestems (*Andropogon, Bothriochloa,* and *Schizachyrium*). Sotol is common, but many other shrubs and herbs are also present.

■ Pinyon-juniper-oak woodland— Woodlands begin to intersperse with the upper grasslands above 3000 feet, depending on the slope and rainfall. Woodlands occupy all the middle and upper slopes of the Chisos Mountains except a few of the higher places that are covered by forest. Along with the pinyon pine there are three species of juniper, several species of oak, and many species of shrubs and herbaceous plants. Attractive trees, such as the Texas madrone (*Arbutus xalapensis*) and bigtooth maple (*Acer grandidentatum*) are present in moist canyons. Pinyon pines, junipers, and various oaks, such as Emory's oak (*Quercus emoryi*) dot the hillsides. The densest woodlands are found in valleys and on north- and east-facing slopes.

■ **Ponderosa pine-Douglas fir-Arizona cypress forest**—The forest community is rather limited in extent but occurs on some of the higher parts of the Chisos Mountains, especially where it is somewhat protected in the heads of canyons.

■ **Riparian communities**—A small area of the Park supports riparian communities found along the Rio Grande, smaller streams and near springs. Trees and shrubs such as honey mesquite, desert willow (*Chilopsis*), cottonwood, false willow (*Baccharis*), and little walnut (*Juglans microcarpa*) are present. Along the Rio Grande and other waterways, plants introduced from the Old World, including tamarisk (*Tamarix*), giant reed (*Arundo donax*), and common reed (*Phragmites australis*) compete with native plants.

PLANT STRUCTURES

Although we have attempted to make this book as nontechnical as possible, it is helpful to know something of the language that the botanist uses in describing plants. The **Glossary** (page 291) will be useful in becoming acquainted with many of the terms, but some of the more frequently used terms are detailed below (figures below refer to Figures 1–5, pages 14–18).

■ **Leaves**—A typical, complete leaf (fig. 2) consists of three parts: the more or less expanded portion, which is called the **blade**; the stemlike portion, called the **petiole**; and two little appendages at the base of the petiole, called **stipules**. Very often the stipules are lacking, and frequently the petiole is also lacking. When the petiole is lacking and the blade is thus attached directly to the stem, the leaf is said to be **sessile**. When the blade is all in one piece and undivided the leaf is a **simple leaf**, but if it is divided so that the leaf appears to have several blades instead of only one it is **compound**. These several parts of a compound leaf are called **leaflets**. Leaflets or the blades of simple leaves may be variously lobed or toothed, or their margins may be completely without teeth or lobes, in which case they are said to be **entire**. Some compound leaves, such as those of the rose or the elder, have a central axis like a feather, and the leaflets are attached along two sides of this axis. Such a leaf is said to be **pinnate** or **pinnately compound** (fig. 2). Others, such as the lupine, have the leaflets all attached to the end of the petiole, and such a leaf is said to be **palmate** or **palmately compound** (fig. 2). These same terms, pinnate and palmate, are sometimes used to describe the arrangement of the veins of a leaf.

There are several terms used to describe the general shape of a leaf (fig. 3). One of them is **lanceolate**, or lance-shaped, which refers to a leaf that is rather long, widest near the base, and gradually tapering to a rather long tip, like a spearhead. Another much-used term is **linear**, which refers to a leaf that is uniformly narrow and with parallel edges like a grass leaf. Only a little less frequently used are the terms ovate, oval, and elliptical. **Ovate** is like a longitudinal section through an egg with the larger end downward, while **oval** and **elliptical** have exactly the same meaning that they have in geometry or in common language. Frequently the prefix **ob-** is used with lanceolate and ovate and means inversely. Thus oblanceolate means lance-shaped, but with the narrower part toward the base, and obovate means inversely ovate.

■ Flowers—A complete flower consists of four sets of parts (fig. 4). Beginning at the outside, the first set consists of leaflike parts, which are usually green and are called **sepals**. The sepals may be entirely separate or more or less grown together, and all the sepals collectively, whether united or not, make up the **calyx**. The parts of the second set of organs are also more or less leaflike but usually are some other color than green and are called **petals**. These, like the sepals, may or may not be united, and they collectively make up the **corolla**. The parts of the third set are called **stamens**. in most cases they are not at all leaflike. Each one consists, as a general rule, of a stalklike portion called the **filament** and a headlike portion called the **anther**. Within the anther are found the numerous minute pollen grains that contain the male elements of the plant. The number of stamens, varying from one to many in the different kinds of plants, is very important in the identification of plants. Finally, the fourth set of parts consists of one or more **pistils**, each pistil consisting ordinarily, of three parts: a more or less slender portion called the **style**; an enlarged basal portion called the **ovary**, within which are the ovules that contain the female elements, and that later may develop into seeds; and a somewhat enlarged upper end to which pollen grains readily adhere and which is called the **stigma**.

Any one or more of these sets of parts may be missing, in which case the flower is said to be **incomplete**. More important, however, than the terms complete and incomplete are the terms **perfect** and **imperfect**. Any flower that has both stamens and pistils is perfect regardless of whether it has a calyx or a corolla or not, while if either stamens or pistils are lacking the flower is imperfect. This is due to the fact that the stamens and pistils are the organs that are directly concerned in reproduction.

Regular and **irregular** are also important terms (fig. 5). These refer especially to the corolla. If the petals or parts of the corolla are all the same size and shape the flower is said to be regular, whereas if they differ in either size or shape, or both, the flower is irregular.

The stem of a flower is called a **pedicel**, and a stem bearing a cluster of flowers is called a **peduncle**. The end of the pedicel to which the parts of the flower are attached is called the **receptacle**. Figure 5 illustrates the various arrangements of flowers on the stem.

HOW TO USE THIS BOOK

To identify an unknown plant, some knowledge of plant structure and names of parts is helpful. Especially helpful is the ability to observe a plant and place it into its family. This quickly narrows down the list of possible choices as to its proper identity. To this end, a **Family Conspectus**, beginning on page 19, provides an illustration of a typical member of each family found in the Park. Once a family is determined, turn to the pages featuring members of that family. Families and genera within families are presented in alphabetical order of their scientific name (e.g., Asteraceae for the Aster Family), with the Park's fern families starting on page 278. For large families such as the Asteraceae, a key is given to identify genera, and similarly, for large genera, a key is provided for the species. Remember that this book does not include every plant found in the Park, but a large percentage of those most often seen by the visitor are described in this book (apart from the grasses and other grass-like families—these are worthy of their own book!). Finally, remember that all plant life in our national parks is protected by law; please do not pick or dig up plants.

PLANT WITH AXILLARY
FLOWERS, LEAFY STEM
AND FIBROUS ROOTS

PLANT WITH FLOWERS
IN A RACEME, LEAVES
BASAL AND TAP ROOT

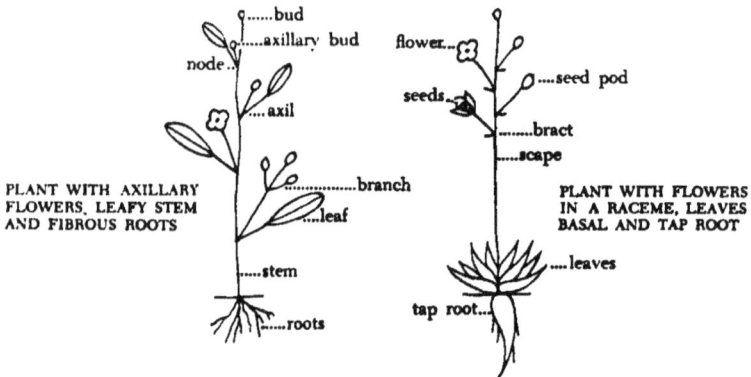

PLANTS AND THEIR PARTS

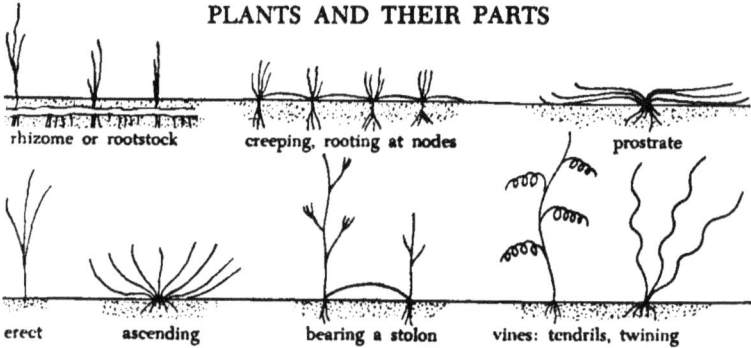

rhizome or rootstock   creeping, rooting at nodes   prostrate

erect   ascending   bearing a stolon   vines: tendrils, twining

GROWTH PATTERNS OF STEMS

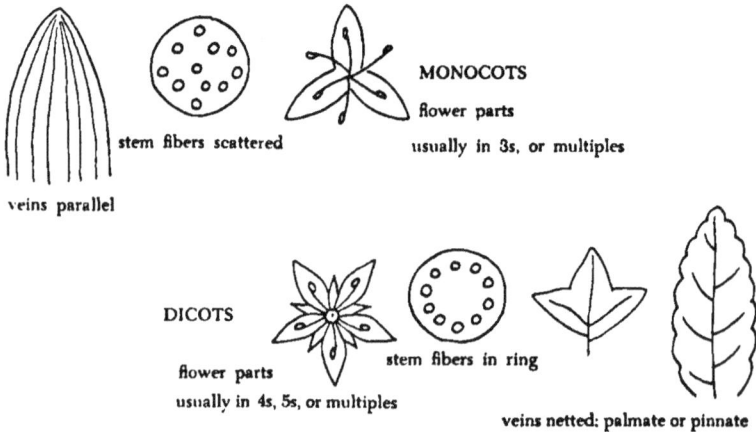

stem fibers scattered

MONOCOTS
flower parts
usually in 3s, or multiples

veins parallel

DICOTS
flower parts
usually in 4s, 5s, or multiples

stem fibers in ring

veins netted: palmate or pinnate

MONOCOT AND DICOT CONTRASTS

Figure 1—Plant characteristics.

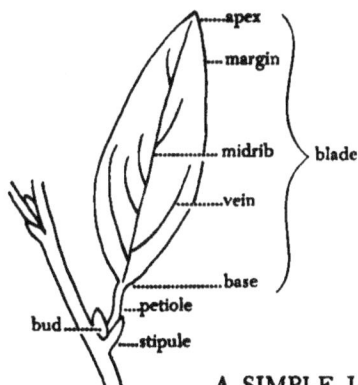

····apex

···margin

···midrib   } blade

·······vein

·······base
····petiole
bud·····
····stipule

A SIMPLE LEAF

pinnate   twice-pinnate   palmate   trifoliolate   twice-palmate

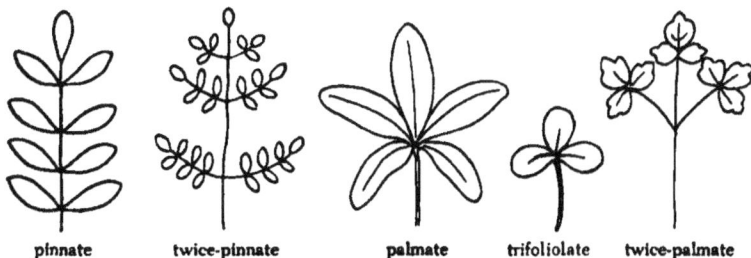

COMPOUND LEAVES

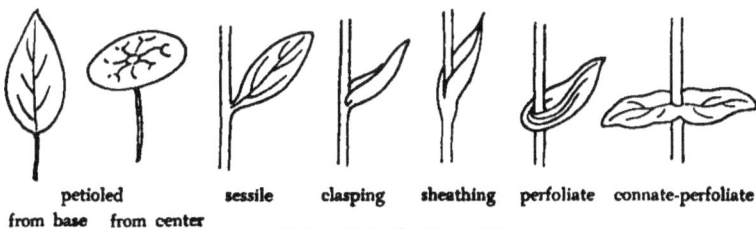

petioled   sessile   clasping   sheathing   perfoliate   connate-perfoliate
from base   from center

LEAF ATTACHMENTS

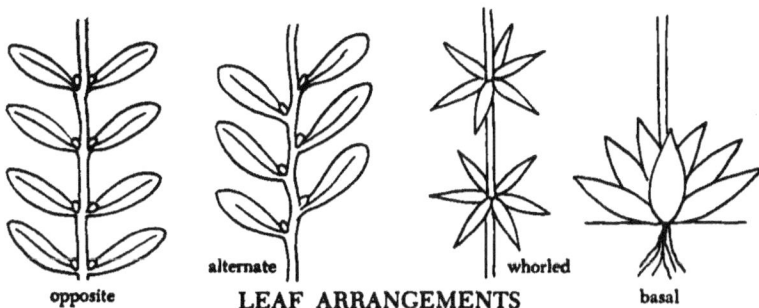

opposite   alternate   whorled   basal

LEAF ARRANGEMENTS

Figure 2—Leaf characteristics.

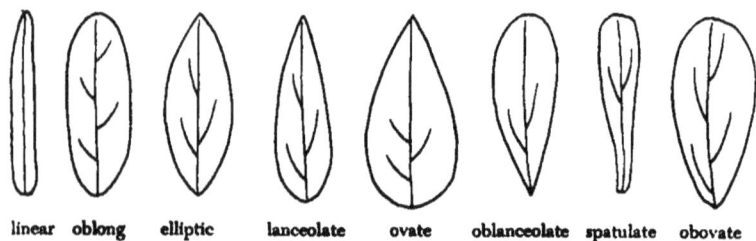

linear   oblong   elliptic   lanceolate   ovate   oblanceolate   spatulate   obovate

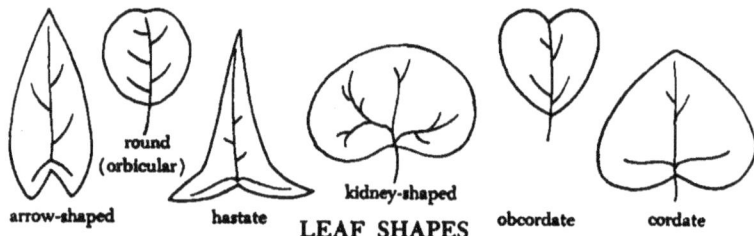

round
(orbicular)

kidney-shaped

arrow-shaped   hastate   **LEAF SHAPES**   obcordate   cordate

pointed   obtuse   rounded   truncate   obcordate   mucronate

LEAF APICES

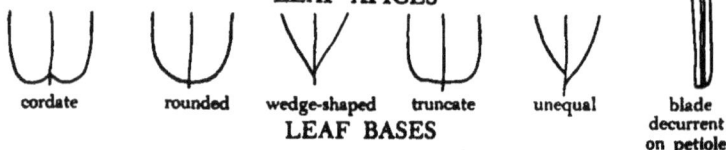

cordate   rounded   wedge-shaped   truncate   unequal   blade
decurrent
on petiole

LEAF BASES

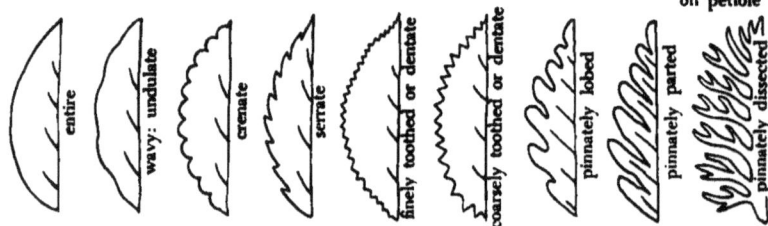

entire   wavy: undulate   crenate   serrate   finely toothed or dentate   coarsely toothed or dentate   pinnately lobed   pinnately parted   pinnately dissected

LEAF MARGINS

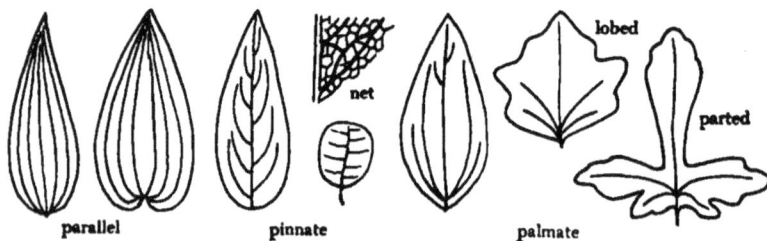

net

lobed

parted

parallel   pinnate   palmate

LEAF VENATION

Figure 3—Leaf characteristics (continued).

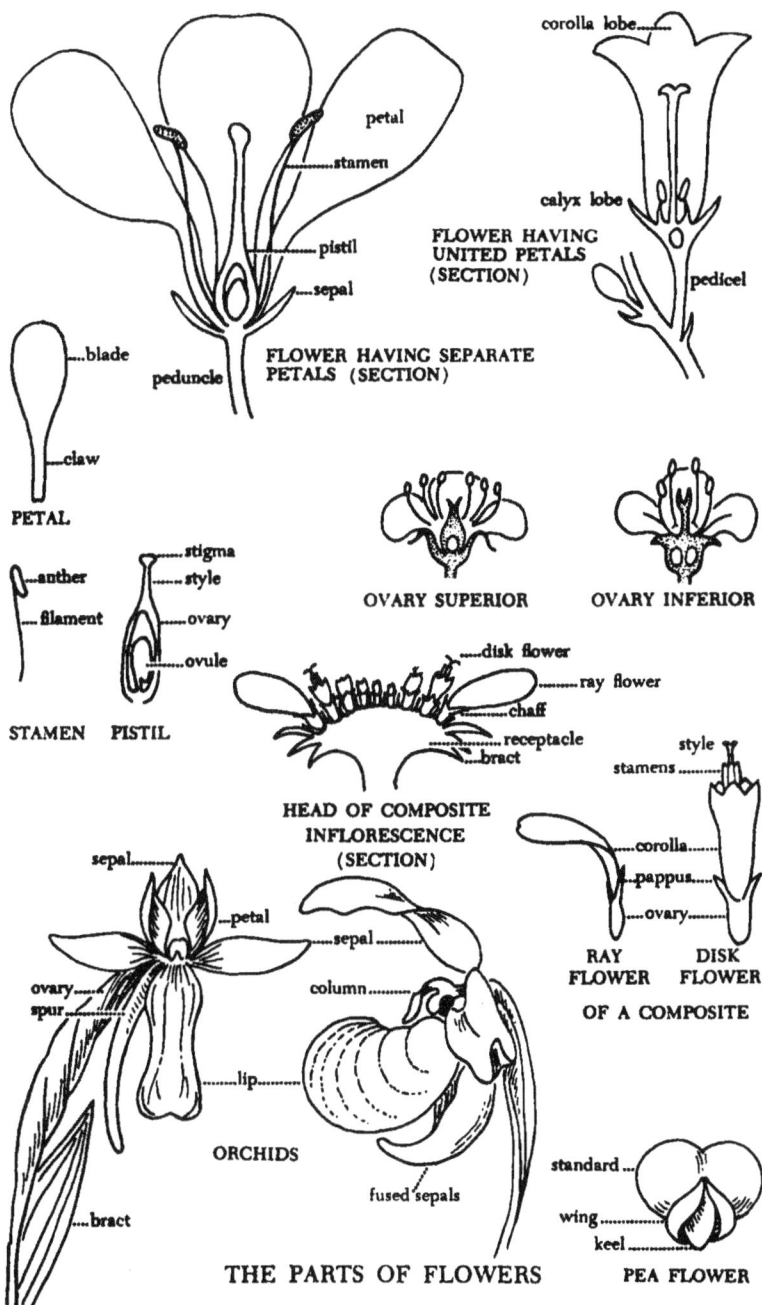

Figure 4—Flower characteristics.

corolla regular,
petals separate

corolla irregular,
petals separate   petals united

corolla irregular,
2-lipped   –with spur

COROLLA TYPES

tubular   bell-shaped   urn-shaped   funnel-shaped   salverform   rotate
        (campanulate)   **COROLLA TYPES,** all regular, petals united

solitary   solitary on   solitary in   raceme   panicle   spike   spathe and   heads
on scape   leafy stem   leaf axil   spadix

cyme   compound cyme   corymb   umbel   compound umbel

INFLORESCENCE TYPES

berry   drupe   achenes   capsule   follicle   legume or pod   nutlets

FRUIT TYPES

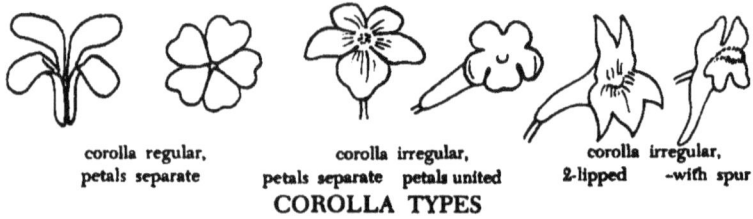

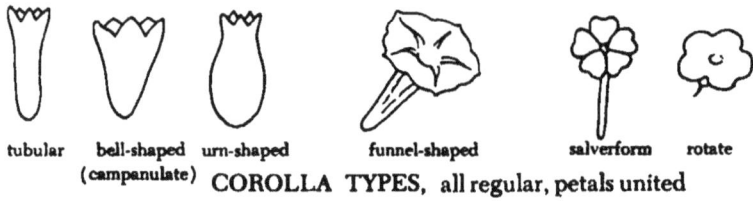

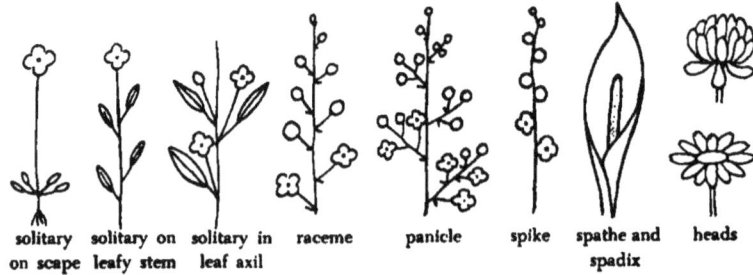

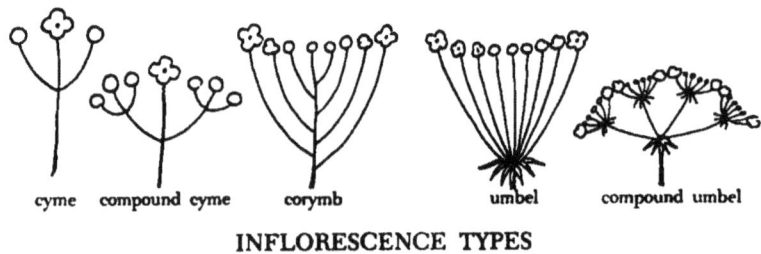

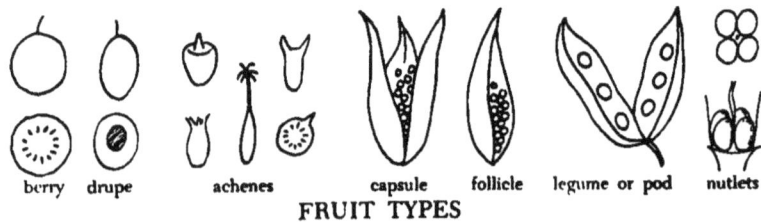

Figure 5—Flower and fruit characteristics.

Acanthus Family
(**ACANTHACEAE**, p. 45)

Amaranth Family
(**AMARANTHACEAE**, p. 46)

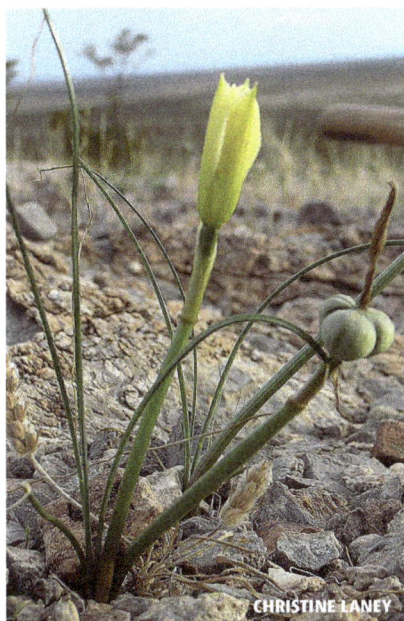

Daffodil Family
(**AMARYLLIDACEAE**, p. 52)

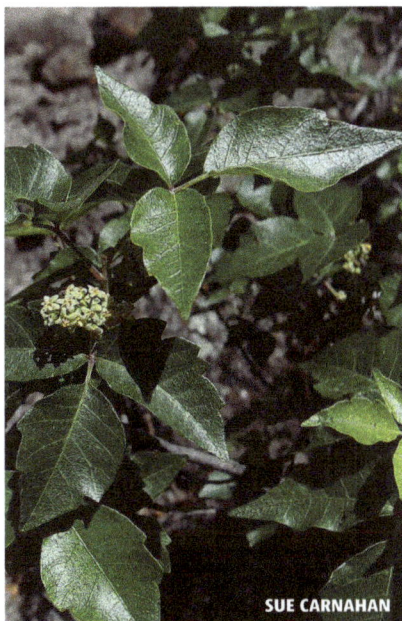

Cashew Family
(**ANACARDIACEAE**, p. 53)

Carrot Family
(**APIACEAE**, p. 54)

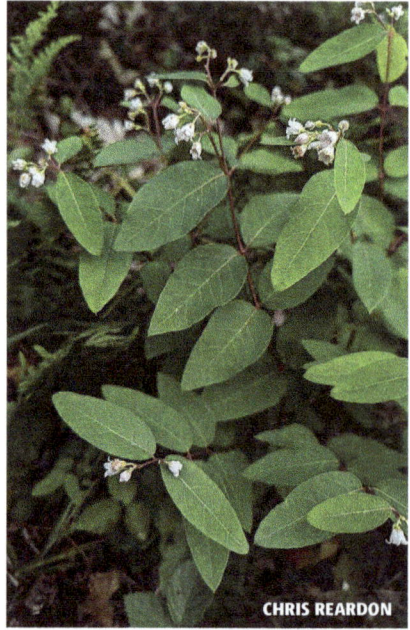

Dogbane Family
(**APOCYNACEAE**, p. 55)

Birthwort Family
(**ARISTOLOCHIACEAE**, p. 61)

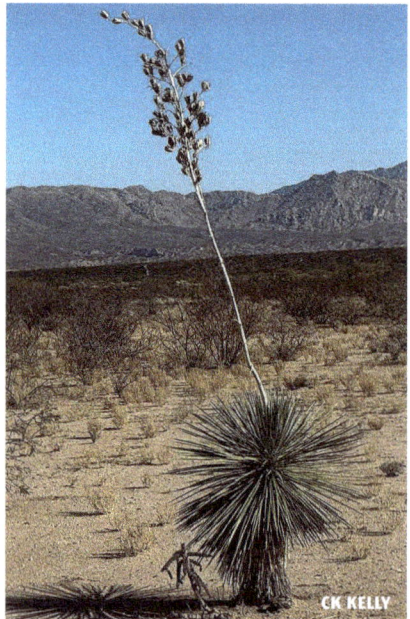

Asparagus Family
(**ASPARAGACEAE**, p. 61)

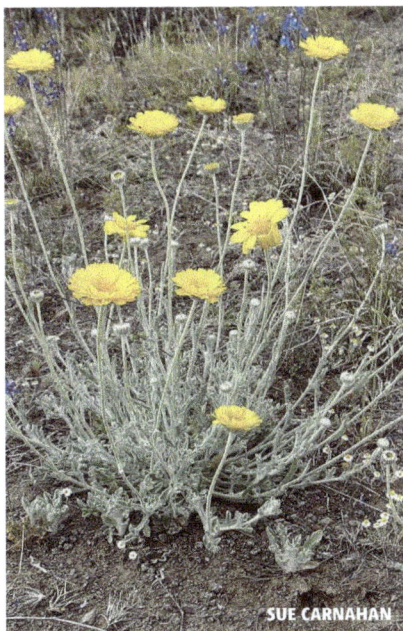
SUE CARNAHAN

Aster Family
(**ASTERACEAE**, p. 65)

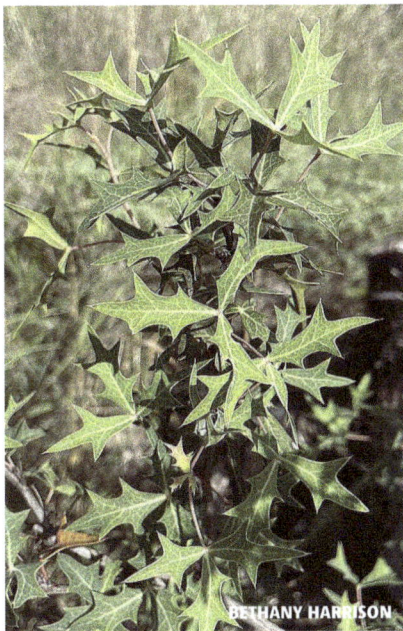
BETHANY HARRISON

Barberry Family
(**BERBERIDACEAE**, p. 108)

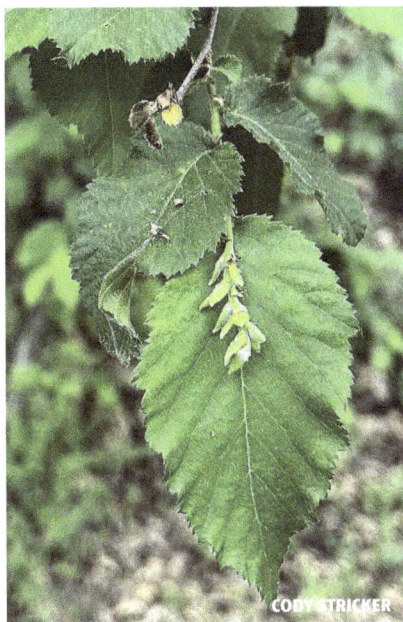
CODY STRICKER

Birch Family
(**BETULACEAE**, p. 109)

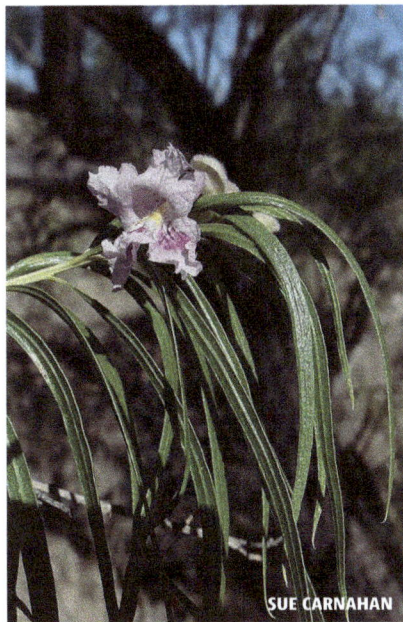
SUE CARNAHAN

Trumpet-Creeper Family
(**BIGNONIACEAE**, p. 110)

WENDY MCCRADY

Borage Family
(**BORAGINACEAE**, p. 111)

SUE CARNAHAN

Mustard Family
(**BRASSICACEAE**, p. 113)

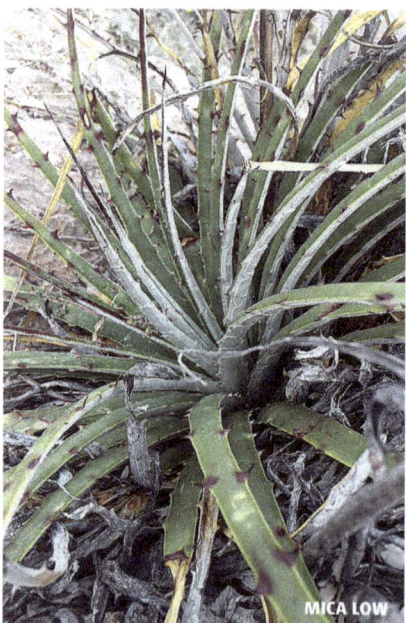

MICA LOW

Pineapple Family
(**BROMELIACEAE**, p. 120)

ULISES PINEDO

Cactus Family
(**CACTACEAE**, p. 121)

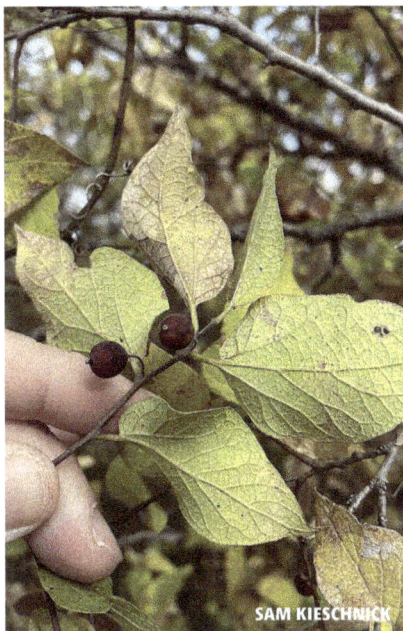
SAM KIESCHNICK

Hemp Family
(**CANNABACEAE**, p. 143)

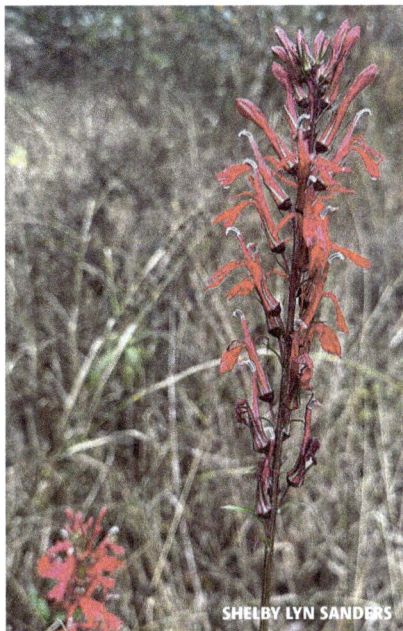
SHELBY LYN SANDERS

Bluebell Family
(**CAMPANULACEAE**, p. 144)

INDIO BROWN

Honeysuckle Family
(**CAPRIFOLIACEAE**, p. 145

CK KELLY

Pink Family
(**CARYOPHYLLACEAE**, p. 146)

SAM KIRSCHNICK

Bittersweet Family
(**CELASTRACEAE**, p. 148)

GUILLERMO HUERTA RAMOS

Rock-Rose Family
(**CISTACEAE**, p. 149)

ALEXIS LÓPEZ HERNÁNDEZ

Spider-Flower Family
(**CLEOMACEAE**, p. 150)

MATT BERGER

Spiderwort Family
(**COMMELINACEAE**, p. 151)

Morning-Glory Family
(**CONVOLVULACEAE**, p. 152)

Stonecrop Family
(**CRASSULACEAE**, p. 154)

Gourd Family
(**CUCURBITACEAE**, p. 156)

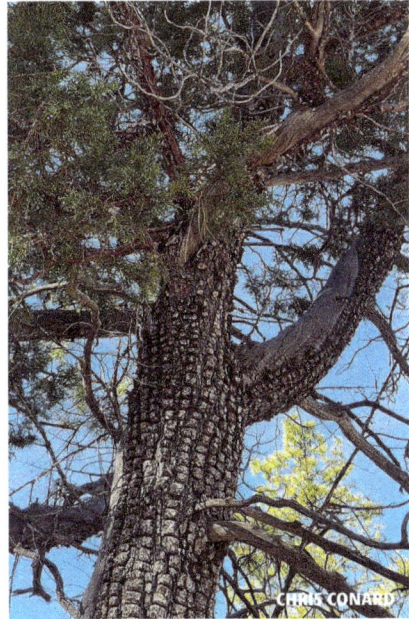

Cypress Family
(**CUPRESSACEAE**, p. 157)

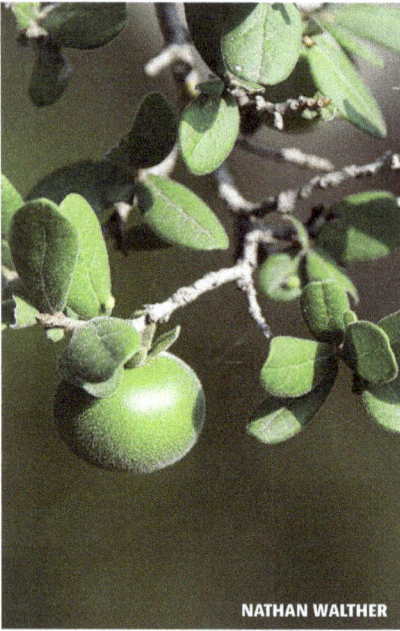
NATHAN WALTHER

Ebony Family
(**EBENACEAE**, p. 159)

ERIC KNIGHT

Scorpion-Bush Family
(**EHRETIACEAE**, p. 159)

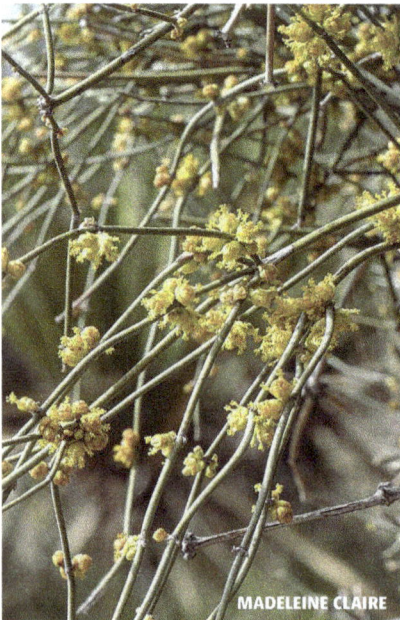
MADELEINE CLAIRE

Mormon-Tea Family
(**EPHEDRACEAE**, p. 160)

NEPTALÍ MARCIAL

Heath Family
(**ERICACEAE**, p. 161)

MICHELLE W.

Spurge Family
(**EUPHORBIACEAE**, p. 162)

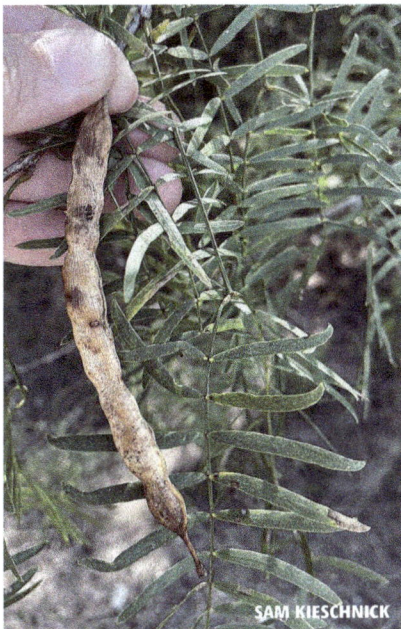

SAM KIESCHNICK

Pea Family
(**FABACEAE**, p. 170)

ERIC KNIGHT

Oak Family
(**FAGACEAE**, p. 182)

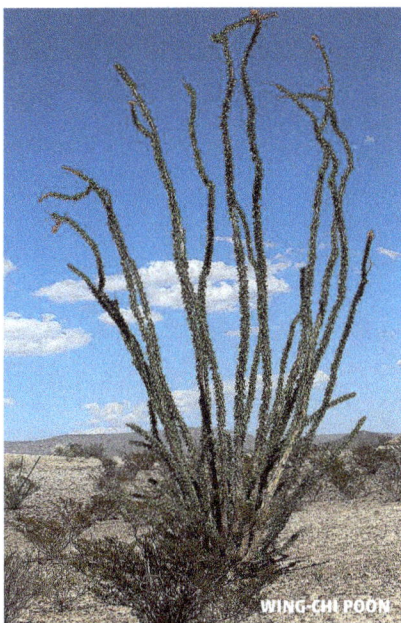

WING-CHI POON

Ocotillo Family
(**FOUQUIERIACEAE**, p. 184)

PATRICK ALEXANDER

Silktassel Family
(**GARRYACEAE**, p. 185)

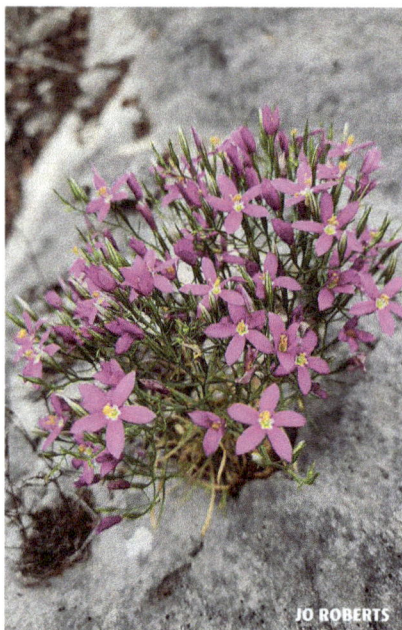

JO ROBERTS

Gentian Family
(**GENTIANACEAE**, p. 185)

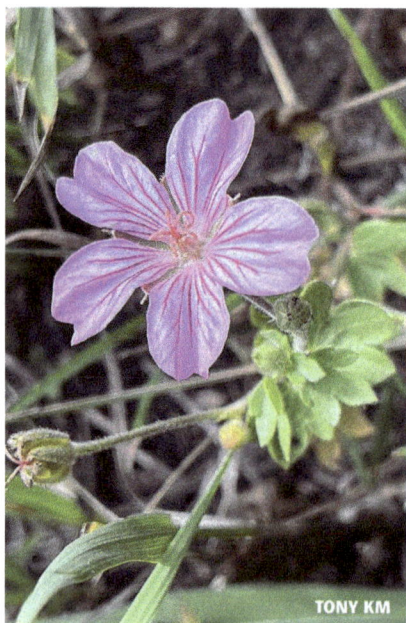

TONY KM

Geranium Family
(**GERANIACEAE**, p. 186)

SAM KIESCHNICK

Heliotrope Family
(**HELIOTROPIACEAE**, p. 188)

MARIN PURDY

Hydrangea Family
(**HYDRANGEACEAE**, p. 190)

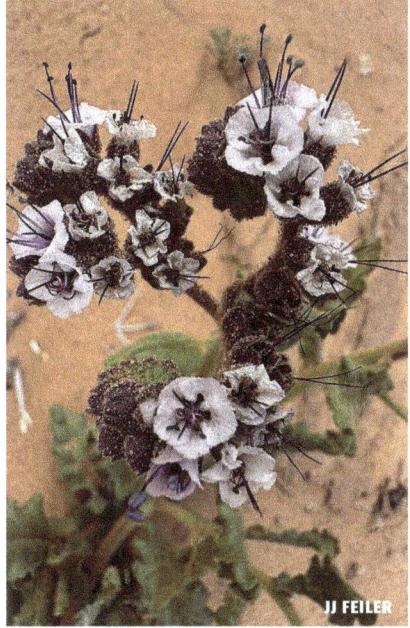

JJ FEILER

Waterleaf Family
(**HYDROPHYLLACEAE**, p. 191)

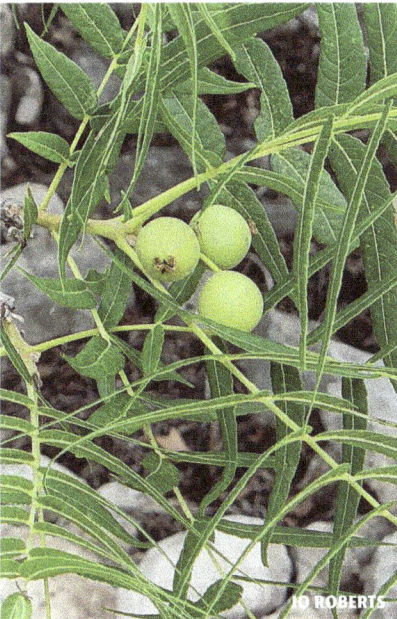

JO ROBERTS

Walnut Family
(**JUGLANDACEAE**, p. 192)

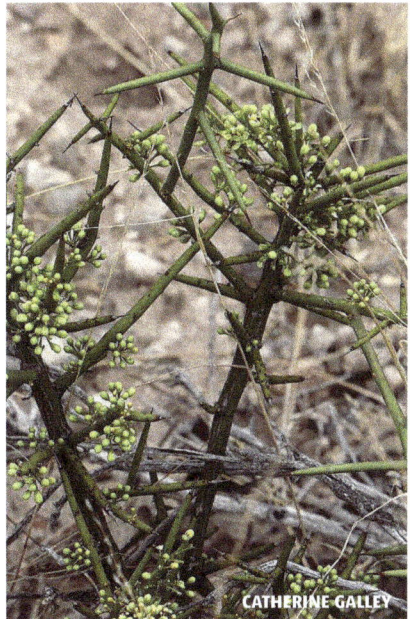

CATHERINE GALLEY

Crown-Of-Thorns Family
(**KOEBERLINIACEAE**, p. 193)

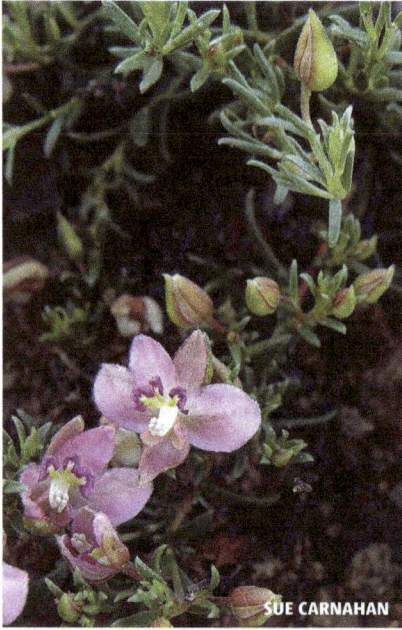

SUE CARNAHAN

Ratany Family
(**KRAMERIACEAE**, p. 193)

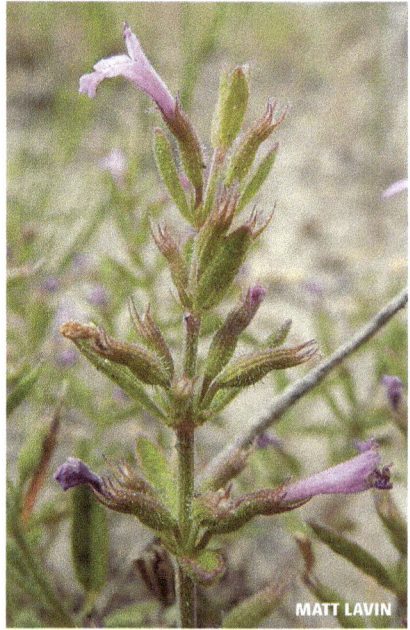

MATT LAVIN

Mint Family
(**LAMIACEAE**, p. 194)

CRICKET RASPET

Flax Family
(**LINACEAE**, p. 200)

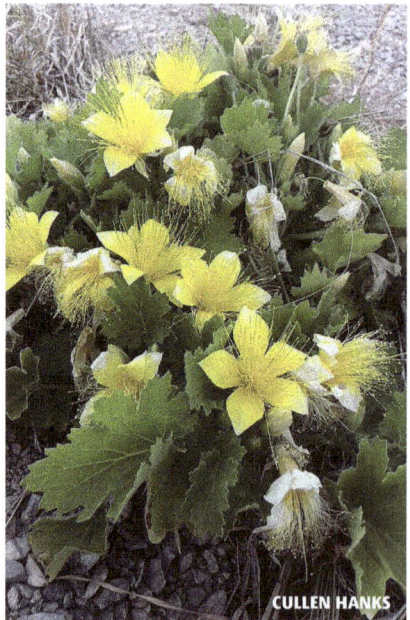

CULLEN HANKS

Blazingstar Family
(**LOASACEAE**, p. 201)

SUE CARNAHAN

Loosestrife Family
(**LYTHRACEAE**, p. 203)

RACHEL STRINGHAM

Barbados-Cherry Family
(**MALPIGHIACEAE**, p. 204)

KATIE RANEY

Mallow Family
(**MALVACEAE**, p. 204)

DOMINIC GENTILCORE

Unicorn-Plant Family
(**MARTYNIACEAE**, p. 209)

SAM KIESCHNICK

Moonseed Family
(**MENISPERMACEAE**, p. 209)

BOBBY MCCABE

Carpetweed Family
(**MOLLUGINACEAE**, p. 210)

CODY STRICKER

Mulberry Family
(**MORACEAE**, p. 211)

HARRIER

Fiddleleaf Family
(**NAMACEAE**, p. 212)

MICHELLE W.

Four-O'clock Family
(**NYCTAGINACEAE**, p. 213)

NORTHCUT

Olive Family
(**OLEACEAE**, p. 219)

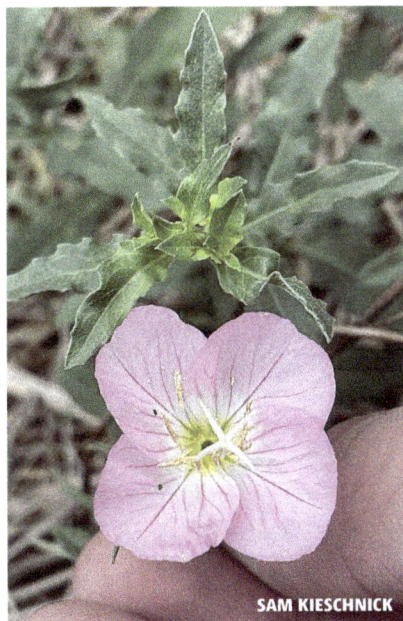

SAM KIESCHNICK

Evening-Primrose Family
(**ONAGRACEAE**, p. 221)

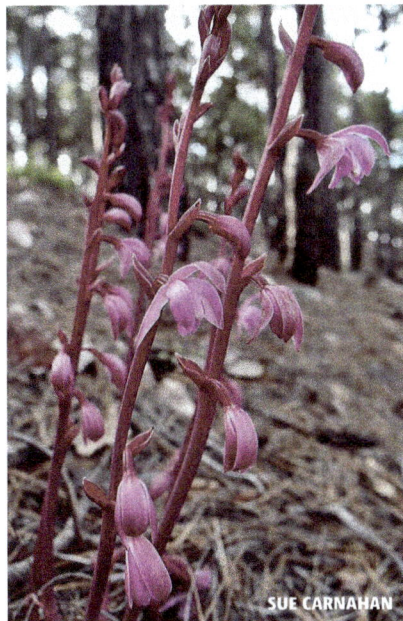

SUE CARNAHAN

Orchid Family
(**ORCHIDACEAE**, p. 224)

Broomrape Family
(**OROBANCHACEAE**, p. 226)

Wood-Sorrel Family
(**OXALIDACEAE**, p. 228)

Poppy Family
(**PAPAVERACEAE**, p. 228)

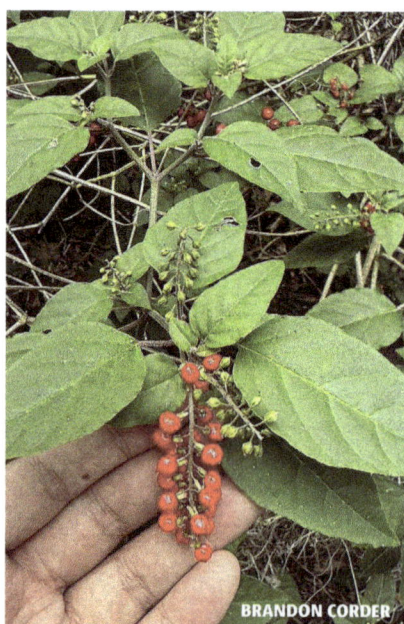

Petiveria Family
(**PETIVERIACEAE**, p. 229)

ALISON NORTHUP

Lopseed Family
(**PHRYMACEAE**, p. 230)

ALEX KARASOULOS

Leaf-Flower Family
(**PHYLLANTHACEAE**, p. 231)

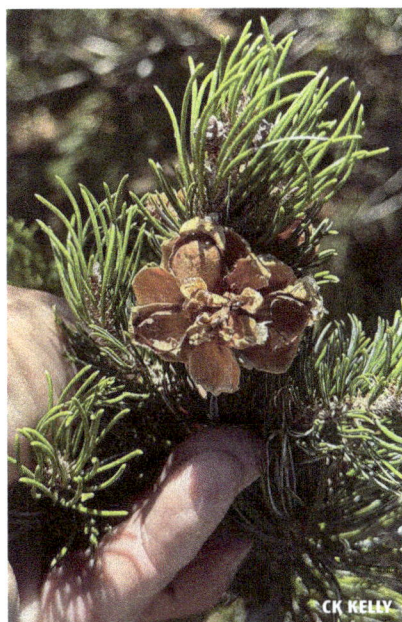

CK KELLY

Pine Family
(**PINACEAE**, p. 231)

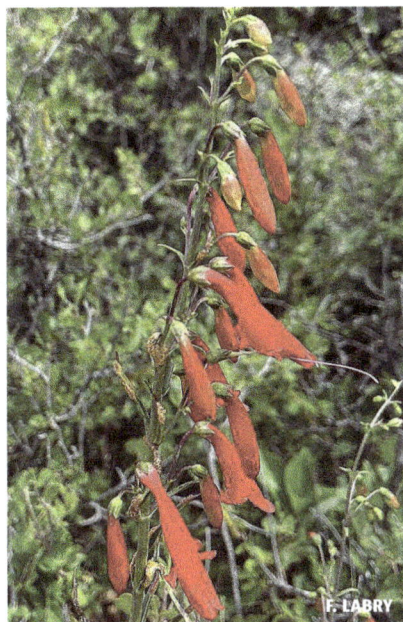

F. LABRY

Plantain Family
(**PLANTAGINACEAE**, p. 233)

SALTYHIKER

Phlox Family
(**POLEMONIACEAE**, p. 235)

ANNIKA LINDQVIST

Milkwort Family
(**POLYGALACEAE**, p. 237)

THOMAS HERMAN

Buckwheat Family
(**POLYGONACEAE**, p. 239)

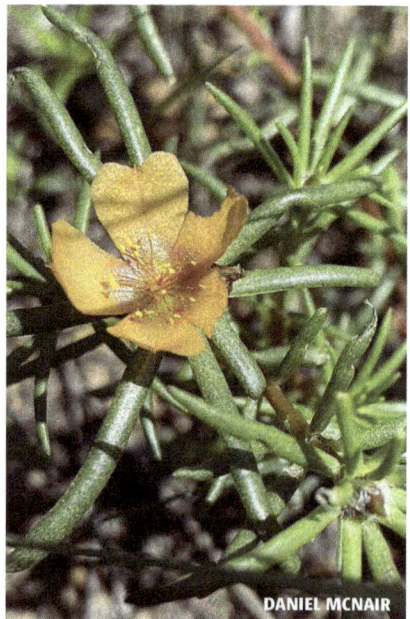

DANIEL MCNAIR

Purslane Family
(**PORTULACACEAE**, p. 242)

ABRAHAM SÁNCHEZ ROMERO

Primrose Family
(**PRIMULACEAE**, p. 243)

BOB NIEMAN

Buttercup Family
(**RANUNCULACEAE**, p. 244)

JASON SCHOEN

Mignonette Family
(**RESEDACEAE**, p. 246)

JO ROBERTS

Buckthorn Family
(**RHAMNACEAE**, p. 246)

GARTH HARWOOD

Rose Family
(**ROSACEAE**, p. 249)

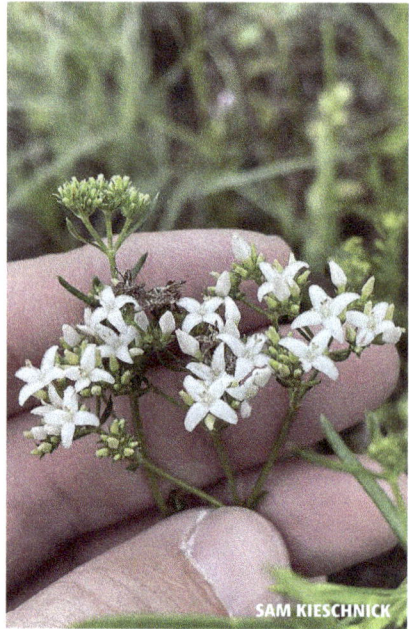

SAM KIESCHNICK

Madder Family
(**RUBIACEAE**, p. 253)

MATT BERGER

Rue Family
(**RUTACEAE**, p. 256)

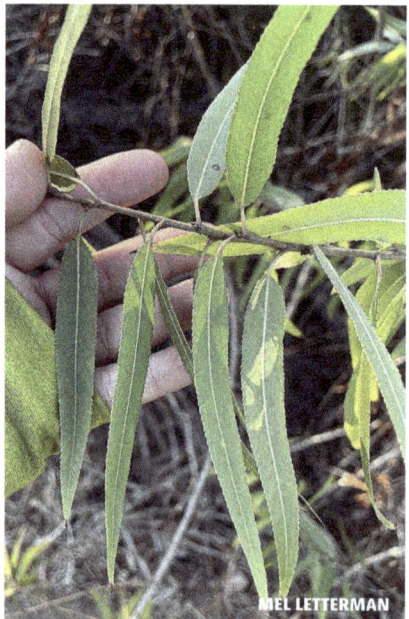

MEL LETTERMAN

Willow Family
(**SALICACEAE**, p. 257)

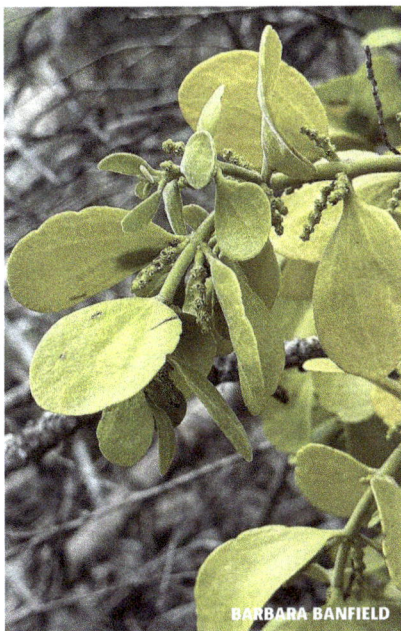

BARBARA BANFIELD

Sandalwood Family
(**SANTALACEAE**, p. 259)

SUE CARNAHAN

Soapberry Family
(**SAPINDACEAE**, p. 260)

MATT BERGER

Saxifrage Family
(**SAXIFRAGACEAE**, p. 262)

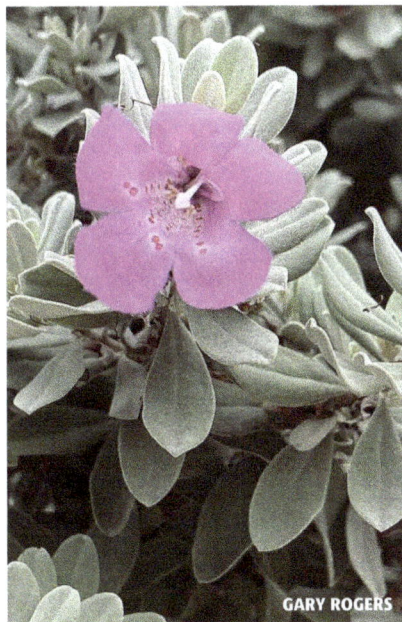

GARY ROGERS

Figwort Family
(**SCROPHULARIACEAE**, p. 262)

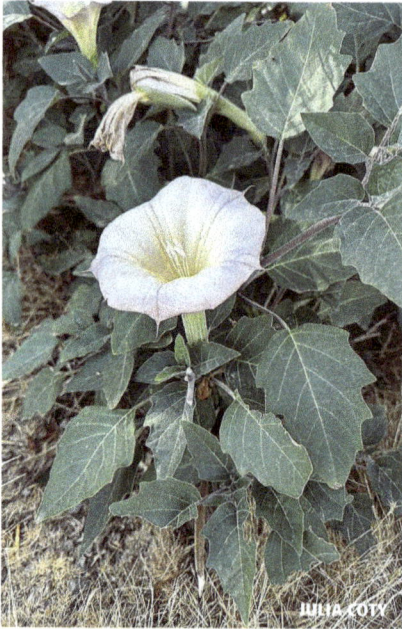

JULIA COTY

Nightshade Family
(**SOLANACEAE**, p. 264)

SUE CARNAHAN

Fameflower Family
(**TALINACEAE**, p. 268)

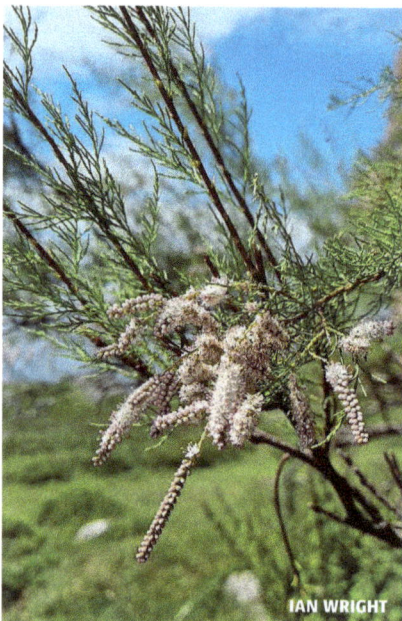

IAN WRIGHT

Tamarisk Family
(**TAMARICACEAE**, p. 269)

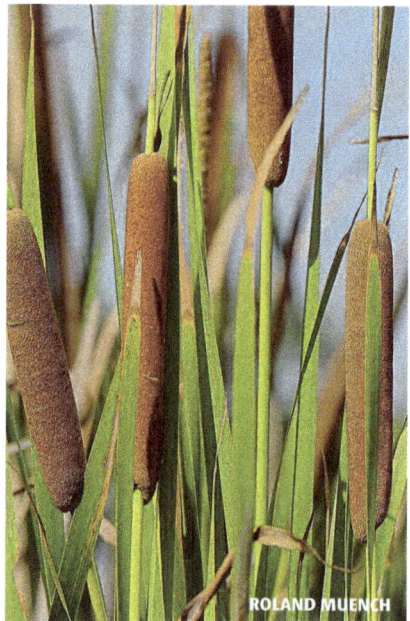

ROLAND MUENCH

Cat-Tail Family
(**TYPHACEAE**, p. 270)

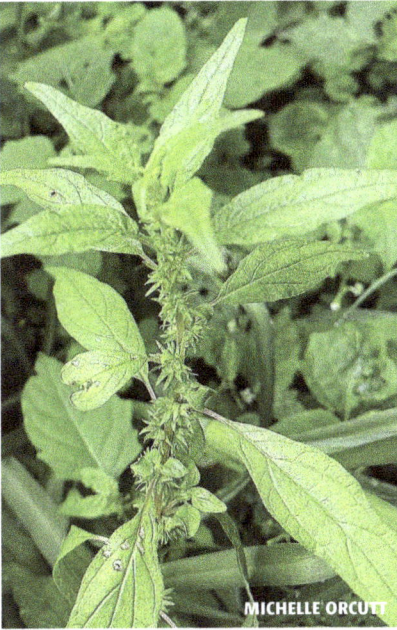
MICHELLE ORCUTT

Nettle Family
(**URTICACEAE**, p. 270)

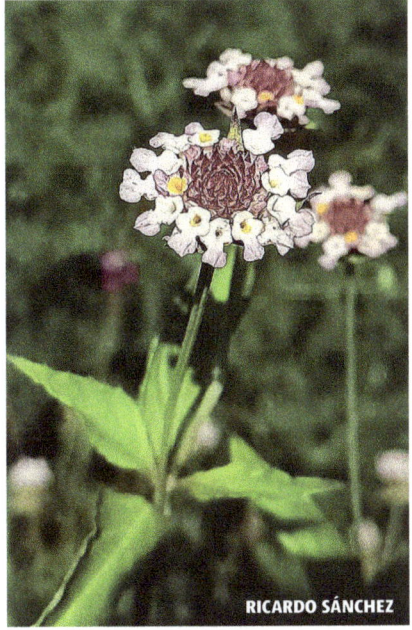
RICARDO SÁNCHEZ

Verbena Family
(**VERBENACEAE**, p. 271)

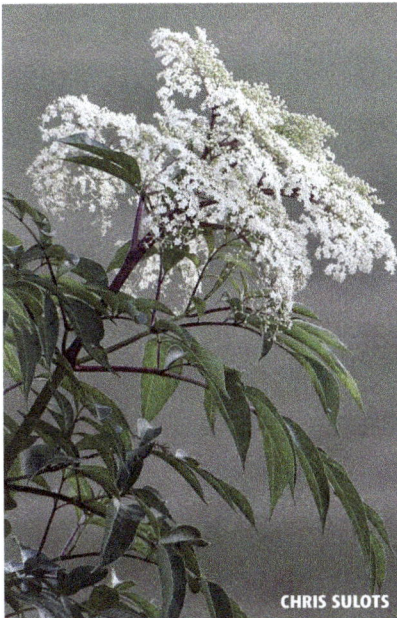
CHRIS SULOTS

Arrow-Wood Family
(**VIBURNACEAE**, p. 274)

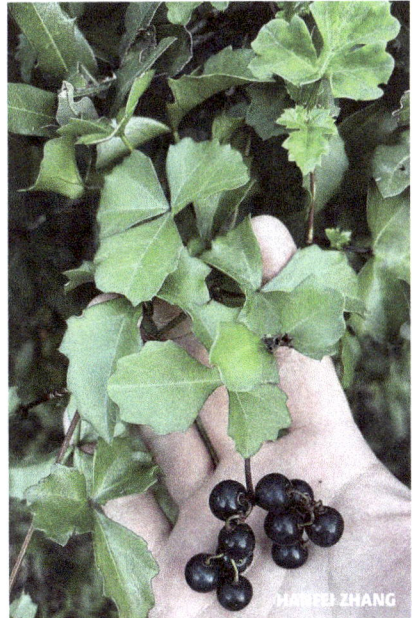
MANEEJ ZHANG

Grape Family
(**VITACEAE**, p. 275)

Creosotebush Family
(**ZYGOPHYLLACEAE**, p. 275)

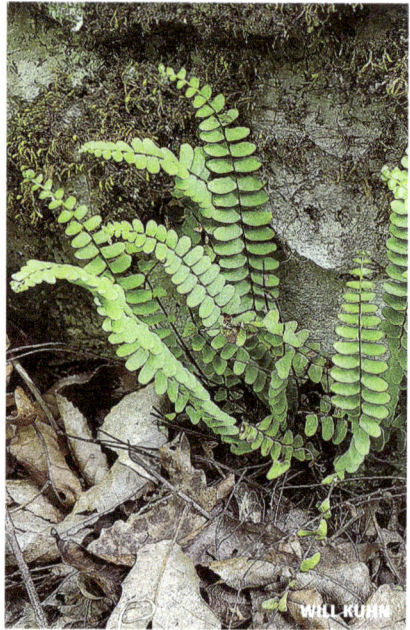

Spleenwort Family
(**ASPLENIACEAE**, p. 279

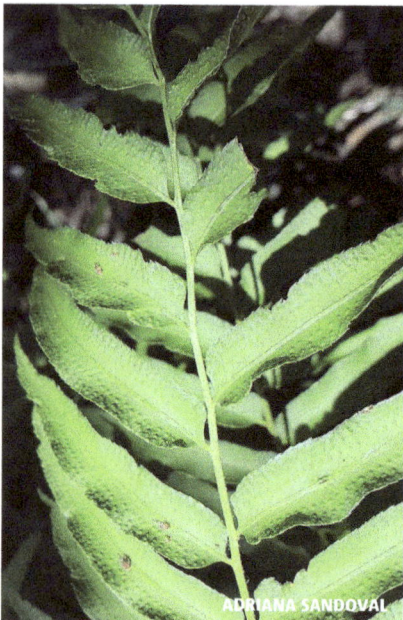

Wood Fern Family
(**DRYOPTERIDACEAE**, p. 280)

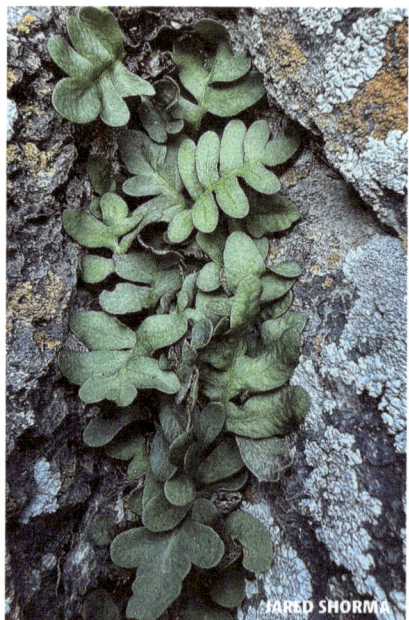

Polypody Fern Family
(**POLYPODIACEAE**, p. 280)

Maidenhair Fern Family
(**PTERIDACEAE**, p. 281)

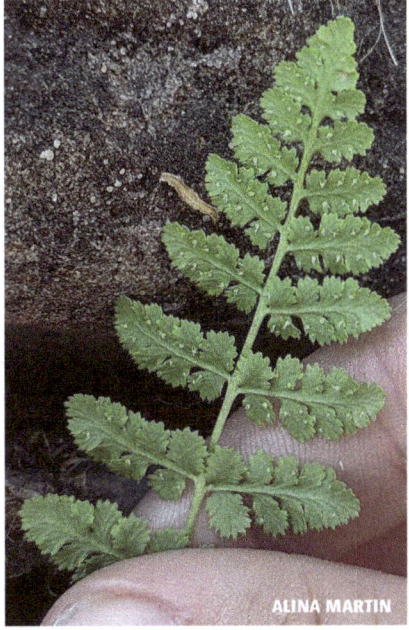

Cliff Fern Family
(**WOODSIACEAE**, p. 286)

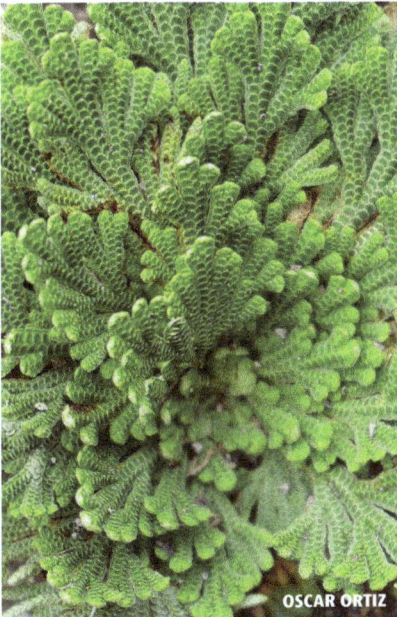

Spike-Moss Family
(**SELAGINELLACEAE**, p. 287)

SAM LUFTY

NARROWLEAF DESERT HONEYSUCKLE
(*Aniscanthus linearis*)

ACANTHUS FAMILY (ACANTHACEAE)

Herbs and shrubs with opposite, simple leaves and flowers with two or four stamens attached to the tube of the corolla, and a tubular, 5-lobed calyx. The fruit is a 2-celled pod with two or more seeds.

1 Stamens 4. 2
  Stamens 2. 4
2 Pods 6- to 20-seeded . . . . PARRY'S WILD PETUNIA
  . . . . (*Ruellia parryi*, p. 46)
  Pods 2- to 4-seeded. 3
3 Plants very hairy with long, white hairs . . . . EARLY SHAGGYTUFT
  . . . . (*Stenandrium barbatum*, p. 46)
  Plants smooth or with short hairs . . . . POLKADOTS
  . . . . (*Dyschoriste linearis*, p. 45)
4 Corolla 2-lipped, with long, narrow tube and short lobes . . . .
  . . . . HAIRY TUBETONGUE (*Justicia pilosella*, p. 46)
  Corolla not obviously 2-lipped 5
5 Corolla purple, the tube shorter than the lobes . . . WRIGHTWORT
  . . . . (*Carlowrightia*, p. 45)
  Corolla red, the tube longer than the lobes . . . .
  . . . . NARROWLEAF DESERT-HONEYSUCKLE
  . . . . (*Anisacanthus linearis*, p. 45)

❧ Narrowleaf Desert-Honeysuckle (*Anisacanthus linearis*)—A shrubby, nearly smooth plant with opposite, linear leaves and rose-red or salmon-colored corollas about 2 inches long. Frequent along watercourses near the foothills of the Chisos Mountains. Also present is Dwarf Desert-Honeysuckle (*Anisacanthus puberulus*).

■ Wrightwort (*Carlowrightia*)—Low shrubs with slender branches and rather small flowers. Heath Wrightwort (*Carlowrightia linearifolia*) has linear leaves ½ to 3 inches long. Three additional species occur in the Park: Arizona Wrightwort (*Carlowrightia arizonica*), Little-Leaf Wrightwort (*Carlowrightia parviflora*), and Trans-Pecos Wrightwort (*Carlowrightia serpyllifolia*).

❧ Polkadots (*Dyschoriste linearis*)—A branched, nearly smooth, somewhat shrubby perennial with rather stiff leaves that vary from linear to oblong and from ½ to 1½ inches long. The blue or purplish flowers are borne in the axils of leaves and are about one inch long. Spreading Snakeherb (*Dyschoriste decumbens*) is also reported.

POLKADOTS
(*Dyschoriste linearis*)

HAIRY TUBETONGUE
(*Justicia pilosella*)

➷ **Hairy Tubetongue** (*Justicia pilosella*)—A low plant branching from a woody base with opposite, ovate or oval leaves ½ to 1½ inches long and pale blue or purple flowers with very narrow corolla tube about an inch long borne in the axils of the leaves.

Parry's Wild Petunia (*Ruellia parryi*)—A low shrub with oblong leaves that taper to a short petiole and vary from about ½ to 1 inch long. The flowers are solitary in the axils of the leaves and have lilac or pale purple or sometimes white corollas an inch or more in length.

Early Shaggytuft (*Stenandrium barbatum*)—A low, hairy plant only a few inches high, branched from a woody base, with very crowded oblanceolate leaves, and purple flowers in several-flowered, leafy spikes.

AMARANTH FAMILY (AMARANTHACEAE)

Mostly herbs with entire leaves without stipules and small, inconspicuous flowers, either perfect or imperfect, with sepals but without petals, each in the axil of one or more bracts. The number of sepals varies from one to five, and the stamens may be the same number or fewer. Some members of the family are pernicious weeds. A few are used as ornamental plants because of their ornamental foliage.

This family now includes former members of the Goosefoot Family (Chenopodiaceae). The Goosefoot Family as formerly described was a large family of weedlike herbs and shrubs with simple, alternate leaves and small, greenish flowers. Many of them are adapted to growing in deserts or in sandy or saline soils. Most of them are wind-pollinated and produce pollen rather abundantly. For this reason they are listed prominently among plants that cause hay fever. Common genera and species found in the Park may be distinguished as follows:

1   Calyx dry and chaffy...2
    Calyx not dry and chaffy (former Chenopdiaceae, Goosefoot Family)...10
2   Leaves alternate 3
    Leaves opposite 4
3   Shrubs .... TEXAS-SHRUB (*Iresine leptoclada*, p. 51)
    Herbs, or woody only at the base   AMARANTH (*Amaranthus*, p. 48)
4   Flowers all perfect, in panicles .... BLOODLEAF
    .... (*Iresine heterophylla*, p. 51)
    Flowers perfect, not in panicles 5
5   Hairs of leaves branched and star-shaped .... HONEYSWEET
    .... (*Tidestromia*, p. 51)
    Hairs of leaves unbranched 6
6   Flowers in spikes .... SNAKE-COTTON (*Froelichia*, p. 50)
    Flowers not in spikes 7
7   Flowers in heads 8
    Flowers clustered in the leaf axils 9
8   Heads stalked, about an inch in diameter; erect herbs ....
    .... GLOBE-AMARANTH (*Gomphrena nitida*, p. 50)
    Heads sessile, less than ½ inch in diameter; prostrate herbs ......
    .... WASHER-WOMAN (*Alternanthera caracasana*, p. 48)
9   Leaves with long, straight hairs beneath ....
    ... WOOLLY COTTON-FLOWER (*Gossypianthus lanuginosus*, p. 50)
    Leaves with curled, densely matted hairs beneath ....
    .... SMALL MATWEED (*Guilleminea densa*, p. 50)
10 Leaves cylindrical or fleshy .... SHRUBBY SEEPWEED
    .... (*Suaeda nigra*, p. 51)
    Leaves flat 11
11 Flowers imperfect .... SALTBUSH (*Atriplex*, p. 48)
    Flowers perfect 12

12 Fruiting calyx transversely winged . . . . WINGED PIGWEED
. . . . (*Cycloloma atriplicifolium*, p. 49)
   Fruiting calyx not winged 13
13 Flowers with 1 sepal and 1 stamen . . NUTTALL'S POVERTY-WEED
. . . . (*Blitum nuttallianum*, p. 49)
   Flowers with 3 to 5 sepals and 3 to 5 stamens . . . . GOOSEFOOT
. . . . (*Chenopodium, Dysphania*, p. 49)

Washer-Woman (*Alternanthera caracasana*)—Herb with prostrate stems and oval or ovate leaves which are narrowed into a petiole. The flowers have five sepals and five stamens; they are borne in dense heads with conspicuous, white bracts.

■ **Amaranth** (*Amaranthus*)—Also called pigweed and careless-weed. Rather coarse, annual herbs with imperfect flowers subtended by spine-tipped, greenish or reddish bracts. The flowers have five or fewer transparent or greenish sepals, five or fewer stamens, and one pistil with two or three styles. Both the leaves and the seeds of some of the amaranths were formerly used for food by the Indians. Eleven species have been found in the Park, five of the more common are keyed below:

1 Staminate and pistillate flowers on separate plants. . . . .
. . . . **Careless Weed** (*Amaranthus palmeri*)
   Staminate and pistillate flowers on the same plant 2
2 Plants erect 3
   Plants prostrate . . . . . . ⌐ **Mat Amaranth** (*Amaranthus blitoides*)
3 Sepals of the pistillate flowers, or some of them, sharp-pointed at
   the tip 4
   Sepals of the pistillate flowers blunt at the tip; capsules usually
   shorter than the calyx; stamens 5 . . . . **Red-Root Amaranth**
. . . . (*Amaranthus retroflexus*)
4 Stamens mostly 3; spikes stout . . . . **Green Amaranth**
. . . . (*Amaranthus powellii*)
   Stamens usually 5; spikes slender . . . . **Smooth Amaranth**
. . . . (*Amaranthus hybridus*)

■ **Saltbush** (*Atriplex*)—Five members of this genus are present in Big Bend; two typical species are: ⌐ **Four-Wing Saltbush** (*Atriplex canescens*) is found in various places in the desert scrub areas. It is an erect, bushy, grayish, scurfy shrub with narrow, 1-nerved leaves and imperfect flowers. The staminate and pistillate flowers are on separate plants. **New Mexico Saltbush** (*Atriplex obovata*) is less frequent and

MAT AMARANTH
(*Amaranthus blitoides*)

FOUR-WING SALTBUSH
(*Atriplex canescens*)

can be distinguished by the fact that it is only slightly shrubby and has sessile or nearly sessile leaves.

Nuttall's Poverty-Weed (*Blitum nuttallianum*, synonym *Monolepis nuttalliana*)—A low, spreading or partly prostrate, slightly fleshy, nearly smooth, annual herb with flowers in small clusters in the axils of leaves.

■ **Goosefoot, Pigweed** (*Chenopodium, Dysphania*)—Weedy plants with greenish, bractless flowers in little, sessile clusters, which are arranged in spiked panicles. **Lamb's-Quarters** (*Chenopodium album*) is a more or less mealy plant with leaves that vary from angular-ovate at the base to lanceolate or linear above. Usually most or all of them have a few angular teeth. The seeds are smooth and shining. **Pit-Seed Goosefoot** (*Chenopodium berlandieri*) is very similar but the seeds are minutely pitted and not shining. **Field Wormseed** (*Dysphania graveolens*, synonym *Chenopodium graveolens*) differs from the other two species in being somewhat glandular and aromatic and in having leaves that are pinnately lobed or at least conspicuously toothed.

Winged Pigweed (*Cycloloma atriplicifolium*)—An annual herb with much branched stems and ovate or lanceolate, coarsely toothed leaves. The flowers are sessile in spikes that are arranged to form a panicle.

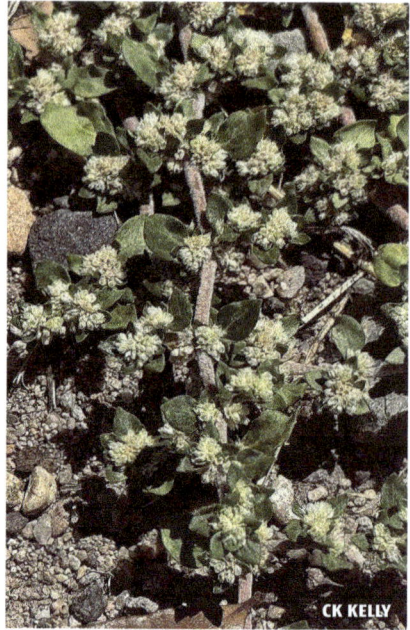

SLENDER SNAKE-COTTON
(*Froelichia gracilis*)

SMALL MATWEED
(*Guilleminea densa*)

■ Snake-Cotton (*Froelichia*)—Hairy or woolly herbs with perfect, 3-bracted flowers in spikes. The densely woolly calyx is tubular and 5-cleft at the summit. Arizona Snake-Cotton (*Froelichia arizonica*) is a perennial with a thick, woody root and stout stems that often branch sparingly. The leaf blades are commonly inverted lance-shaped and rather thick. ⌖ Slender Snake-Cotton (*Froelichia gracilis*) is an annual with a leafless flowering stem. The leaves are lanceolate and covered with silky down on the underside.

Globe-Amaranth (*Gomphrena nitida*)—A hairy, annual herb growing 8 to 20 inches high with perfect flowers borne in large heads, the flowers subtended by white or pinkish bracts and the heads subtended by leaves. Not common.

Woolly Cotton-Flower (*Gossypianthus lanuginosus*)—Perennial herb with partly prostrate, woolly stems. The basal leaves are long spatula-shaped, while those on the stem are ovate, sessile, and silky-woolly. This species has been found in lower Willow Creek Canyon but may occur elsewhere in the Park.

⌖ Small Matweed (*Guilleminea densa*)—A prostrate, white-hairy, leafy herb, which has a perennial root and forms thick mats on the

SUE CARNAHAN

MADELEINE CLAIRE

BLOODLEAF
(*Iresine heterophylla*)

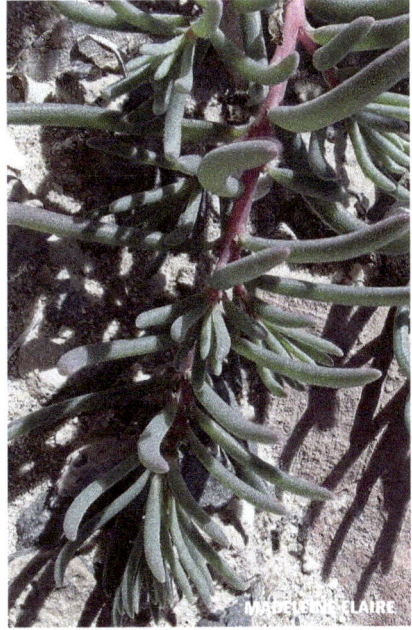

SHRUBBY SEEPWEED
(*Suaeda nigra*)

ground. The leaves are opposite, ovate, and entire; the very small flowers are perfect and are borne in the axils of the leaves. Found on the lower parts of the Chisos Mountains.

↗ Bloodleaf (*Iresine heterophylla*)—Herb with opposite leaves and flowers subtended by three dry, whitish bracts. The five slender stamens are united below into a short cup. Found in the Chisos Mountains.

Texas-Shrub (*Iresine leptoclada*)—A white-hairy shrub with small, scattered, alternate leaves and small, imperfect flowers, which are immersed in long wool in branched, terminal clusters. The leaves are ovate or lance-shaped, entire, and taper to a short petiole.

↗ Shrubby Seepweed (*Suaeda nigra*)—A perennial, fleshy plant usually somewhat woody at the base. The leaves are cylindrical and fleshy. The inconspicuous flowers are sessile in the axils of leaflike bracts. Each flower has a 5-parted calyx and five stamens. The little 1-seeded fruit is permanently enclosed by the calyx. Frequent in the desert in the western part of the Park.

■ Honeysweet (*Tidestromia*)—Plants with small, round or nearly round, entire, petioled leaves and very small, axillary flowers, each subtended by three concave, transparent bracts. ↗ Shrubby Honeysweet

SHRUBBY HONEYSWEET
(*Tidestromia suffruticosa*)

WOOLLY HONEYSWEET
(*Tidestromia lanuginosa*)

(*Tidestromia suffruticosa*) is somewhat woody at the base, and the stems are erect and very much branched. **Woolly Honeysweet** (*Tidestromia lanuginosa*) is an annual species, and the stems are wholly or partly prostrate. The leaves are a little larger than those of the other species but they are often in threes with two of them smaller.

DAFFODIL FAMILY (AMARYLLIDACEAE)

A rather large and important group, the Daffodil Family contains some edible plants, the most notable of which is the onion, and many ornamental flowers. Species found in the Park include:

■ **Wild Onion** (*Allium*)—The wild onions can easily be recognized by their odor, which is the same as that of cultivated onions. The flowers are produced in umbels. **Nodding Onion** (*Allium cernuum*) has the umbel nodding, while **Kunth's Onion** (*Allium kunthii*) has the umbel upright.

False Garlic (*Nothoscordum bivalve*)—Readily identified because it looks like an onion but does not have the onion odor and taste.

Evening Rain-Lily (*Zephyranthes chlorosolen*)—The rainlily grows from a bulb about an inch in diameter. The leaves are very narrow and

F. LABRY

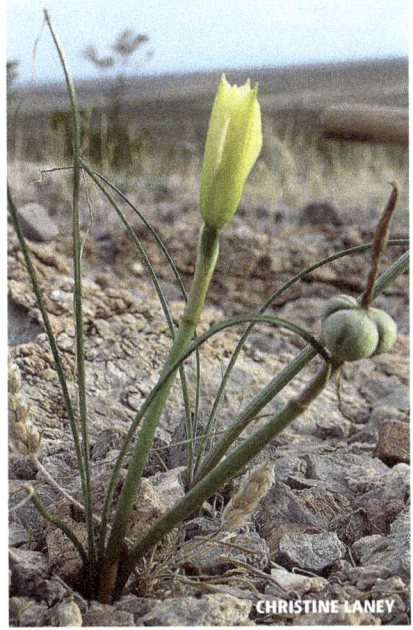

CHRISTINE LANEY

NODDING ONION
(*Allium cernuum*)

ZEPHYR-LILY
(*Zephyranthes longifolia*)

grasslike, and the slender flowering stalk, 6 to 12 inches long, bears a single white, lilylike flower with a slender tube 3 to 5 inches long. Found in the Chisos Mountains but not common.

➤ **Zephyr-Lily** (*Zephyranthes longifolia*)—Closely related to the Rain-Lily and is most frequently observed on flats of the desert scrub following rainy periods. The flowering stem is from a bulb similar to that of an onion and bears a large, solitary, yellow flower. The leaves are grasslike and somewhat fleshy.

CASHEW FAMILY (ANACARDIACEAE)

A family of shrubs and small trees with alternate, compound leaves and small flowers. Usually the fruits are more conspicuous than the flowers. Some of the white-fruited species are very poisonous to the touch, and one should be very cautious about handling any shrub whose leaves have three leaflets until one has become familiar with poison-ivy. Whenever one suspects that they have been in contact with one of these poisonous plants, they should, as soon as possible, wash their hands and face thoroughly in strong soapsuds or, better still, in a solution of ferric chloride. The family is represented in the Park by four species of

SUE CARNAHAN

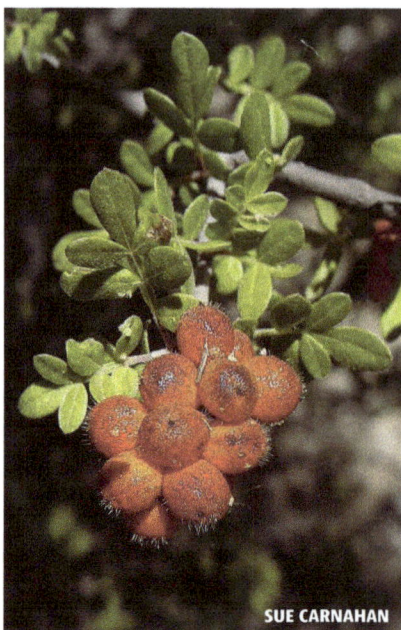

SUE CARNAHAN

EASTERN POISON-IVY
(*Toxicodendron radicans*)

LITTLE-LEAF SUMAC
(*Rhus microphylla*)

Rhus (non-toxic) and one of *Toxicodendron* (toxic), most of which are included in the following key:

1   Leaflets 3, lobed and toothed 2
    Leaflets more than 3, entire 3
2   Leaflets 4 or 5 inches long; fruits white, smooth or nearly so .....
    .... ⤝ **Eastern Poison-Ivy** (*Toxicodendron radicans*)
    Leaflets ½ to 1½ inches long; fruits covered with crimson hairs ..
    .... **Fragrant Sumac** (*Rhus aromatica*)
3   Leaflets 5 to 9, 3 inches or less long .... ⤝ **Little-Leaf Sumac**
    .... (*Rhus microphylla*)
    Leaflets usually 5 or 7, 1 to 1½ inches long . ⤝ **Evergreen Sumac**
    .... (*Rhus virens*)

CARROT FAMILY (APIACEAE)

This is a large family and contains some valuable, edible plants, such as the parsnip and the carrot, and others, such as the water-hemlock, that are deadly poisonous if eaten. Most members of the family are herbs with hollow stems and alternate leaves. The leaves are usually com-

 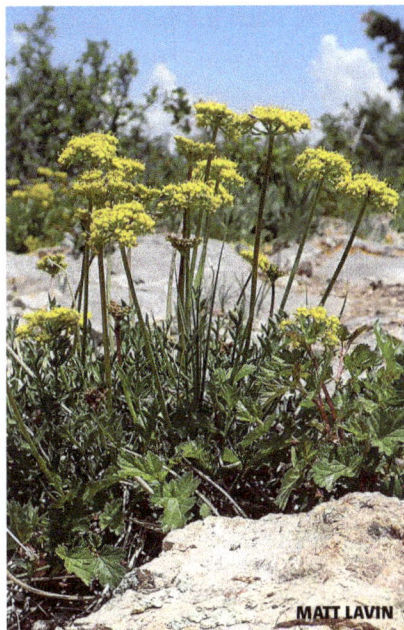

EVERGREEN SUMAC
(*Rhus virens*)

HALL'S SPRING-PARSLEY
(*Cymopterus hallii*)

pound and often two or three times compound. The ovary is below the other parts of the flower, and there are usually five calyx teeth, five petals, five stamens, and two styles. The fruits are dry and may be flat or cylindrical, but in any case consist of two 1-seeded parts, which are attached face to face and the backs of which are provided with five or more ribs, some or all of which are sometimes winged.

The flowers are so nearly alike in many members of the family that often it is necessary to have mature fruits in order to make identification certain. However, only four species have been reported from the Park. One, ✈ Hall's Spring-Parsley (*Cymopterus hallii*), is a low plant with all the leaves basal and with a naked stem 4 to 6 inches high with an umbel of small, yellow flowers at the summit. The leaves are pinnately compound with more or less wedge-shaped leaflets, which are variously toothed or cleft.

DOGBANE FAMILY (APOCYNACEAE)

A family of herbs or rarely shrubs, most of which have a milky juice containing, among other things, some rubber. The flower structure is much like that of a gentian except that there are two pistils. The fruit consist of two pods with large numbers of seeds, and the seeds are usually provided with long hairs, which aid in wind dissemination.

The Milkweed Family (Asclepiadaceae) is now incorporated into the Dogbane Family. Former members are characterized by opposite or whorled leaves, ordinarily abundant, milky juice, and curiously shaped flowers. Some of the flowers are beautiful and pleasantly fragrant, while others are ill-smelling, but all have much the same highly specialized form designed to bring about cross pollination through the aid of insects. From the base of the stamens grows a corollalike structure called the crown. The five lobes of the crown are united at the base into a column or collar whose height varies in different species. At varying heights on their inner surfaces the lobes bear spurs that may or may not extend beyond the crown. The lobes are usually called hoods, and the spurs are called horns. The whole structure surrounds the stamens and forces the anthers to touch in a circle around the pistil. In most cases the filaments are united into a column and the sepals are turned back when the flower is in full bloom. If you insert a pin into one of the slits of the crown of a milkweed flower and pull upward you will find two pollen masses hanging to the pin. When a bee alights on the crown for the purpose of obtaining nectar its foot is very likely to slip into one of these slits, and, when the foot is withdrawn, the pollen masses cling to it just as they did to the pin. If the bee now flies to another flower the pollen masses may come in contact with the stigmatic surfaces, and pollination is thus accomplished. The fruits of milkweeds are pods containing many seeds; the seeds are usually provided with silky hairs, which aid in wind dissemination.

Most members of the Dogbane Family found in the Park may be distinguished as follows:

1 Styles united throughout 2
   Styles separate below, united at the top (former Asclepiadaceae, Milkweed Family). 3
2 Plants perennial herbs . . . . DOGBANE
   . . . . (*Apocynum androsaemifolium*, p. 57)
   Plants woody, at least at their base . . . . ROCKTRUMPET
   . . . . (*Mandevilla macrosiphon*, p. 59)
3 Crown of 5 inflated bags . . . . TWINEVINE (*Funastrum*, p. 59)
   Crown not as above 4

CHRIS REARDON

CK KELLY

SPREADING DOGBANE
(*Apocynum androsaemifolium*)

TUFTED MILKWEED
(*Asclepias nummularia*)

4   Stems not twining 5
      Stems twining 6
5   Stems erect; corolla reflexed .... MILKWEED (*Asclepias*, p. 57)
      Stems decumbent; corolla rotate .... ANTELOPEHORN
      .... (*Asclepias asperula*, p. 58)
6   Lobes of crown sharp-pointed TALAYOTE (*Pattalias palmeri*, p. 60)
      Lobes of crown not sharp-pointed 7
7   Crown consisting of 5 flat or slender and distinct scales or processes
      ..... BEARDED SWALLOW-WORT (*Cynanchum barbigerum*, p. 59)
      Crown a fleshy, 5- to 10-lobed ring or disk ... NETTED MILKVINE
      .... (*Matelea reticulata*, p. 60)

➷ Spreading Dogbane (*Apocynum androsaemifolium*)—A branched herb growing 1 to 4 feet high with simple, entire, opposite leaves, white milky juice, and clusters of pink, bell-shaped flowers with darker stripes. The slender pods are 3 to 4 inches long. The stem is usually stained red on one side. Found in moist places in the Chisos Mountains.

■ Milkweed (*Asclepias*)—This is the largest and most typical genus of the family; its members can usually be recognized by the abundant

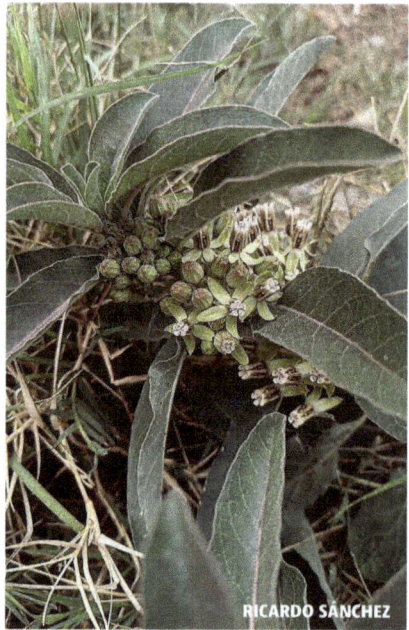

TERESA MAYFIELD

RICARDO SÁNCHEZ

HORSETAIL MILKWEED
(*Asclepias subverticillata*)

ZIZOTES MILKWEED
(*Asclepias oenotheroides*)

milky juice and the typical milkweed flowers arranged in many-flow-ered umbels. Five species (plus Antelopehorn) are reported:

1   Plants only a few inches high, with 2 or 4, rarely 6, leaves and 2 clus-ters of pink or white flowers. . . . . ❧ **Tufted Milkweed**
. . . . (*Asclepias nummularia*)
Plants more than a few inches tall and with more than 6 leaves . . **2**
2   Leaves linear, whorled in 3's or 6's . . . . ❧ **Horsetail Milkweed**
. . . . (*Asclepias subverticillata*)
Leaves not linear, opposite **3**
3   Leaves sessile. . . . . **Nodding Milkweed** (*Asclepias elata*)
Leaves petioled **4**
4   Flowers yellowish green; hoods long-stalked ❧ **Zizotes Milkweed**
. . . . (*Asclepias oenotheroides*)
Flowers white; hoods sessile . **Texas Milkweed** (*Asclepias texana*)

Antelopehorn (*Asclepias asperula*, synonym *Asclepiodora decum-bens*)—A frequent plant of open grassy slopes. This species differs from other members of *Asclepias* by a rotate, somewhat spreading corolla. The crown is of five-hooded fleshy bodies, each with a salient crest. The leaves are alternate.

CRAIG HENSLEY

CODY STRICKER

ROCKTRUMPET
(*Mandevilla macrosiphon*)

BEARDED SWALLOW-WORT
(*Cynanchum barbigerum*)

❧ Rocktrumpet (*Mandevilla macrosiphon*)—A perennial plant usually at least partly shrubby. The leaves are opposite, oblong, oval or nearly round and somewhat woolly beneath. The large white flowers are very showy and conspicuous during the early part of the day but they soon wither. The corolla tube may be 3 to 4 inches long, and the open part of the corolla may be 2 to 3 inches across. The flowers are borne in the axils of the upper leaves. Found in several places in the lower parts of the Chisos Mountains, especially on the more open slopes.

❧ Bearded Swallow-Wort (*Cynanchum barbigerum*, synonym *Metastelma barbigerum*)—A perennial, twining herb with small, opposite leaves and small, whitish flowers in umbels in the axils of leaves. The plant is smooth, except that the narrow leaves of the corolla are densely white-hairy on the inner side.

■ Twinevine (*Funastrum*, synonym *Sarcostemma*)—Twining plants with petioled leaves and fragrant flowers in stalked umbels. Three species have been found in the Park. ❧ Wavy-Leaf Twinevine (*Funastrum crispum*, synonym *Sarcostemma crispum*) has the umbel stalks much shorter than the leaves, and the leaves are narrow, almost linear.

SUE CARNAHAN

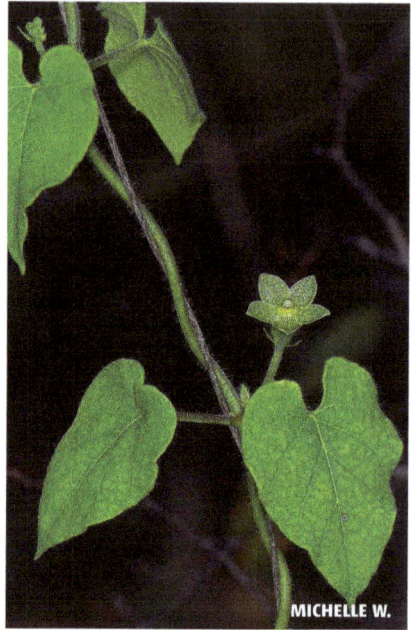

MICHELLE W.

WAVY-LEAF TWINEVINE
(*Funastrum crispum*)

NETTED MILKVINE
(*Matelea reticulata*)

Hartweg's Twinevine (*Funastrum heterophyllum*, synonym *Sarcostemma heterophyllum*) is smooth, with the umbel stalks nearly as long as the leaves and the flowers purplish. Soft Twinevine (*Funastrum torreyi*, synonym *Sarcostemma torreyi*) is densely short-hairy, with the umbel stalks nearly as long as the leaves and the flowers white.

➤ Netted Milkvine (*Matelea reticulata*, synonym *Vincetoxicum reticulatum*)—A hairy, twining plant with heart-shaped leaves and green, 5-lobed flowers in long-stalked umbels in the axils of leaves. The corolla is green, but has a network of purplish veins. This plant is sometimes called pearl-milkweed because each flower has a silvery crown in the center that resembles a pearl.

Talayote (*Pattalias palmeri*, synonym *Cynanchum racemosum*)—A twining plant with heart-shaped or arrow-shaped, pointed, opposite leaves and small, greenish-white flowers in clusters that are more like racemes than umbels. The pods are oblong, thick, and 3 to 4 inches long.

MICHELLE W.

ALEXIS HERNÁNDEZ

CORY'S DUTCHMAN'S PIPE
(*Aristolochia coryi*)

WRIGHT'S DUTCHMAN'S PIPE
(*Aristolochia wrightii*)

BIRTHWORT FAMILY (ARISTOLOCHIACEAE)

Plants with short-petioled, somewhat heart-shaped, entire leaves and curious flowers without petals but with a tubular calyx shaped like a pitcher or a pipe. The flower has five stamens more or less united with the style. The fruit is a many-seeded pod. The family is represented in the Park by two species of Dutchman's Pipe (*Aristolochia*), both having small, yellowish-green, black, or purplish-black flowers and five-celled pods with very flat seeds. ⚘ Cory's Dutchman's Pipe (*Aristolochia coryi*) is sparsely hairy and the lip of the pitcherlike calyx is broadly elliptic in shape. ⚘ Wright's Dutchman's Pipe (*Aristolochia wrightii*) is more hairy, usually somewhat velvety and yellowish, and the lip of the calyx is very long and narrow.

ASPARAGUS FAMILY (ASPARAGACEAE)

Plants with grasslike or fleshy, basal leaves, and showy flowers on long, bracted, leafless stalks. The flowers have 3 sepals, 3 petals, 6 stamens, and one pistil with the ovary below the other parts of the flowers.

LECHIGUILLA
(*Agave lechuguilla*)

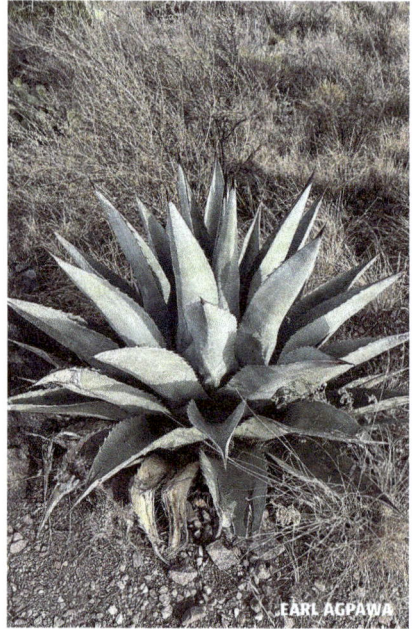

HAVARD'S CENTURY-PLANT
(*Agave havardiana*)

■ Century-Plant (*Agave*)—The century-plants have very thick, fleshy leaves, which, in ours, are spiny-toothed along the margins. Four species have been found in the Park. ➷ Lechiguilla (*Agave lechuguilla*) is by far the most common. It covers the ground over extensive areas so thickly that it is difficult to walk through. The flowering stalk, which is several feet tall, is unbranched and bears a long, spikelike panicle of flowers. Parry's Century-Plant (*Agave parryi*) and Chisos Mountain Century-Plant (*Agave × glomeruliflora*, synonym *Agave chisosensis*) are much larger plants. ➷ Havard's Century-Plant (*Agave havardiana*) also occurs.

Like all the large century-plants they require 10 to 20 years of preparation for producing the immense flowering stalk, which may grow 15 feet tall in a short time by using the food stored in the leaves. These plants bloom but once. After the seeds have been matured the mother plant dies. As the plants approach maturity, offsets are often formed around the base of the mother plant, these continuing to grow after the mother plant has flowered and died. Agave parryi is the larger and commoner century-plant in the Chisos Mountains. The flowers are produced on branches extending from the central stalk, producing a

SOTOL
(*Dasylirion leiophyllum*)

BEARGRASS, BASKETGRASS
(*Nolina erumpens*)

paniclelike inflorescence. *Agave* × *glomeruliflora* is a smaller plant. The branches producing the flowers in *Agave* × *glomeruliflora* are short and give the inflorescence a spikelike appearance.

➤ Sotol (*Dasylirion leiophyllum*)—The sotol produces a basal cluster of ribbonlike leaves, which are 1 to 3 feet long and about ½ inch wide and spiny-toothed along the margin. The unbranched flower stalk is 5 to 15 feet tall and produces a long, dense panicle of small, white flowers at the upper end. This plant is limited in the United States to Texas and southern New Mexico, but it extends also into Mexico. When the leaves are burned off and the cabbagelike base split open it is relished by cattle, especially during a drought period when other food is scarce. When the basal portion is baked and allowed to ferment it is found to be rich in alcohol, and from this is distilled a fiery beverage called *sotol*.

➤ Beargrass, Basketgrass (*Nolina erumpens*)—This plant resembles sotol in its habit of growth, but the leaves are very minutely toothed along the margins instead of being spiny-toothed. The flower cluster is much more open and bushy than is that of sotol. The whole leaves are used for weaving basketry and are especially good for making basket handles.

SOAPTREE YUCCA
(*Yucca elata*)

THOMPSON'S YUCCA
(*Yucca thompsoniana*)

■ **Spanish Bayonet, Spanish Dagger, Soapweed** (*Yucca*)—The yuccas are classed as trees or shrubs because they have woody stems, although in some the stem is so short as to be scarcely noticeable. The large, white flowers are borne in a loose panicle. They are pollinated by a little, white, woolly moth belonging to the genus *Pronuba*, which collects pollen from the stamens and places some of it on the receptive end of the pistil after each act of laying an egg in the ovary of the flower.

Five species of Yucca are found in the Park: ⇗ **Soaptree Yucca** (*Yucca elata*), ⇗ **Thompson's Yucca** (*Yucca thompsoniana*), and **Beaked Yucca** (*Yucca rostrata*) have narrow, stiff leaves and capsular fruit. In *Y. elata* the margins of the leaf blades separate into whitish fibers, and the fruit is large, symmetrical, and pale tan. In *Y. thompsoniana* and *Y. rostrata* the margins of the leaf are horny, pale yellow, and more or less toothed with very small teeth. The fruit of the former is usually oblong with short, fragile tips and a rather thin wall, while that of the latter is rounded below and has long, thick beaks and a thick wall. When mature, *Y. elata* and *Y. rostrata* form tall, treelike plants and are very similar in general appearance, while *Y. thompsoniana* does not attain the height of the other two but forms a small tree of neat and striking appearance.

KEVIN FLOYD

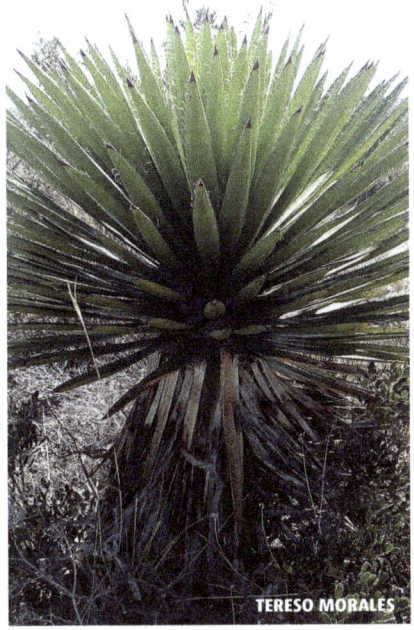
TERESO MORALES

TORREY'S YUCCA
(*Yucca torreyi*)

EVE'S-NEEDLE
(*Yucca faxoniana*)

➤ Torrey's Yucca (*Yucca torreyi*) and ➤ Eve's-Needle (*Yucca faxoniana*) have broad, large, fleshy leaves and fleshy fruits. *Y. torreyi* is nearly stemless and the flower cluster is produced near the ground. *Y. faxoniana* forms large, handsome trees with tall stems, symmetrical clusters of leaves, and large, beautiful flower clusters.

ASTER FAMILY (ASTERACEAE)

The Aster Family, a very large group, is believed to be one of the youngest of plant families, that is, recent in its origin, but at the same time one of the most successful. More than 130 species of plants in the Park's flora belong to this family. Many members of the aster family are used as ornamental plants, and still larger numbers are prized as wild-flowers. The family also contains many pernicious weeds, but relatively few plants that are used as food by man. Lettuce is undoubtedly the most widely used food plant belonging to this family. The great majority of the members of the family are herbs, although there are also many shrubs, and the success of the family in spreading to all parts of the earth is due largely to the remarkable adaptations for seed dissemination, mostly by wind or animals, possessed by many of its members.

The chief characteristic of the family that distinguishes it from practically all others as they are represented in our flora is that the relatively small flowers are borne in a dense head, all on one receptacle, and are surrounded by an involucre of bracts. What we commonly call a flower of a dandelion, sunflower, or aster, is not a single flower but a whole "bouquet" of flowers. Each of the little petal-like parts of a dandelion, for example, is an individual flower. In such a flower the ovary is inferior, that is, the other parts of the flower are attached above the ovary. At the top of the ovary is a cluster of white hairs called the pappus, which represents the calyx. In some members of the family the pappus consists of bristles, awns, scales, or teeth, and in some it is entirely lacking. Within and above the pappus is the yellow, strap-shaped part of the dandelion flower which is the corolla and is made up of five very narrow, united petals. In the center of the flower is a single style with two stigmas at the end, and around this are the five stamens with the filaments distinct but the anthers united around the style.

The advantage of having a large number of flowers together on one receptacle is obvious. They can be small and still conspicuous enough to attract insects, and once an insect has been attracted it is likely to visit a number of flowers before leaving. In the aster and many other members of the family there are two kinds of flowers in each head. The outer ones are similar to those of the dandelion and are called ray flowers, while the inner ones have tubular corollas and are called disk flowers. Often the ray flowers differ in color from the disk flowers, and in some cases the ray flowers do not produce any fruits, their purpose being to attract insects, while the less conspicuous disk flowers produce the fruits. The insects, of course, visit the flowers for food, that is, for the nectar, which they use either directly for food or for making honey, and while obtaining this food they accidentally bring about a transfer of pollen from anthers to stigmas.

There are also some members of the family in which all the flowers have tubular corollas. The members of the family, therefore, may be divided into three groups: those whose flowers all have tubular corollas; those whose flowers all have strap-shaped corollas; and those having both tubular and strap-shaped corollas, or both ray and disk flowers. The fruits, in all cases, are achenes. Most Aster Family members found in the Park may be distinguished as follows:

1   Corollas all strap-shaped 2
    Corollas all tubular or corollas of the ray flowers strap-shaped and those of the disk flowers tubular............................. 5

2   Bristles of the pappus feathery .... WIRE-LETTUCE .... (*Stephanomeria pauciflora*, p. 103)
    Bristles of the pappus not feathery 3

3   Fruits flattened .... SOW-THISTLE (*Sonchus oleraceus*, p. 103)
    Fruits not flattened.. 4

4   Flowers pink-tinged or nearly white...... WHITE ROCK-LETTUCE .... (*Pinaropappus roseus*, p. 98)
    Flowers yellow or orange .... ROUGH-STEM HAWKWEED .... (*Hieracium schultzii*, p. 91)

5   Corollas of disk flowers more or less irregular 6
    Corollas of disk flowers regular............................. 8

6   Ray flowers present........ SILVERPUFF (*Chaptalia texana*, p. 81)
    Ray flowers lacking.. 7

7   Flowers yellow AMERICAN THREEFOLD (*Trixis californica*, p. 106)
    Flowers rose-purple to white ... DESERT-PEONY (*Acourtia*, p. 73)

8   Ray flowers lacking.. 9
    Ray flowers present 37

9   Pappus none 10
    Pappus present 13

10   Heads one-flowered .... CLUSTERED YELLOWTOPS .... (*Flaveria trinervia*, p. 84)
    Heads with more than one flower 11

11   Receptacle without chaffy bracts between the flowers; plants with odor of sage.................... SAGEBRUSH (*Artemisia*, p. 74)
    Receptacle with chaffy bracts between the flowers; plants without odor of sage 12

12   Flowers imperfect, the outer ones in each head pistillate and the inner ones staminate . SUMPWEED (*Hedosyne ambrosiifolia*, p. 88)
    Flowers perfect.......... GREENTHREAD (*Thelesperma*, p. 104)

13   Pappus of awns or scales or both, these sometimes united into a crown.. 14
    Pappus of hairlike bristles 20

14   Receptacle with chaffy scales between the flowers........... 15
    Receptacle without chaffy scales between the flowers........ 16

15   Plants shrubby.............. TARBUSH (*Flourensia cernua*, p. 85)
    Plants herbaceous .... GREENTHREAD (*Thelesperma*, p. 104)

16 Pappus of about 20 awns. . . . . LEAFY ROCK DAISY
. . . . (*Perityle rupestris*, p. 98)
Pappus of about 12 scales or awns. . . . BIGELOW'S BRISTLEHEAD
. . . . (*Carphochaete bigelovii*, p. 80)
Pappus of fewer than 12 scales or awns 17

17 Flowers not yellow. 18
Flowers yellow 19

18 Pappus of 1 to 5 awns or scales or both; flowers rose-pink . . . .
. . . . SAW-TOOTH CANDYLEAF (*Stevia serrata*, p. 104)
Pappus of 6 to 8 scales; flowers purple PALAFOX (*Palafoxia*, p. 95)

19 Heads with 3 to 5 flowers . . . . MANY-FLOWER FALSE BAHIA
. . . . (*Picradeniopsis multiflora*, p. 98)
Heads with more than 5 flowers . . . . MOUNTAIN LEAFTAIL
. . . . (*Pericome caudata*, p. 97)

20 Receptacle densely bristly 21
Receptacle naked or chaffy 22

21 Both leaves and involucre prickly. . . . . WAVY-LEAF THISTLE
. . . . (*Cirsium undulatum*, p. 81)
Only the involucre prickly . . . . BASKETFLOWER
. . . . (*Plectocephalus americanus*, p. 99)

22 Bracts of involucre partly or wholly dry and lacking green color 23
Bracts of involucre green, at least in the center 25

23 Flowers all imperfect, the staminate and pistillate heads on separate
plants. . . . . FALSE WILLOW (*Baccharis*, p. 76)
Marginal flowers of each head pistillate; those of the central part of
the head perfect 24

24 Flowers purplish; plants not hairy . . . . ARROW-WEED
. . . . (*Pluchea sericea*, p. 99)
Flowers not purplish; plants hairy or woolly . . . .
. . . . . . CUDWEED, RABBIT-TOBACCO (*Pseudognaphalium*, p. 100)

25 Flowers imperfect, the staminate and pistillate flowers on separate
plants. . . . . FALSE WILLOW (*Baccharis*, p. 76)
Flowers perfect or imperfect but the same on all plants 26

26 Plants low, annual and hairy . . . . MOCK TURTLEBACK
. . . . (*Psathyrotopsis scaposa*, p. 100)
Plants perennial or, if annual, then not low and hairy 27

27 Bracts of involucre and leaves bearing conspicuous, partly transparent oil glands . . . . PORELEAF (*Porophyllum*, p. 100)

Bracts of involucre and leaves sometimes glandular but not with partly transparent oil glands **28**

28 Pappus bristles feathery **29**

Pappus bristles not feathery **31**

29 Plants annual . . . . **PLUMEWEED** (*Carminatia tenuiflora*, p. 80)

Plants perennial **30**

30 Flowers whitish; leaves not linear . . . . **BRICKELLBUSH**

. . . . (*Brickellia*, p. 79)

Flowers rose-purple; leaves linear . . . . **DOTTED GAYFEATHER**

. . . . (*Liatris punctata*, p. 93)

31 Pappus double, the outer of short scales, the inner of hairlike bristles

. . . . **PLAINS IRONWEED** (*Vernonia marginata*, p. 107)

Pappus not double, of hairlike bristles **32**

32 Heads with the outer flowers pistillate and the inner ones perfect

. . . . **33**

Heads with all the flowers perfect **34**

33 Corollas purplish . . . . **ARROW-WEED** (*Pluchea sericea*, p. 99)

Corollas whitish . . . . **WOOLWORT** (*Laennecia*, p. 92)

34 Flowers not yellow. **35**

Flowers yellow **36**

35 Achenes 5-ribbed or 5-angled. . . . . . . **BONESET, THROUGHWORT**

. . . . (former *Eupatorium*, p. 83)

Achenes 10-ribbed . . . . **BRICKELLBUSH** (*Brickellia*, p. 79)

36 Bracts of the involucre in a single series of equal length or with a few much shorter outer bractlets . . . . **GROUNDSEL, RAGWORT**

. . . . (*Packera, Senecio*, p. 94)

Bracts of the involucre unequal and in more than one principal series. . . . . **BAILEY'S RABBITBRUSH** (*Lorandersonia baileyi*, p. 93)

37 Pappus none **38**

Pappus present **47**

38 Ray flowers white, sometimes with yellow base **39**

Ray flowers yellow, sometimes partly purple or maroon **41**

39 Rays not remaining attached to the fruits **40**

Rays remaining attached to the fruits, becoming papery . . . .

. . . . **WHITE ZINNIA** (*Zinnia acerosa*, p. 108)

40 Outer achenes completely surrounded by the bracts of the involucre

. . . . **PLAINS BLACKFOOT** (*Melampodium leucanthum*, p. 93)

Outer achenes not completely surrounded by the bracts of the in-volucre . . . . **YERBA-DE-TAJO** (*Eclipta prostrata*, p. 82)

41 Receptacle without chaffy bracts between the flowers **42**

Receptacle with chaffy bracts between the flowers **44**

42 Leaves 1 to 3 times palmately divided into linear lobes.... **BAHIA**

.... (former *Bahia*, p. 77)

Leaves not palmately divided **43**

43 Heads small; plant covered with a glutinous material . **GUMHEAD**

.... (*Gymnosperma glutinosum*, p. 86)

Heads large; plant woolly................. **DESERT-MARIGOLD**

.... (*Baileya multiradiata*, p. 78)

44 Ray flowers pistillate and producing fruits; disk flowers perfect but not producing fruits .... **LYRE-LEAF GREENEYES**

.... (*Berlandiera lyrata*, p. 78)

Both ray and disk flowers perfect and producing fruits........ **45**

45 Rays not remaining attached to the fruits nor becoming papery ..

.... **GREENTHREAD** (*Thelesperma*, p. 104)

Rays remaining attached to the fruits and becoming papery... **46**

46 Achenes very much flattened .... **WHITE ZINNIA**

.... (*Zinnia acerosa*, p. 108)

Achenes plump... **MOUNTAIN OXEYE** (*Heliopsis parvifolia*, p. 90)

47 Pappus of hairlike bristles, rarely with a few outer scales in addition

....**48**

Pappus of awns or scales which are sometimes united into a crown

....**58**

48 Ray flowers not yellow **49**

Ray flowers yellow...................................... **51**

49 Pappus double, the outer of hairlike bristles, the inner of 5 very narrow but long scales with the midrib extended into an awn ....

EDWARDS' HOLE-IN-THE-SAND PLANT (*Nicolletia edwardsii*, p. 94)

Pappus not double...................................... **50**

50 Bracts of the involucre in several series and unequal; rays relatively broad .... **ASTER** (former *Aster*, p. 75)

Bracts of the involucre nearly equal and in one series; rays mostly very narrow....................... **FLEABANE** (*Erigeron*, p. 82)

51 Leaves opposite **52**

Leaves alternate **53**

52 Leaves and bracts of the involucre bearing prominent, partly transparent oil glands.................. **LEMONSCENT** (*Pectis*, p. 96)

Leaves and glands of the involucre without prominent oil glands .

.... **FALSE BROOMWEED** (*Haploesthes greggii*, p. 87)

53 Pappus double, the inner part of hairlike bristles, the outer of short bristles or scales **54**

Pappus single, of hairlike bristles **55**

54 Ray achenes smooth or nearly so and without pappus; disk achenes hairy and with double pappus . . . . CAMPHORWEED . . . . (*Heterotheca subaxillaris*, p. 90)

Achenes all alike and with double pappus FALSE GOLDEN-ASTER . . . . (*Heterotheca*, p. 91)

55 Bracts of the involucre mostly equal and in one series. **56**

Bracts of the involucre unequal and in several series **57**

56 Leaves linear . . . . DAMIANITA (*Chrysactinia mexicana*, p. 81)

Leaves not linear GROUNDSEL, RAGWORT (*Packera, Senecio*, p. 94)

57 Heads usually small and numerous; plants herbaceous. . . . . GOLDENROD (*Solidago*, p. 102)

Heads usually few and relatively large or, if small, then the plants shrubby . . . . GOLDENSHRUB (former *Haplopappus*, p. 87)

58 Receptacle with chaffy bracts between the flowers **59**

Receptacle without chaffy bracts between the flowers **68**

59 Ray flowers white or rose-color **60**

Ray flowers yellow **61**

60 Ray flowers producing fruits; disk flowers not producing fruits . . . . FEVERFEW (*Parthenium*, p. 95)

Both ray and disk flowers producing fruits . . . . SOUTHWESTERN COSMOS (*Cosmos parviflorus*, p. 81)

61 Involucre distinctly double, the outer bracts narrow and leaflike, the inner ones broader and membranous. **62**

Involucre not distinctly double **64**

62 Inner bracts of the involucre grown together to the middle or higher . . . . GREENTHREAD (*Thelesperma*, p. 104)

Inner bracts of the involucre separate or nearly so clear to the base **63**

63 Achenes of 2 sorts, the outer ones with a more or less winged margin, the inner ones narrower and not winged . . . . WINGPETAL . . . . (*Heterosperma pinnatum*, p. 90)

Achenes all alike . . . . BEGGARTICKS (*Bidens*, p. 79)

64 Leaves, at least the lower ones, pinnately lobed. . . . . PRAIRIE CONEFLOWER (*Ratibida columnifera*, p. 100)

Leaves entire or merely toothed. **65**

65 Ray flowers with pistils SHORT-LEAF JEFEA (*Jefea brevifolia*, p. 92)
   Ray flowers without pistils **66**
66 Achenes very flat............. CROWNBEARD (*Verbesina*, p. 106)
   Achenes more or less thickened........................... **67**
67 Pappus awns or scales falling from the fruit at maturity ....
   .... SUNFLOWER (*Helianthus*, p. 89)
   Pappus awns or scales persistent on the fruit .... GOLDENEYE
   .... (*Viguiera*, others, p. 107)
68 Involucre and leaves with partly transparent oil glands........ **69**
   Involucre and leaves without partly transparent oil glands..... **71**
69 Bracts of the involucre somewhat unequal and in two series .....
   .... PRICKLYLEAF, DOGWEED (*Thymophylla*, p. 105)
   Bracts of the involucre equal and in one series **70**
70 Bracts of involucre united to form a toothed cup or tube.........
   .... LICORICE MARIGOLD (*Tagetes micrantha*, p. 104)
   Bracts of involucre not united ...... LEMONSCENT (*Pectis*, p. 96)
71 Ray flowers white or purplish.................... WHITE-DAISY
   .... (*Aphanostephus ramosissimus*, p. 74)
   Ray flowers yellow.. **72**
72 Bracts of involucre in several series......................... **73**
   Bracts of involucre in one or two series **74**
73 Involucres sticky; heads medium sized .... GUMWEED
   .... (*Grindelia havardii*, p. 85)
   Involucres not sticky; heads small .... SNAKEWEED
   .... (*Gutierrezia*, p. 85)
74 Rays remaining attached to the achenes, becoming papery.... **75**
   Rays not remaining attached to the achenes.................. **76**
75 Rays 3 to 5................ PAPERFLOWER (*Psilostrophe*, p. 102)
   Rays 10 or more .... STEMMED BITTERWEED
   .... (*Tetraneuris scaposa*, p. 104)
76 Achenes strongly flattened, 2-edged . ROCK DAISY (*Perityle*, p. 97)
   Achenes not strongly flattened or 2-edged **77**
77 Bracts of the involucre spreading or turned back **78**
   Bracts of the involucre erect **79**
78 Receptacle naked SNEEZEWEED.............. (*Helenium*, p. 88)
   Receptacle beset with fibers .... BLANKETFLOWER
   .... (*Gaillardia pinnatifida*, p. 85)
79 Ray flower only one .... MANY-FLOWER FALSE BAHIA
   .... (*Picradeniopsis multiflora*, p. 98)

DWARF DESERT-PEONY
(*Acourtia nana*)

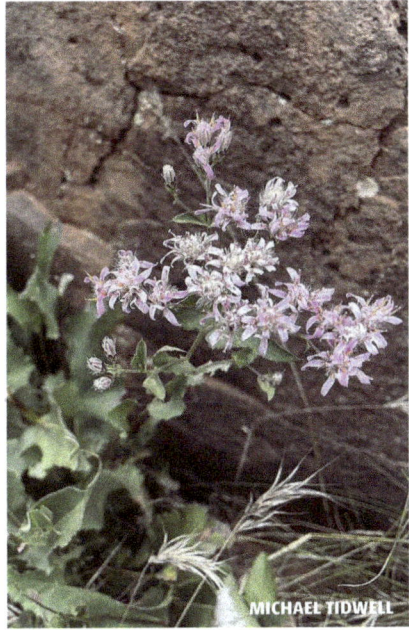

BROWNFOOT
(*Acourtia wrightii*)

Ray flowers more than one 80
80 Involucre more or less hairy. . . . . **STEMMED BITTERWEED**
. . . . (*Tetraneuris scaposa*, p. 104)
Involucre not at all hairy . . . . **BAHIA** (former *Bahia*, p. 77)

■ **Desert-Peony** (*Acourtia*, synonym *Perezia*)—Perennial herbs with alternate or all basal leaves and solitary or clustered heads of fragrant, rose-purple to white disk flowers. The fruits are oblong or nearly cylindrical, and the pappus consists of an abundance of rough, hairlike bristles. Three species occur in the Park: ⅋ **Dwarf Desert-Peony** (*Acourtia nana*, synonym *Perezia nana*) is a low plant with nearly round or ovate leaves, which are 1 to 2 inches long and coarsely toothed. The heads are ½ to 1 inch long and 20- to 30-flowered. **Feather-Leaf Desert-Peony** (*Acourtia runcinata*, synonym *Perezia runcinata*) has the leaves all basal; they are pinnately lobed and 4 to 8 inches long. The heads are like those of the preceding species. ⅋ **Brownfoot** (*Acourtia wrightii*, synonym *Perezia wrightii*) is a taller plant, 1 to 3 feet high, with oblong or ovate leaves densely spiny-toothed, the heads about half as large as those of the other two species.

WHITE-DAISY
(*Aphanostephus ramosissimus*)

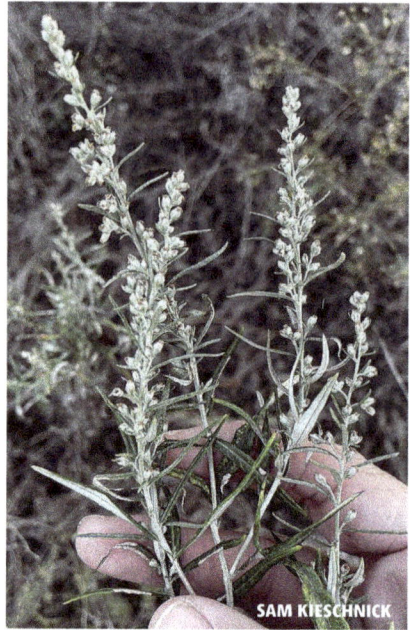

SAGEWORT
(*Artemisia ludoviciana*)

❧ **White-Daisy** (*Aphanostephus ramosissimus*)—A branched herb growing 3 to 12 inches high and bearing heads with yellow disk flowers and a fringe of small, white or purplish ray flowers. The leaves are entire or toothed, and the small fruits have a crown of fine, short hairs.

■ **Wormwood, Sagebrush** (*Artemisia*)—Herbs or shrubs with odor of sage. The heads are small and numerous with no ray flowers. There is no pappus, and the receptacle is nearly flat and naked. Three species occur in the Park: **Wormwood** (*Artemisia dracunculus*, synonym *Artemisia dracunculoides*) is mostly herbaceous but somewhat woody at the base and grows 2 to 6 feet tall. The leaves are linear and entire. ❧ **Sagewort** (*Artemisia ludoviciana*) is perennial from creeping underground stems, is white-woolly throughout, and has linear or narrowly lance-shaped leaves, the upper ones entire and the lower variously toothed or cut-lobed; it is very aromatic. **Carruth's Sagebrush** (*Artemisia carruthii*), is rhizomatous and spreads in loose patches. It grows to several feet tall, is most often silvery hairy, and usually has leaves with very narrow divisions. Plants are quite similar to *A. ludoviciana*.

SUE CARNAHAN

MEXICAN DEVIL-WEED
(*Chloracantha spinosa*)

MICHELLE W.

TAKHOKA DAISY
(*Machaeranthera tanacetifolia*)

■ **Aster** (former *Aster*)—Mostly herbs with several to many heads with white, purple, or blue ray flowers and yellow disk flowers, which sometimes change to purple with age. The bracts of the involucre overlap like shingles and usually have green, leaflike tips. The receptacle is flat, the fruits somewhat flattened, and the pappus consists of simple, hairlike bristles. Formerly placed in genus *Aster*, our species are now assigned to different genera as indicated below.

Rose-Heath (*Chaetopappa ericoides*, synonym *Aster leucelene*) has a crowded cluster of stems from a woody base with usually a single head on each stem. The numerous leaves are linear to spatula-shaped, the ray flowers are white, and the fruits are hairy.

❧ **Mexican-Devilweed** (*Chloracantha spinosa*, synonym *Aster spinosus*) is entirely herbaceous, with reedlike stems and almost leafless branches. The few leaves are linear and have spines in or above their axils. The heads are usually solitary at the ends of branches and have white ray flowers. The fruits are not hairy.

❧ **Takhoka Daisy** (*Machaeranthera tanacetifolia*, synonym *Aster tanacetifolius*) has numerous leaves, one to three times pinnately cleft

ANNUAL SALTMARSH ASTER
(*Symphyotrichum expansum*)

BIG BEND WOODY-ASTER
(*Xylorhiza wrightii*)

or parted. The heads are rather large with numerous, bright-violet rays nearly ½ inch long. The bracts of the involucre are narrowly linear with slender, spreading, leaflike tips.

☙ **Annual Saltmarsh Aster** (*Symphyotrichum expansum*, synonym *Aster exilis*) is an annual herb with linear or inversely lance-shaped leaves and rather small heads with white to light pink rays.

☙ **Big Bend Woody-Aster** (*Xylorhiza wrightii*, synonym *Aster wrightii*) is a somewhat sticky-hairy plant with oblong or spatula-shaped leaves which are entire or nearly so. The heads are very large, about an inch broad exclusive of the 30 or 40 purple rays, which are themselves about ¾ inch long.

■ **False Willow** (*Baccharis*)—Smooth and somewhat resinous shrubs with alternate leaves and heads of imperfect, whitish flowers, the pistillate and staminate flowers on separate plants. The corollas of the pistillate flowers are very slender and threadlike, those of the staminate larger and 5-lobed. The pappus is composed of hairlike bristles, scanty in the staminate flowers, more abundant in the pistillate.

Five species occur in the Park; four are described below: ☙ **Mule's-Fat** (*Baccharis salicifolia*) grows 4 to 12 feet high and has stems that are

MULE'S-FAT
(*Baccharis salicifolia*)

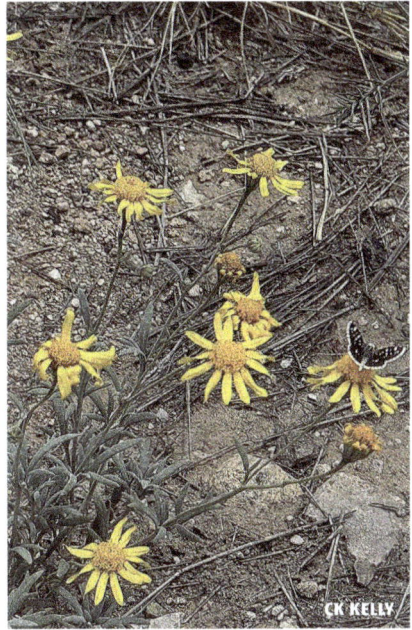

HAIRYSEED BAHIA
(*Picradeniopsis absinthifolia*)

herbaceous above but woody toward the base. The leaves are long and lance-shaped and usually have a few teeth on each side. The heads are rather small but numerous and have yellowish involucres.

Havard's False Willow (*Baccharis havardii*) has slender but much-branched stems; the upper leaves are narrowly linear and entire or nearly so, while the lower ones are somewhat broader and variously cut and lobed.

Yerba-de-Pasmo (*Baccharis pteronioides*) may be distinguished from other species by its very small, linear leaves crowded into clusters.

Great Plains False Willow (*Baccharis salicina*) grows 3 to 15 feet high and has smooth, green, angled branches and oblong or lance-shaped leaves 1 to 2 inches long and either toothed or entire. The heads are in small clusters.

■ Bahia (former *Bahia*)—Mostly herbs with alternate or opposite leaves and small or middle-sized heads of yellow flowers, both disk and ray. The receptacle is nearly flat and the fruits are 4-angled. The pappus, when present, consists of several dry scales each with a thickened base which is sometimes extended as a strong midrib. ✈ Hairyseed Bahia (*Picradeniopsis absinthifolia*, synonym *Bahia absinthifolia*) differs from

BLUNTSCALE BAHIA
(*Hymenothrix pedata*)

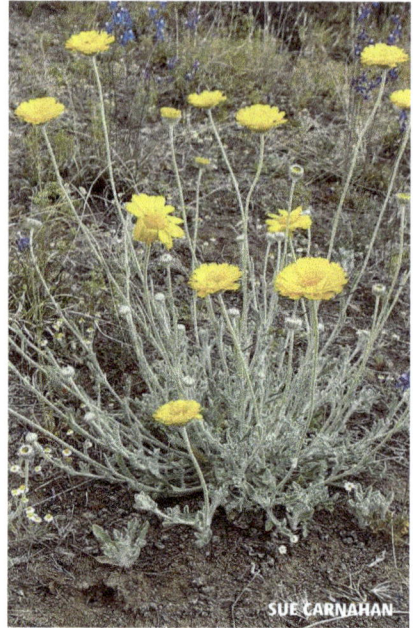

DESERT-MARIGOLD
(*Baileya multiradiata*)

all the others in having opposite leaves 3- to 5-parted into narrow divisions or lobes. The pappus consists of very broad scales, which have a thickened base but no midrib. **Ragleaf Bahia** (*Hymenothrix dissecta*, synonym *Bahia dissecta*) has alternate leaves, heads about ½ inch broad and no pappus. ❧ **Bluntscale Bahia** (*Hymenothrix pedata*, synonym *Bahia pedata*) has alternate leaves, heads about ¼ inch broad, and pappus scales with midribs not reaching the tips of the scales. The leaves are palmately lobed into three main divisions of which the lateral are 2-parted and the middle 3- to 7-lobed.

❧ **Desert-Marigold** (*Baileya multiradiata*)—This is a densely woolly, common herb with alternate, pinnately lobed leaves and heads of yellow flowers, the rays of which become pale and papery with age. The upper leaves are usually small and entire. The large heads are usually more than an inch across.

❧ **Lyre-Leaf Greeneyes** (*Berlandiera lyrata*)—Low plants, usually less than a foot high, with both stems and leaves more or less whitish with very fine, white hairs. Leaves variously lobed or toothed and often are mostly basal. The 5 to 12 ray flowers are yellow, and there is no pappus. The medium-sized heads are borne singly at the ends of stems.

LYRE-LEAF GREENEYES
(*Berlandiera lyrata*)

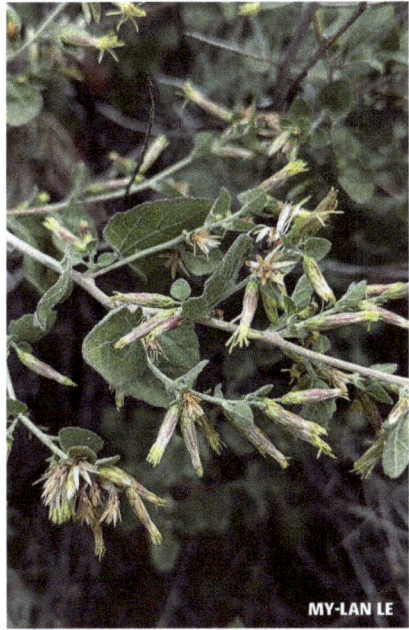

CALIFORNIA BRICKELLBUSH
(*Brickellia californica*)

■ **Beggarticks** (*Bidens*)—Herbs with opposite, pinnately or bipinnately divided leaves, and few- or many-flowered heads. The disk flowers are yellow; the rays are whitish and small, or sometimes lacking. The slender, 4-sided fruits are provided with two to four awns furnished with barbs that cause fruits to cling readily to clothing or to the fur of animals. Two species occur in the Park:

1   Heads cylindric, few-flowered (5-9, rarely 15) . . . .
. . . . **Few-Flower Beggarticks** (*Bidens leptocephala*)
Heads bell-shaped, many-flowered (more than 15) . . . .
. . . . **Bigelow's Beggarticks** (*Bidens bigelovii*)

■ **Brickellbush** (*Brickellia*)—Shrubs with veiny, resinous-dotted leaves and whitish flowers in narrow heads with no rays. The receptacle is naked, the fruits are 10-nerved or ribbed, and the pappus usually consists of a single series or rough or somewhat feathery bristles. Species occurring in the Park can be distinguished most readily by their leaves. ⤴ **California Brickellbush** (*Brickellia californica*) has triangular-ovate leaves varying from ½ to 1½ inches long and rather coarsely toothed with blunt, rounded teeth. **Gravelbar Brickellbush** (*Brickellia cylin-*

CARLOS MARTÍNEZ

ALINA MARTIN

PLUMEWEED
(*Carminatia tenuiflora*)

BIGELOW'S BRISTLEHEAD
(*Carphochaete bigelovii*)

dracea) has oblong to lanceolate leaves 1 to 2 inches long and blunt-toothed. Split-Leaf Brickellbush (*Brickellia laciniata*) has rather small, thin leaves, which are ovate to oblong and rather deeply cut into sharp teeth or lobes. Speedwell Brickellbush (*Brickellia veronicifolia*) has small, ovate or rounded leaves, which are usually less than ½ inch long and entire or with very small teeth.

➳ Plumeweed (*Carminatia tenuiflora*)—An annual, somewhat hairy plant with opposite or partly alternate, thin, veiny, long-petioled leaves, which are triangular-ovate, about as broad as long, and blunt-toothed. The heads contain whitish disk flowers only, and the pappus consists of 10 to 18 bristles, which are feathery with long, cobwebby hairs.

➳ Bigelow's Bristlehead (*Carphochaete bigelovii*)—A shrubby plant with opposite, sessile, entire leaves and clusters of 4- to 6-flowered heads with disk flowers only. The flowers are rose-colored, as is also the involucre, and the pappus consists of several long, sharp-pointed scales and one or more small, pointless ones. The lower leaves are oblong, about 1 inch long, and have clusters of smaller ones in the axils. The upper leaves are smaller and vary from oblong to linear.

CYNTHIA ROUSH

BOB NIEMAN

SILVERPUFF
(*Chaptalia texana*)

DAMIANITA
(*Chrysactinia mexicana*)

↣ **Silverpuff** (*Chaptalia texana*)—A low, woolly-hairy plant with a cluster of basal, oblong leaves, green above and white beneath, and a naked stem bearing a solitary head of white or purplish ray and disk flowers. The pappus consists of abundant, soft, hairlike bristles, and the fruits have slender beaks as long as the body.

↣ **Damianita** (*Chrysactinia mexicana*)—A low, much-branched, very leafy shrub with thick or almost cylindrical, short, linear, entire leaves and heads of golden-yellow flowers, both ray and disk. The pappus consists of abundant rough, hairlike bristles, and the fruits are shorter than the pappus. The involucre consists of 10 or more short, distinct bracts, and usually each one bears a large and prominent oil gland just below the tip.

Wavy-Leaf Thistle (*Cirsium undulatum*)—A very prickly plant, the leaves and involucre being armed with long prickles, with large heads of reddish-purple flowers. This plant is fairly common in some of the canyons of the Chisos Mountains. Several other thistle species occur in the Park.

↣ **Southwestern Cosmos** (*Cosmos parviflorus*)—This plant is not common in the Park but has been found along streams in canyons of

SUE CARNAHAN

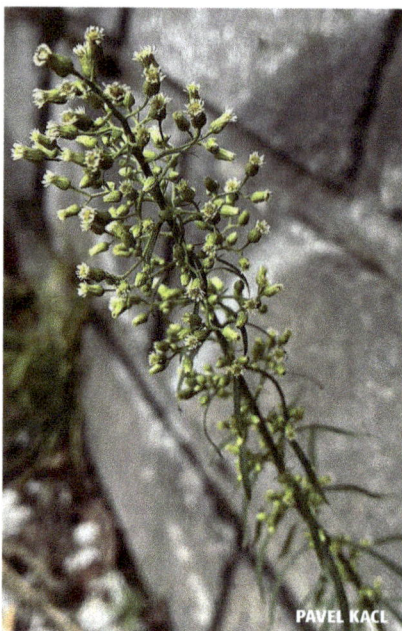
PAVEL KACL

SOUTHWESTERN COSMOS
(*Cosmos parviflorus*)

HORSEWEED
(*Erigeron canadensis*)

the Chisos Mountains. In general appearance it is very similar to beggarticks (*Bidens*) except that the ray flowers are white or rose instead of yellow.

Yerba-de-Tajo (*Eclipta prostrata*)—A low annual with weak, partly trailing stems and opposite, lance-shaped or oblong leaves. The flowers are white, both disk and ray, in small, solitary heads. The rays are short; the involucre consists of 10 to 12 green bracts; the receptacle is flat; the fruits are short, 3- or 4-angled and hairy at the tip; there is no pappus.

■ **Fleabane** (*Erigeron*)—Annual or perennial herbs with entire or toothed leaves, mostly sessile, and solitary or clustered heads often quite showy. The disk flowers are yellow, and the ray flowers vary from white to purple. The bracts of the involucre are narrow and of nearly equal length. The pappus consists of hairlike bristles. This is a very large genus, but only a handful of species have been found in the Park including: the introduced ➷ **Horseweed** (*Erigeron canadensis*) has numerous leaves varying from lance-shaped to linear and mostly entire, though the lower ones are sometimes toothed. The heads are small and very numerous, with very short and inconspicuous white rays. This is a common weed in waste places throughout the United States.

SPREADING FLEABANE
(*Erigeron divergens*)

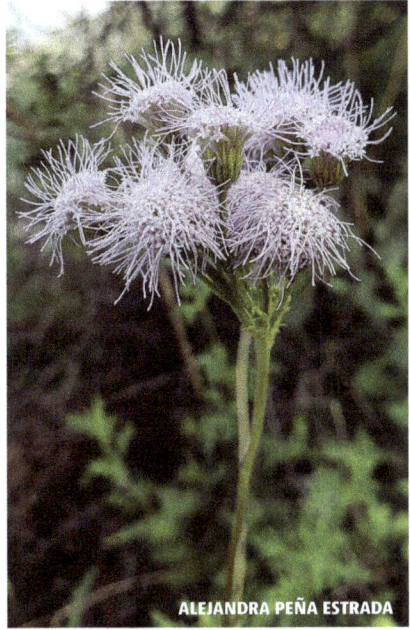

PALMLEAF THROUGHWORT
(*Conoclinium dissectum*)

🌱 Spreading Fleabane (*Erigeron divergens*) is much branched from the base with the basal leaves spatula-shaped and entire or few-lobed and the upper ones linear. The heads are numerous with hairy involucres and bluish-purple or lilac rays. Trailing Fleabane (*Erigeron flagellaris*) is branched from the base and has the lower leaves spatula-shaped, coarsely toothed, and long petioled, while the upper leaves are linear, entire, and sessile. The heads are large, few in number, and have ray flowers that vary from pink to white.

◼ Boneset, Throughwort (former *Eupatorium*)—Erect, perennial herbs or shrubs, the leaves usually opposite but sometimes alternate, the heads of disk flowers only and these white, bluish, or purple. The fruits are 5-angled, and the pappus consists of slender, hairlike bristles. Most species that occur in the Park may be distinguished as follows:

1   Leaves deeply cleft; flowers purple .... 🌱 Palmleaf Throughwort .... (*Conoclinium dissectum*, synonym *Eupatorium greggii*) Leaves entire or merely toothed 2
2   Heads sessile, clustered; leaves lanceolate Shrubby Throughwort .... (*Koanophyllon solidaginifolium*, ... synonym *Eupatorium solidaginifolium*)

MATT BERGER

ERIC KNIGHT

FRAGRANT SNAKEROOT
(*Ageratina herbacea*)

ROTHROCK'S SNAKEROOT
(*Ageratina rothrockii*)

Heads stalked; leaves ovate 3

3   Leaves mostly alternate .... **Chisos Mountain Brickellbush**
.... (*Flyriella parryi*, synonym *Eupatorium parryi*)
Leaves mostly opposite 4

4   Shrubs; leaves mostly less than 1 inch long, obtuse at apex ......
.... **Wright's Snakeroot**
.... (*Ageratina wrightii*, synonym *Eupatorium wrightii*)
Herbs; leaves larger, acute at apex 5

5   Larger leaves heart-shaped at base; corolla lobes without hairs ...
.... ❧ **Fragrant Snakeroot**
.... (*Ageratina herbacea*, synonym *Eupatorium herbaceum*)
Larger leaves acute or obtuse at base; corolla lobes without hairs .
.... ❧ **Rothrock's Snakeroot**
.... (*Ageratina rothrockii*, synonym *Eupatorium rothrockii*)

Clustered Yellowtops (*Flaveria trinervia*)—A low, stout, herbaceous
plant with opposite, lanceolate, 3-nerved, slightly toothed leaves and
dense, sessile clusters of very small 1-flowered heads of yellowish flowers. This plant grows in water or in very wet places.

TARBUSH
(*Flourensia cernua*)

BLANKETFLOWER
(*Gaillardia pinnatifida*)

↗ **Tarbush** (*Flourensia cernua*)—A very leafy and much-branched shrub growing 3 to 7 feet high and bearing clusters of small heads of whitish or yellowish disk flowers. The leaves are alternate, entire, and ovate or oblong. Frequent on the dry, flat areas north of the Chisos Mountains.

↗ **Blanketflower** (*Gaillardia pinnatifida*)—A branched herb, 1 to 2 feet high, with alternate, pinnately lobed leaves, and a solitary large, long-stalked head with purplish disk flowers and yellow ray flowers at the end of each stem. The fruits are densely long-hairy, and the pappus consists of 5 to 10 lance-shaped scales each tipped with an awn.

Gumweed (*Grindelia havardii*)—A fairly stout herb with alternate, oblong, sharply toothed leaves ½ to 2 inches long and medium-sized heads of yellow flowers, both ray and disk, with the involucre somewhat gummy or sticky.

■ **Snakeweed** (*Gutierrezia*)—Herbs or shrubs with narrowly linear, alternate leaves and small heads of yellow flowers, both ray and disk. The fruits are short-cylindrical and 5- to 10-ribbed, and the pappus consists of numerous, chaffy scales, which are shorter than the achenes or

JOHN POWERS

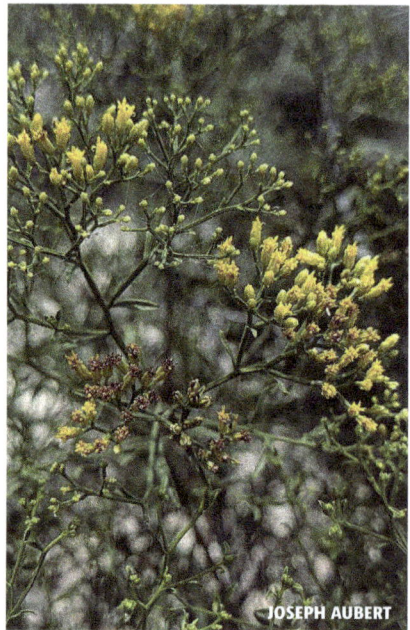

JOSEPH AUBERT

BROOM SNAKEWEED
(*Gutierrezia sarothrae*)

GUMHEAD
(*Gymnosperma glutinosum*)

are sometimes lacking in the ray flowers. The four species occurring in the Park may be distinguished as follows:

1 Plants annual, herbaceous .... Round-Leaf Snakeweed
.... (*Gutierrezia sphaerocephala*)
Plants perennial, more or less shrubby 2
2 Ray flowers 1 or 2 .... Small-Head Snakeweed
.... (*Gutierrezia microcephala*)
Ray flowers 3 to 8. 3
3 Disk flowers 1 or 2 or sometimes 3 ..... Small-Head Snakeweed
.... (*Gutierrezia microcephala*)
Disk flowers 3 to 12 ⤧ Broom Snakeweed (*Gutierrezia sarothrae*)

⤧ Gumhead (*Gymnosperma glutinosum,* synonym *Selloa glutinosa*)—
This is a perennial plant, but the parts above ground are annual. The several stems grow about 4 feet high and bear numerous, narrowly lance-shaped or linear leaves and clusters of small heads of yellow flowers. There are both ray and disk flowers; the rays are no longer than the disk corollas. There is no pappus. The entire plant is covered with a glutinous material.

FALSE BROOMWEED
(*Haploesthes greggii*)

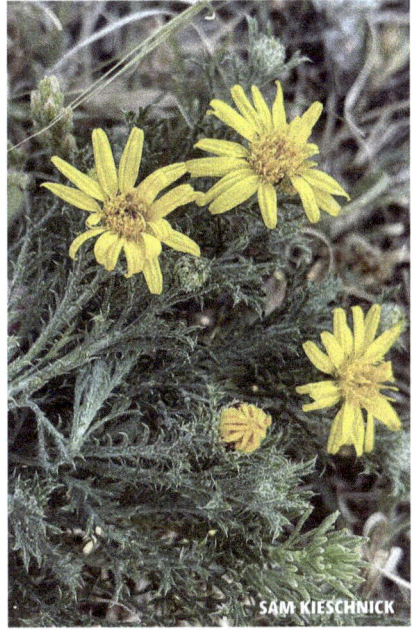

TANSY-ASTER
(*Xanthisma spinulosum*)

⭢ **False Broomweed** (*Haploesthes greggii*)—A somewhat fleshy, herbaceous or shrubby plant with opposite, linear leaves and medium-sized heads with both ray and disk flowers. The flowers are yellow, and the four or five broad bracts that make up the involucre are tinged with yellow. The receptacle is flat and the fruits are slender and smooth. The pappus is composed of rather rigid, rough bristles which are about as long as the corollas of the disk flowers. Usually growing in rather salty soil.

■ Goldenshrub (former *Haplopappus*)—Herbs or shrubs with alternate leaves and yellow flowers in several- or many-flowered heads, either with or without ray flowers. The hemispherical involucre consists of closely overlapping bracts in several series, the receptacle is flat, and the pappus consists of numerous unequal bristles. Three species formerly grouped as *Haplopappus* occur in the Park: ⭢ Tansy-Aster (*Xanthisma spinulosum*, synonym *Haplopappus spinulosus*) is quite variable but is herbaceous and the leaves are more or less toothed or lobed. ⭢ Jimmyweed (*Iscoma pluriflora*, synonym *Haplopappus heterophyllus*) is shrubby and has linear leaves, which may be 1 or 2 inches long. Its

MICHELLE W.

ERIC KNIGHT

JIMMYWEED
(*Iscoma pluriflora*)

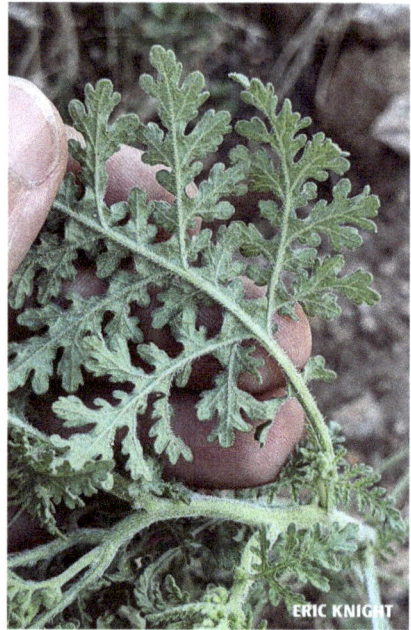

SUMPWEED
(*Hedosyne ambrosiifolia*)

heads have no ray flowers. **Trans-Pecos Desert Goldenrod** (*Gundlachia triantha*, synonym *Haplopappus trianthus*) is a low shrub with very narrow, linear leaves usually not more than ¼ inch long. Its tiny heads are composed of only three or four flowers.

⌇ **Sumpweed** (*Hedosyne ambrosiifolia*, synonym *Iva ambrosiifolia*)— This is a common weed in low places. The leaves are alternate and two or three times pinnately parted into small, oblong lobes somewhat resembling the leaves of a ragweed. All the flowers in the very small, greenish-white heads are disk flowers; they are imperfect, the marginal ones in each head being pistillate and the others staminate. There is no pappus, but the small receptacle bears a few chaffy scales.

▪ **Sneezeweed** (*Helenium*)—Upright, branching herbs with alternate, narrow leaves usually extending down on the angled stems. The branches at terminated by single or clustered heads of yellow or sometimes purple flowers. The ray flowers are wedge-shaped and 3- to 5-cleft. The receptacle is oblong or nearly spherical, and the narrow bracts of the involucre are usually turned downward. The fruits are top-shaped, and the pappus consists of five to eight thin, one-nerved, chaffy scales, the nerve usually extended to form a bristle or tip. The species

SMALL-HEAD SNEEZEWEED
(*Helenium microcephalum*)

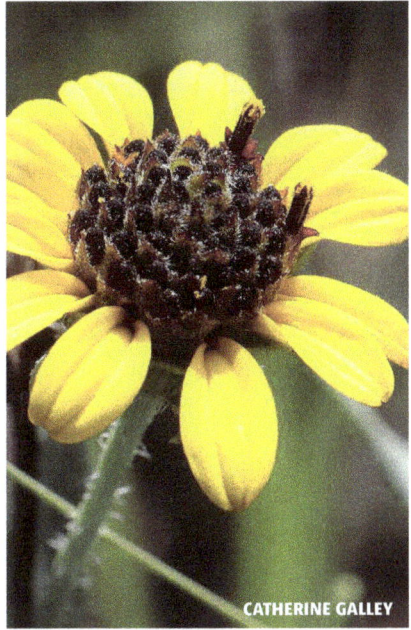

TEXAS-BLUEWEED
(*Helianthus ciliaris*)

occurring in the Park are all much alike in general appearance. Swollen-Stalk Sneezeweed (*Helenium amphibolum*) and Pretty Sneezeweed (*Helenium elegans*) both have purple disks and yellow rays, but in the latter species the bases of the rays are often brownish purple. In both species the pappus scales are very small and shorter than the width of the fruits. ⤷ Small-Head Sneezeweed (*Helenium microcephalum*) has yellow disks and yellow rays, with pappus scales varying from half as long as the fruits to almost as long as the fruits.

■ Sunflower (*Helianthus*)—Coarse herbs with petioled, mostly alternate leaves and rather showy heads. Sometimes the lowermost leaves are opposite and in some species nearly all of them are. The ray flowers are yellow, while the disk flowers, in our species, are dark brown or purple. The receptacle is flat or convex and each of the 4-sided fruits is embraced by a chaffy scale. The pappus consists of pointed scales at the angles of the fruits. Three species have been found in the Park: Common Sunflower (*Helianthus annuus*) is the species from which the large, cultivated sunflower is derived. It is tall and rough. In the wild state the disk is usually an inch or more broad and the rays are about an inch long. Prairie Sunflower (*Helianthus petiolaris*) has the stems

WINGPETAL
(*Heterosperma pinnatum*)

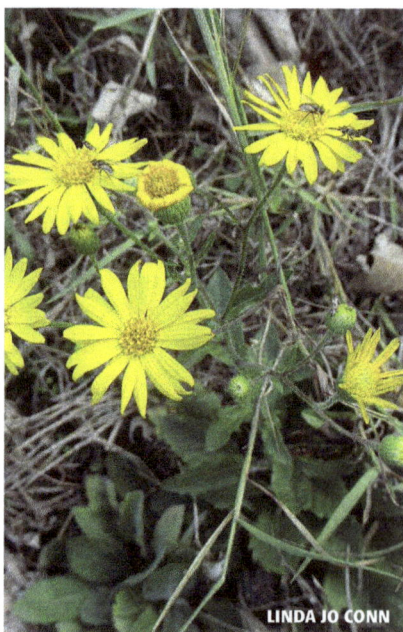

CAMPHORWEED
(*Heterotheca subaxillaris*)

and leaves whitened by white hairs, and the heads are about half as large as those of the preceding species. ❧ **Texas-Blueweed** (*Helianthus ciliaris*) is smooth and nearly all the leaves are opposite, sessile, and lance-shaped. The ray flowers are few and very short.

Mountain Oxeye (*Heliopsis parvifolia*)—A perennial herb, often somewhat woody at the base, with opposite, lance-shaped, toothed leaves, about 1 to 2 inches long, and large showy heads of yellow flowers. The ray flowers are ½ to nearly 1 inch long. The receptacle is conical and chaffy, and the fruits are 4-angled, but there is no pappus.

❧ **Wingpetal** (*Heterosperma pinnatum*)—An annual plant with opposite leaves, which are pinnately parted into a few very narrowly linear divisions, and small heads of yellow ray and disk flowers. The fruits are of two forms, the outer more or less winged and the inner narrow and wingless, but armed with two barbed awns. The involucre consists of 3 to 5 linear, leaflike outer bracts and several oval, thin, inner bracts.

❧ **Camphorweed** (*Heterotheca subaxillaris*)—A tall, hairy, and somewhat sticky plant growing 2 to 5 feet tall. The leaves are lance-shaped or oblong, ½ to 1½ inches long, partly clasping the stem at the

STIFF-LEAF FALSE GOLDEN ASTER
(*Heterotheca stenophylla*)

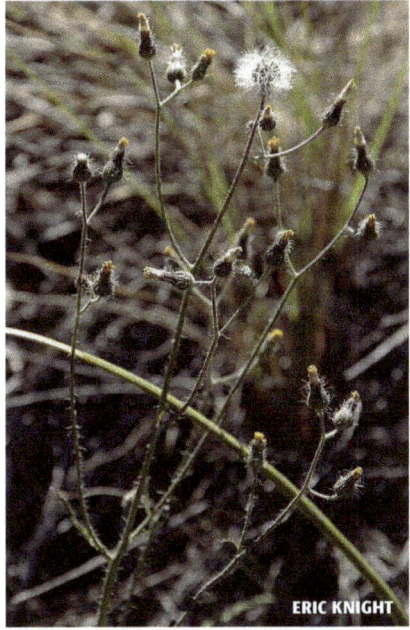

ROUGH-STEM HAWKWEED
(*Hieracium schultzii*)

base, and having a peculiar camphorlike odor when crushed. The heads are medium-sized, and both ray and disk flowers are yellow. The fruits of the ray flowers are more or less triangular and without any pappus, while those of the disk flowers are flattened and have a double pappus, the inner part of long bristles and the outer of short, stout bristles.

■ **False Golden-Aster** (*Heterotheca*, synonym *Chrysopsis*)—Low, perennial, hairy herbs with alternate, oblong, or lance-shaped, entire leaves and rather large heads with both ray and disk flowers yellow. The receptacle is flat; the fruits are flattened and hairy; and the pappus is double, the outer part of very short and somewhat chaffy bristles and the inner of long, hairlike bristles. Four species occur in the Park. They are quite similar in general appearance, but *Heterotheca fulcrata* (synonym *Chrysopsis fulcrata*) has the involucre densely glandular and not densely hairy while ⚹ **Stiff-Leaf False Golden Aster** (*Heterotheca stenophylla*, synonym *Chrysopsis villosa*) has the involucre densely hairy and the glands inconspicuous or none. See also p. 90 for **Camphorweed** (*Heterotheca subaxillaris*).

⚹ **Rough-Stem Hawkweed** (*Hieracium schultzii*, synonym *Hieracium wrightii*)—This is an uncommon herb not likely to be seen by

COULTER'S WOOLWORT
(*Laennecia coulteri*)

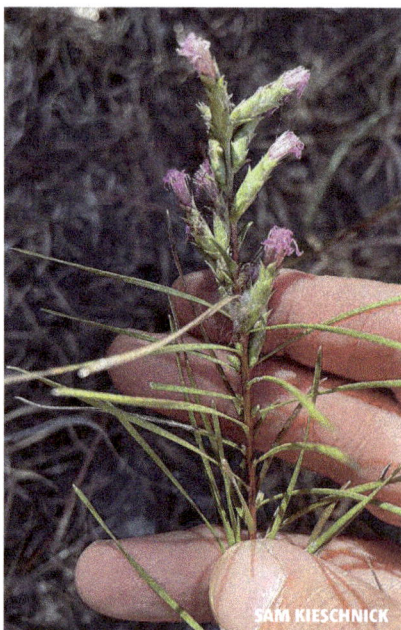

DOTTED GAYFEATHER
(*Liatris punctata*)

most Park visitors. It grows 1 to 2 feet high and is more or less hairy, especially toward the base. The basal leaves are petioled and may be as much as 8 inches long. Those on the stem are smaller and sessile, the upper ones being reduced to mere scales. The heads are medium-sized; all the flowers are yellow and have strap-shaped corollas.

Short-Leaf Jefea (*Jefea brevifolia*)—A much-branched, shrubby plant with ovate or oval leaves, which are less than 1 inch long and short-petioled. The medium-sized heads are solitary at the ends of the branches; both ray and disk flowers are yellow.

■ Woolwort (*Laennecia*, synonym *Conyza*)—Annual herbs with alternate leaves and rather small heads of dull white or yellowish flowers in a dense cluster. There are no ray flowers, but the two or more outer circles of flowers in the head are somewhat irregular and have a pistil but no stamens, while the central flowers are perfect. The fruits are small and the pappus consists of a single series of bristles. ➷ Coulter's Woolwort (*Laennecia coulteri*, synonym *Conyza coulteri*) has oblong or lance-shaped, coarsely toothed leaves 1 to 2 inches long, while Cut-Leaf Woolwort (*Laennecia sophiifolia*, synonym *Conyza sophiifolia*) has

BAILEY'S RABBITBRUSH
(*Lorandersonia baileyi*)

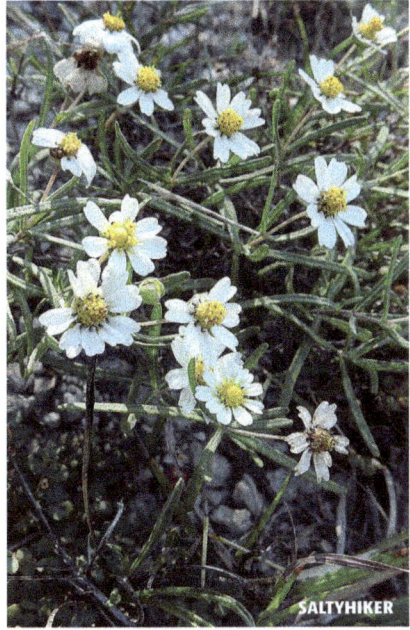

PLAINS BLACKFOOT
(*Melampodium leucanthum*)

small leaves about ¼ inch long and deeply cut into numerous narrow divisions.

⫷ Dotted Gayfeather (*Liatris punctata*)—A stout plant growing 8 to 30 inches high with alternate, linear leaves varying from 1 to 4 inches long, and a spike of purple heads occupying the upper third of the stem. The bracts of the involucre, the corollas, and the stigmas, which extend beyond the corollas, are all rose-purple, and, since the heads are ½ to 1 inch long, the plant is very attractive when in bloom. Each head contains four to six disk flowers but no ray flowers; and the pappus is composed of very feathery, hairlike bristles.

⫷ Bailey's Rabbitbrush (*Lorandersonia baileyi*, synonym *Chrysothamnus baileyi*)—A densely branched shrub, 1 to 2 feet high, with smooth branches, linear leaves and small heads of yellow disk flowers. The fruits are slender and hairy, and the pappus consists of an abundance of soft, hairlike bristles.

⫷ Plains Blackfoot (*Melampodium leucanthum*)—A low perennial, sometimes slightly shrubby at the base, growing from a few inches to a foot high, with opposite leaves that vary from linear to lance-shaped,

EDWARDS' HOLE-IN-THE-SAND PLANT
(*Nicolletia edwardsii*)

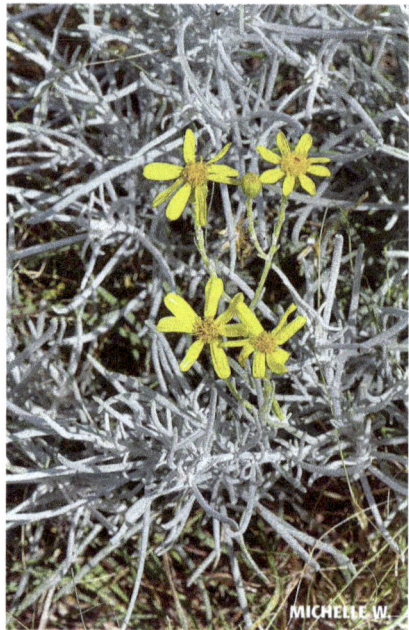

THREAD-LEAF RAGWORT
(*Senecio flaccidus*)

from entire to blunt-toothed or lobed, and from ½ to 2 inches in length. The heads are medium-sized with yellowish disk flowers and conspicuous, white ray flowers.

↗ **Edwards' Hole-in-the-Sand Plant** (*Nicolletia edwardsii*)—This is a low annual plant growing only a few inches high with leaves pinnately divided into a few very narrowly linear lobes. The heads are large in proportion to the size of the plant, with yellowish disk flowers and flesh-colored or purplish ray flowers. The pappus is double, the outer part of numerous hairlike bristles and the inner part of five lance-shaped, very thin scales with the midrib extended to form a rough awn.

■ **Groundsel, Ragwort** (*Packera, Senecio*)—Herbs or shrubs with alternate leaves and many-flowered heads with both ray and disk flowers yellow. The involucre is cylindrical to bell-shaped and consists of one or two rows of nearly equal bracts, sometimes with a few little bracts at the base. The fruits are cylindrical and the pappus consists of numerous soft, white bristles. The several species that occur in the Park can readily be distinguished by their leaves. ↗ **Thread-Leaf Ragwort** (*Senecio flaccidus*, synonym *Senecio longilobus*) is gray and shrubby and

SMALL PALAFOX
(*Palafoxia callosa*)

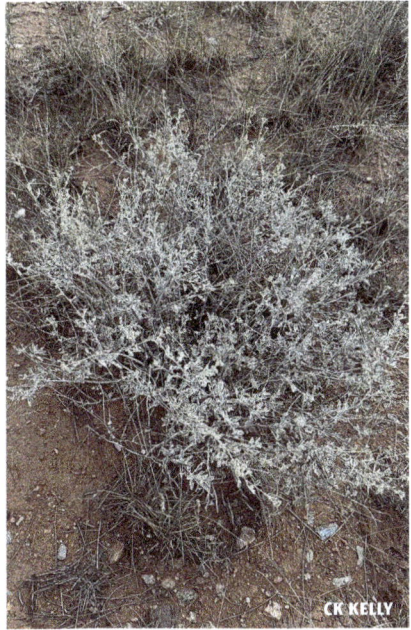

MARIOLA
(*Parthenium incanum*)

the leaves are pinnately parted into a few long, linear, entire lobes. Uinta Groundsel (*Packera millelobata*, synonym *Senecio millelobatus*) is a green herb with leaves pinnately divided into rather short, toothed lobes. Mountain Ragwort (*Senecio parryi*) has rather large, broad leaves which are toothed but not lobed, except sometimes at the base, and which have their bases clasping the stem. The whole plant is glandular.

➤ Small Palafox (*Palafoxia callosa*)—A short-hairy plant, a foot or more high, with alternate, linear leaves 1 to 2 inches long and medium-sized heads of purple disk flowers with corollas ½ inch or more long, but no ray flowers. The pappus consists of six to eight scales.

■ Feverfew (*Parthenium*)—Herbs or shrubs with alternate, pinnately lobed leaves and clusters of small heads of whitish flowers. There are five ray flowers with short, inconspicuous corollas and several disk flowers in each head, but only the ray flowers produce fruits. This is the genus to which Guayule (*Parthenium argentatum*), the Mexican rubber plant, belongs, and this species is reported as occurring in the Park, but it probably is not present in any abundance. Two other species in Big Bend are ➤ Mariola (*Parthenium incanum*), a shrub growing 1 to 3 feet

GRAY'S FEVERFEW
(*Parthenium confertum*)

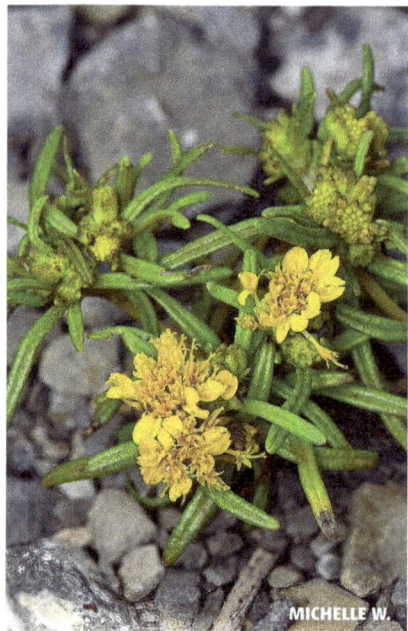

LEMONSCENT
(*Pectis angustifolia*)

high, much-branched, with both stems and leaves whitened by very short, fine, white hairs; and ⚘ Gray's Feverfew (*Parthenium confertum*), an herb with green stems and leaves, somewhat hairy with short, white hairs.

■ Lemonscent (*Pectis*)—Low, branching, heavily scented herbs with opposite, narrow leaves conspicuously dotted with oil glands. Some species are distinctly lemon-scented. The heads are small or medium-sized but often quite conspicuous. Both ray and disk flowers are yellow. Four species that occur in the Park may be distinguished as follows:

1   Plants mostly prostrate or creeping; pappus of a few short-awned scales; bracts of involucre 5 ....Spreading Chinchweed
....(*Pectis prostrata*)
Plants upright **2**
2   Heads in dense clusters and nearly sessile; bracts of involucre 7 to 10 ....⚘ Lemonscent (*Pectis angustifolia*)
Heads scattered and stalked **3**
3   Bracts of involucre 5; pappus usually of 2 or 3 rigid awns with thickened bases, or lacking ....Five-Bract Chinchweed (*Pectis filipes*)

MOUNTAIN LEAFTAIL
(*Pericome caudata*)

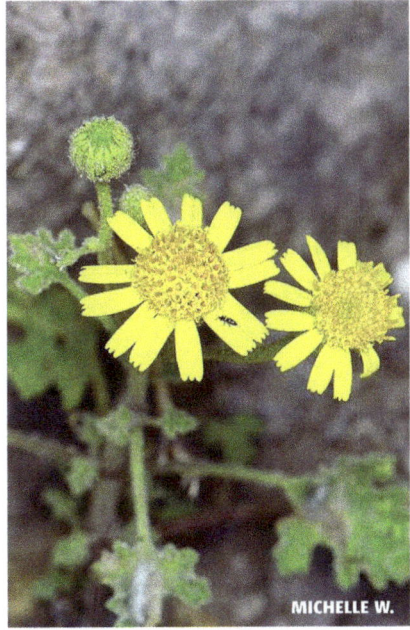

VASEY'S ROCK DAISY
(*Perityle vaseyi*)

Bracts of involucre 7 to 9; pappus of disk flowers consisting of 12 to 18 bristles .... **Many-Bristle Chinchweed** (*Pectis papposa*)

❧ **Mountain Leaftail** (*Pericome caudata*)—A tall, much-branched herb with opposite, petioled, triangular, long-pointed leaves and small or medium-sized heads of yellow disk flowers in terminal clusters. The involucre consists of a single row of numerous narrow bracts, which are lightly connected at their edges to form a cup. The pappus is a short crown, sometimes with two short awns.

■ **Rock Daisy** (*Perityle,* synonym *Laphamia*)—Annual herbs with toothed or lobed leaves, the lower ones opposite and the upper ones alternate and small or medium-sized heads of yellow ray and disk flowers. The bracts of the involucre are narrow and distinct, the fruits are flat, and the pappus is a scaly or cuplike crown, usually with a slender awn from one or both angles. **Parry's Rock Daisy** (*Perityle parryi*) has toothed or only slightly lobed leaves, and the corollas of the disk flowers are slender with long and narrow throat. ❧ **Vasey's Rock Daisy** (*Perityle vaseyi*) has leaves which are divided into three long-stalked, wedge-shaped segments, which are in turn usually 3-lobed. The disk corollas in this species are funnel-shaped.

GUILLERMO DEBANDI

LILIANA RAMÍREZ-FREIRE

MANY-FLOWER FALSE BAHIA
(*Picradeniopsis multiflora*)

WHITE ROCK-LETTUCE
(*Pinaropappus roseus*)

Leafy Rock Daisy (*Perityle rupestris*, synonym *Laphamia rupestris*)—
This is a little, short-hairy, slightly sticky plant, only a few inches high,
found growing in the crevices of rocks. The leaves are ½ inch or less
long and about as wide, toothed and slender-petioled. There are 12 to
15 yellow disk flowers in each head, but no ray flowers. The pappus consists of about 20 unequal, rigid bristles, which are much longer than the
corolla tubes.

❧ **Many-Flower False Bahia** (*Picradeniopsis multiflora*, synonym
Schkuhria multiflora)—A slender, much-branched annual with alternate
leaves pinnately parted into three to seven vary narrow, hairlike divisions. Sometimes the lower leaves are opposite, and often the uppermost are entire. The plant produces very small heads of only three to
five yellow flowers each. Sometimes one flower is a ray flower, but more
often they are all disk flowers. The involucre consists of four or five erect
bracts. The fruits are densely long-hairy on the angles, and the pappus
consists of eight dry scales.

❧ **White Rock-Lettuce** (*Pinaropappus roseus*)—A deep-rooted
perennial with growth habits similar to those of the common dande-

AMERICAN BASKETFLOWER
(*Plectocephalus americanus*)

ARROW-WEED
(*Pluchea sericea*)

lion. The leaves are mostly basal, though there are often a few on the lower part of the stem, and are narrowly lance-shaped or linear and entire or slightly pinnately lobed. At the end of each stem is a solitary, fairly large head of rose-tinged or nearly white flowers all with strap-shaped corollas. The fruits are slender and smooth but 10- to 15-ribbed and taper upward into a slender beak. The pappus consists of an abundance of soft, dirty-white, hairlike bristles.

➤ American Basketflower (*Plectocephalus americanus*, synonym *Centaurea americana*)—An annual herb with alternate, oblong or lanceolate leaves, which are entire or nearly so. The stem is stout, usually unbranched, 2 to 7 feet high, and somewhat thickened under the single naked head. The enlarged outer flowers are rose-color, while the inner flowers are flesh-color or nearly white, and the head is large, 1 to 2 inches broad, with the numerous bracts of the involucre all provided with conspicuously fringed, dry appendages.

➤ Arrow-Weed (*Pluchea sericea*)—A slender, willowlike shrub, 3 to 8 or more feet high, with numerous entire, lance-shaped, silvery-silky leaves, less than an inch long, and clusters of heads of purplish disk flowers. The outermost flowers of the head have narrow corollas, which are entire or 2- or 3-toothed, while the inner flowers have 5-toothed corollas. Most of the outer flowers are pistillate and produce fruits, while the inner ones are perfect but do not produce fruits. The pappus consists of a single series of hairlike bristles.

■ **Poreleaf** (*Porophyllum*)—Smooth herbs or somewhat shrubby plants with simple leaves and medium-sized heads of purple or yellow disk flowers. The involucre consists of 5 to 10 distinct bracts usually dotted or striped with oil glands. There are no ray flowers; the fruits are linear; and the pappus consists of many hairlike bristles. Two species occur in the Park; they are quite different and readily distinguished: **Large-Head Poreleaf** (*Porophyllum macrocephalum*) is an annual herb with petioled, oblong or nearly round, rounded-toothed leaves and heads about an inch high with purplish flowers and an involucre of five bracts. ❧ **Trans-Pecos Poreleaf** (*Porophyllum scoparium*) is a shrubby plant with green, rushlike branches, very narrowly linear, entire leaves, and heads about ½ inch high with yellow flowers and an involucre of seven to nine bracts.

❧ **Mock Turtleback** (*Psathyrotopsis scaposa*)—A low somewhat hairy annual herb with the ovate or roundish, nearly entire leaves all at or near the base and several naked stems each bearing three to seven small heads of yellow disk flowers. The fruits are hairy, and the pappus, which consists of reddish bristles, is about half as long as the corollas.

■ **Cudweed, Rabbit-Tobacco** (*Pseudognaphalium*)—Woolly herbs with alternate, entire, sessile leaves and white, yellowish, or pink heads in terminal clusters. The innermost flowers in each head have 5-lobed, tubular corollas and are perfect, while the outer flowers are pistillate only and have very narrow, almost hairlike corollas. Three species (of six reported) occurring in the Park may be distinguished as follows:

1   Leaves distinctly green on the upper surface . **Macoun's Cudweed**
     ....(*Pseudognaphalium macounii*)
     Leaves white-hairy or gray-hairy on both sides 2
2   Involucre greenish yellow ....**Cotton Cudweed**
     ....(*Pseudognaphalium stramineum*)
     Involucre pearly white .... ❧ **Wright's Rabbit-Tobacco**
     ....(*Pseudognaphalium canescens*)

❧ **Prairie Coneflower** (*Ratibida columnifera*)—This is a very distinctive herb, easily recognized. It is much-branched and grows 1 to 3 feet

TRANS-PECOS PORELEAF
(*Porophyllum scoparium*)

MOCK TURTLEBACK
(*Psathyrotopsis scaposa*)

WRIGHT'S RABBIT-TOBACCO
(*Pseudognaphalium canescens*)

WOOLLY PAPERFLOWER
(*Psilostrophe tagetina*)

MICHELLE W.

CARMAN LANZONE

PRAIRIE CONEFLOWER
(*Ratibida columnifera*)

THREE-NERVE GOLDENROD
(*Solidago velutina*)

tall with alternate leaves, which are deeply cut into five to nine narrow segments. The heads are large with gray or brown disk flowers and yellow or brownish-purple ray flowers. The receptacle is a cylindrical column 1 to 1½ inches long, and the ray flowers droop back against the flower stalk.

■ **Paperflower** (*Psilostrophe*)—Much-branched, somewhat woolly herbs with alternate, spatula-shaped or linear leaves and small or medium-sized heads of yellow flowers, both ray and disk. The ray corollas are persistent and remain with the fruits. The involucre consists of 4 to 10 woolly bracts; the fruits are narrow and cylindrical; and the pappus consists of 4 to 6 transparent scales. Two species, **Dudweed** (*Psilostrophe gnaphalodes*) and ➤ **Woolly Paperflower** (*Psilostrophe tagetina*), occur in the Park; but they are very similar and difficult to distinguish in the field.

■ **Goldenrod** (*Solidago*)—Perennial herbs with wandlike stems, nearly sessile, alternate leaves, and dense clusters of small heads with both ray and disk flowers yellow. The single pappus consists of equal, hairlike bristles. **Julia's Goldenrod** (*Solidago juliae*) has mostly oblong

SOW-THISTLE
(*Sonchus oleraceus*)

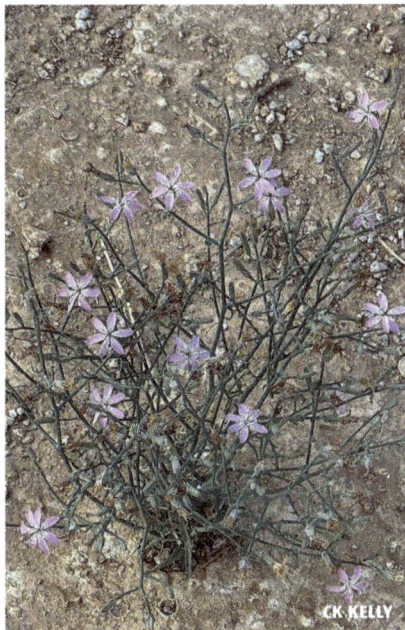

WIRE-LETTUCE
(*Stephanomeria pauciflora*)

leaves, the lower 4 or 5 inches long, an inch or more wide, and toothed, the upper very much smaller and entire. ➤ **Three-Nerve Goldenrod** (*Solidago velutina*) has lance-shaped or elliptical leaves, the widest about ½ inch wide and entire or with a few small, sharp teeth on each side.

➤ **Sow-Thistle** (*Sonchus oleraceus*)—This is a common, exotic weed that was introduced into this country from Europe. It is a stout herb growing 1 to 5 feet tall. The lower leaves are petioled, 4 to 8 inches long, and triangular. The upper leaves are much reduced and sessile. The heads are medium large, and the yellow flowers all have strap-shaped corollas. The pappus consists of numerous fine, soft, white bristles.

➤ **Wire-Lettuce** (*Stephanomeria pauciflora*)—A somewhat shrubby plant, growing about a foot high, with stiff, greenish branches, linear leaves, the lower ones toothed or pinnately lobed, and small heads of pinkish ray flowers. There are no disk flowers. The involucre consists of five narrow bracts; the small fruits are roughened; and the pappus consists of bristles, which are feathery along the upper portions.

SUE CARNAHAN

ERIC KNIGHT

SAW-TOOTH CANDYLEAF
(*Stevia serrata*)

LICORICE MARIGOLD
(*Tagetes micrantha*)

🌿 Saw-Tooth Candyleaf (*Stevia serrata*)—A stout, very leafy herb with narrowly spatula-shaped leaves which may be either alternate or opposite and are usually toothed but sometimes entire. The heads are small but borne in dense clusters. Each head contains three to five white or pale rose-colored disk flowers and no ray flowers. The pappus consists of one to five awns or scales.

🌿 Licorice Marigold (*Tagetes micrantha*)—This plant, not common in the Park, is a small herb with pinnately divided leaves (though the upper leaves may be entire). In either case the leaves or leaf divisions are very narrowly linear. The heads are very small but contain both ray and disk flowers, both yellow or the rays whitish. The pappus consists of two short, blunt scales and two longer awns.

🌿 Stemmed Bitterweed (*Tetraneuris scaposa*)—This plant consists of a rosette of linear, gray leaves and leafless stems 3 to 5 inches high, each topped by a single head of bright yellow flowers.

■ Greenthread (*Thelesperma*)—Perennial, smooth herbs with opposite, usually finely dissected leaves and many-flowered heads on long, naked stalks, the ray flowers yellow or absent and the disk flowers yellow or purple. The involucre is double, the scales of the inner part

MICHELLE W.

MATT BERGER

STEMMED BITTERWEED
(*Tetraneuris scaposa*)

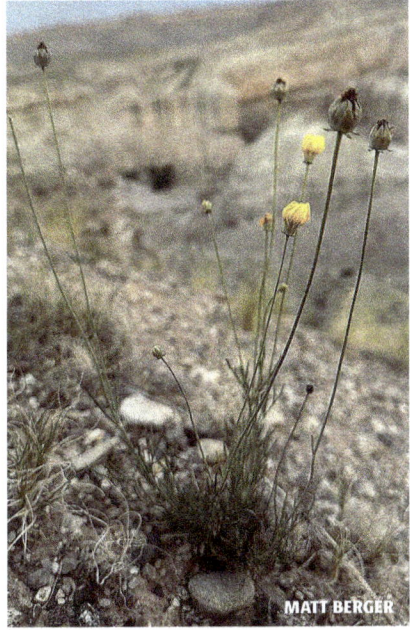

HOPI-TEA
(*Thelesperma megapotamicum*)

grown together part way up and those of the outer part separate. The receptacle is flat and chaffy. The fruits are cylindrical in shape; the pappus consists of two stout, rough awns or is entirely lacking. ❧ **Hopi-Tea** (*Thelesperma megapotamicum*) is leafy well up on the stems; the disk is yellow or purple; the outer involucre consists of four to six bracts; and ray flowers are usually present (sometimes absent) and to nearly ½ inch long. **Long-Stalk Greenthread** (*Thelesperma longipes*) is very leafy only near the woody base and the long, naked flower stalks may be 5 to 10 inches long. The heads are small and ray flowers are lacking. The pappus is also lacking, and the outer involucre is short and small. Several other species are reported from the Park.

■ **Pricklyleaf, Dogweed** (*Thymophylla*, synonym *Dyssodia*)—Annual or perennial herbs with opposite or alternate, pinnately parted leaves and small heads of yellow flowers. The bracts of the involucre are united into a cup; the receptacle is naked; the fruits are slender; and the pappus consists of several or many scales. **Many-Awn Pricklyleaf** (*Thymophylla aurea*, synonym *Dyssodia aurea*) is an annual with the divisions of the leaves linear and not rigid and with the pappus consisting of five to eight unawned scales. *Thymophylla aurea* var. *polychaeta* (syn-

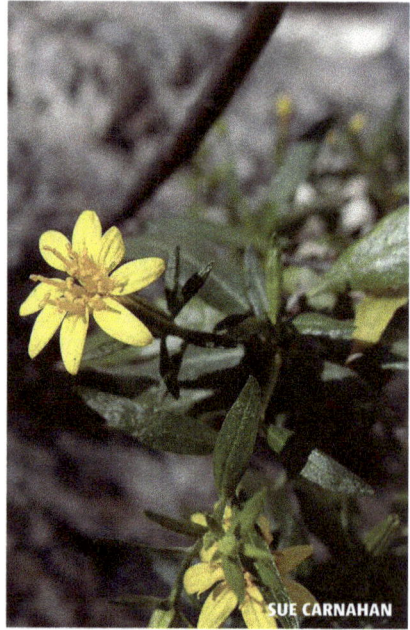

COMMON DOGWEED
(*Thymophylla pentachaeta*)

AMERICAN THREEFOLD
(*Trixis californica*)

onym *Dyssodia polychaeta*) is similar, but the pappus consists of 18 to 20 awned scales. ➢ **Common Dogweed** (*Thymophylla pentachaeta*, synonym *Dyssodia pentachaeta*) is perennial and has the divisions of the leaves hairlike and rigid, and the pappus is in two series of scales, the inner awned and the outer not awned.

➢ **American Threefold** (*Trixis californica*)—A low shrub growing from 8 inches to 2 or more feet in height with alternate, lanceolate, entire or small-toothed leaves and medium-sized, terminal heads of yellow disk flowers with 2-lipped corollas, the inner lip deeply 2-lobed and the outer 3-toothed.

■ **Crownbeard** (*Verbesina*)—Erect, branching herbs with ovate or lance-shaped, toothed leaves and medium-sized heads of bright yellow ray and disk flowers. The receptacle is somewhat cone-shaped and chaffy, the chaff scales being concave and folded about the outer edges of the fruits. The fruits are flattened and winged on each edge, each wing extended to form an awn. Two species occur in the Park: ➢ **Golden Crownbeard** (*Verbesina encelioides*), sometimes called yellowtop, has the leaves green on the upper side but gray from whitish hairs beneath.

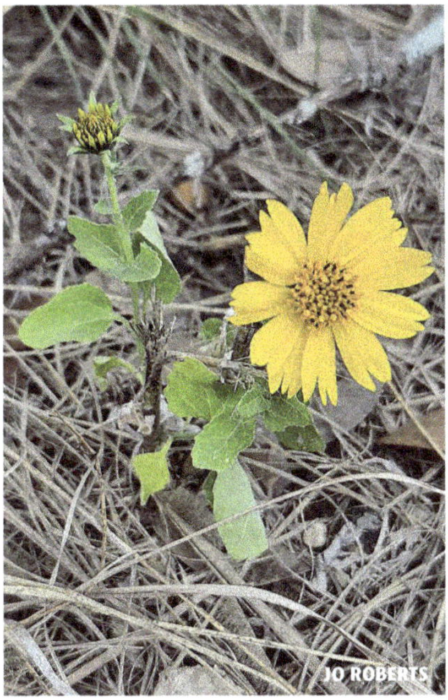

GOLDEN CROWNBEARD
(*Verbesina encelioides*)

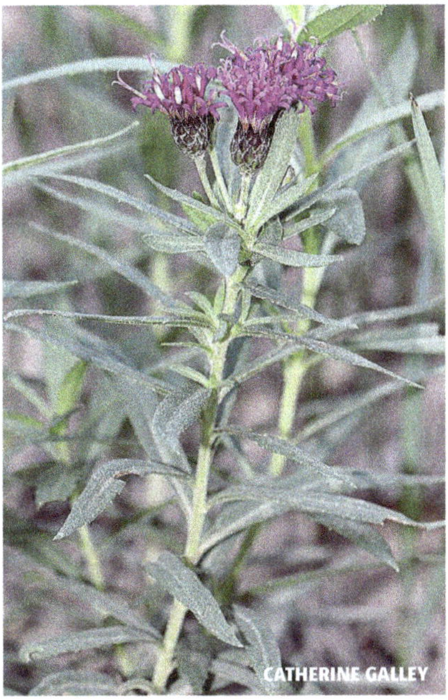

PLAINS IRONWEED
(*Vernonia marginata*)

Mountain Crownbeard (*Verbesina oreophila*) has the leaves short-hairy but green on both sides.

Plains Ironweed (*Vernonia marginata*)—A stout herb growing 1 to 3 feet tall with numerous leaves, which are linear or nearly so, 2 to 6 inches long, and at least the lower ones toothed. The heads of disk flowers clustered at the top of the plant are medium-sized, and both the flowers and the involucre are purple. The very abundant pappus is composed of straw-colored or purple-tinged bristles.

■ **Goldeneye** (*Viguiera*, others)—Herbs or shrubs usually with the lower leaves opposite and the upper alternate, though sometimes all are opposite. The heads are medium-sized; both ray and disk flowers are yellow. The receptacle is convex or cone-shaped and chaffy, the chaff embracing the fruits which usually are hairy. The pappus, when present, consists of two chaffy scales, one at each angle of the fruit, and two or more scales on each side. Four species are found in the Park:

1 Plants, shrubby; leaves pinnately lobed, the lobes linear. . . . . **Resinbush** (*Sidneya tenuifolia*, synonym *Viguiera stenoloba*)
Plants herbaceous 2

ELLIOTT GORDON

CR KELLY

TOOTH-LEAF GOLDENEYE
(*Viguiera dentata*)

WHITE ZINNIA
(*Zinnia acerosa*)

2   Pappus lacking, leaves very narrowly linear, entire. . . . . **Long-Leaf False Goldeneye** (*Heliomeris longifolia*, synonym *Viguiera longifolia*)
     Pappus present; leaves broad and usually toothed 3
3   Leaves sessile or nearly so. . . . . **Heart-Leaf False Goldeneye**
     . . . . (*Aldama cordifolia*, synonym *Viguiera cordifolia*)
     Leaves slender-petioled . . . . ⚹ **Tooth-Leaf Goldeneye**
     . . . . (*Viguiera dentata*)

White Zinnia (*Zinnia acerosa*)—A low, shrubby, much-branched plant, usually about 4 to 6 inches high, with very narrowly linear, 1-nerved leaves ½ inch or less long, and very showy heads borne singly at the ends of branches with yellow disk flowers and pale yellow ray flowers which become white with age.

BARBERRY FAMILY (BERBERIDACEAE)

A small family of woody plants. The Japanese barberry is a valuable ornamental shrub, while the **American Barberry** (*Berberis canadensis*) has been condemned by the Government in all the wheat-growing

AGARITA
(*Alloberberis trifoliolata*)

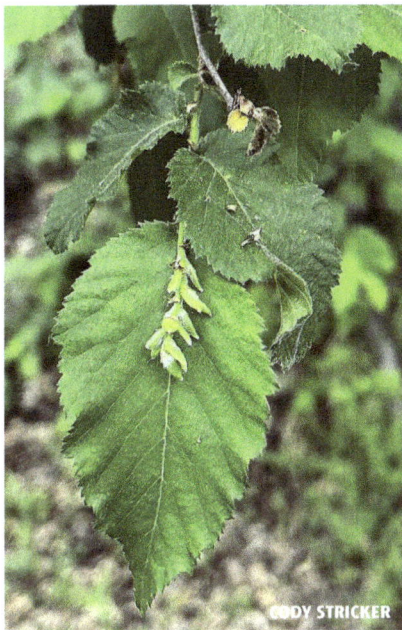

BIG BEND HOP-HORNBEAM
(*Ostrya chisosensis*)

states because it harbors the destructive wheat-rust fungus. A single genus occurs in the Park:

■ **False Oregon-Grape** (*Alloberberis*, synonyms *Berberis, Mahonia*)—Shrubs with spiny-toothed leaves, small, yellow flowers, and bright red berries, which are edible and are often used for making jellies. The plants are very ornamental when loaded with the red fruits. **Red False Oregon-Grape** (*Alloberberis haematocarpa*) has pinnately compound leaves with mostly five or seven leaflets and occurs in canyons and in the Laguna. ➤ **Agarita** (*Alloberberis trifoliolata*) has leaves with only three leaflets and occurs most frequently along arroyos and washes near the mountains.

BIRCH FAMILY (BETULACEAE)

A small family of trees and shrubs with alternate, toothed leaves and w ith staminate flowers in long, slender catkins and pistillate flowers in shorter, spikelike catkins. The edible hazelnuts and filberts belong to this family. The family is represented in the Park only by the ➤ **Big Bend Hop-Hornbean** (*Ostrya chisosensis*), which is a small tree with

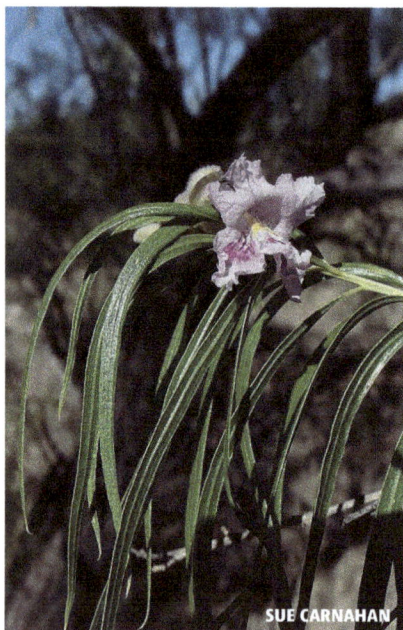

SUE CARNAHAN

DESERT WILLOW
(*Chilopsis linearis*)

ANDREA VILLARREAL RODRÍGUEZ

YELLOW TRUMPETBUSH
(*Tecoma stans*)

oval or ovate leaves 1 to 2 inches long with very fine teeth all along the margins. This uncommon tree is found only in the Chisos Mountains and adjacent northern Chihuahua, Mexico.

TRUMPET-CREEPER FAMILY (BIGNONIACEAE)

Trees or shrubs with opposite leaves and large, showy flowers more or less 2-lipped. There are four stamens in two pairs and one style with two stigmas. The fruit is a long pod containing numerous winged seeds.

➤ Desert Willow (*Chilopsis linearis*)—A large shrub usually 6 to 8 feet high, with opposite, linear, entire leaves 4 to 6 inches long and showy flowers with white, pink, or purplish corollas about 1½ inches long. The fruits are 6 to 10 inches long. Growing mostly along washes and arroyos in the desert.

➤ Yellow Trumpetbush (*Tecoma stans*, synonym *Stenolobium incisum*)—A shrub, usually about 3 or 4 feet high, with opposite, pinnate leaves having sharply toothed leaflets and large, showy, bright yellow flowers with corollas up to 2 inches long.

BORAGE FAMILY (BORAGINACEAE)

Mostly rough-hairy herbs or small shrubs with simple, entire, alternate leaves and flowers either solitary or clustered, often in spikes, that tend to be somewhat coiled or one-sided. The flowers usually have a 5-toothed or 5-lobed calyx, which may be somewhat irregular, and a 5-lobed corolla which is regular or nearly so. There are five stamens and one pistil, but sometimes the pistil is lobed and often the ovary is deeply 4-lobed. The fruit is 1- to 4-seeded and often splits up into one to four 1-seeded nutlets.

1 Ovary unlobed or only slightly lobed 2
   Ovary deeply 4-lobed. 3
2 Flowers in terminal heads or axillary . . . . TIQUILIA
   . . . . (see **Scorpion-Bush Family**, Ehretiaceae, p. 159)
   Flowers in scorpioid spikes or racemes . . (see **Heliotrope Family**,
   . . . . Heliotropaceae, p. 188)
3 Fruit burlike; nutlets armed with hooked prickles 4
   Fruit not burlike; nutlets smooth or rough but not armed with hooked prickles 5
4 Fruiting stalks erect . . . . WESTERN STICKSEED
   . . . . (*Lappula occidentalis*, p. 112)
   Fruiting stalks recurved . . . . LIVERMORE STICKSEED
   . . . . (*Hackelia pinetorum*, p. 112)
5 Nutlets attached at the very base GROMWELL (*Lithospermum*, p. 112)
   Nutlets attached on the inner side from the base to or above the middle . . . . CAT'S-EYE (former *Cryptantha*, p. 111)

■ Cat's-Eye (former *Cryptantha*)—Very hairy plants with small, usually white flowers and four or fewer nutlets, which are not armed with prickles. New Mexico Nievitas (*Johnstonella albida*, synonym *Cryptantha albida*) is a low plant which is much branched from the base and has leaves that are less than an inch long. ⌇ Perennial Cat's-Eye (*Oreocarya palmeri*, synonym *Cryptantha coryi*) is a much larger and stouter plant, growing from a few inches to a foot or more high, with few branches and leaves that vary up to 2 inches or more long. Mexican Nievitas (*Johnstonella mexicana*, synonym *Cryptantha mexicana*) is a low and much-branched plant, but its leaves are intermediate in size between those of the two preceding species. Panamint Nievitas (*Johnstonella angustifolia*, synonym *Cryptantha angustifolia*), which occurs

MATT BERGER

WENDY MCCRADY

PERENNIAL CAT'S-EYE
(*Oreocarya palmeri*)

WESTERN STICKSEED
(*Lappula occidentalis*)

quite frequently in the desert scrub areas, is a stout, leafy plant having a great abundance of stiff hairs. The racemes are not bracted and the calyx lobes are very narrow. The plant is usually prostrate or partly so.

Livermore Stickseed (*Hackelia pinetorum*)—This plant somewhat resembles *Lappula occidentalis*, but it is perennial and has bracted flower-stalks which recurve in fruit.

➤ **Western Stickseed** (*Lappula occidentalis*)—An erect, annual plant growing from 6 inches to 2 or 3 feet tall, the larger plants branched above the middle. The plant is somewhat hairy, the hairs being short and ash-colored. The leaves vary from linear to oblong or lance-shaped, the lower ones often more than an inch long, the upper ones shorter. The flowers vary from blue to yellowish and are borne opposite the reduced leaves along the upper parts of the stems. The nutlets are armed with a single row of prickles on the back.

■ **Gromwell** (*Lithospermum*)—Somewhat hairy, perennial herbs with alternate, sessile leaves and flowers in the axils of upper leaves or in leafy spikes. The flowers have tubular corollas, and the fruit consists of four bony, white nutlets attached by the base. ➤ **Many-Flower Gromwell** (*Lithospermum multiflorum*) has orange flowers with corolla

ERIC KNIGHT

MARTIN PURDY

MANY-FLOWER GROMWELL
(*Lithospermum multiflorum*)

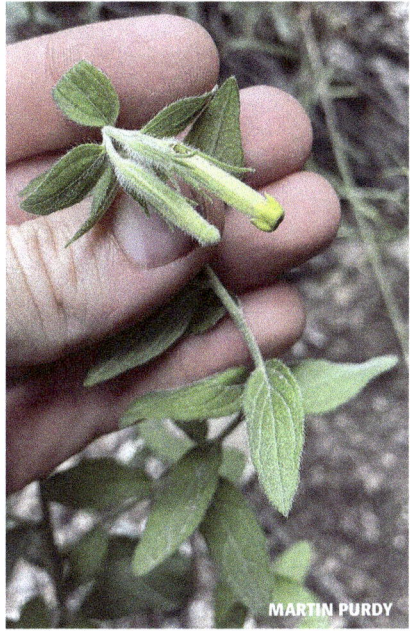

GREEN GROMWELL
(*Lithospermum viride*)

tubes about ½ inch long, while ⤳ Green Gromwell (*Lithospermum viride*) has dull-green flowers with corolla tubes about 1 inch long. Fringed Gromwell (*Lithospermum incisum*) has also been found in the Park.

MUSTARD FAMILY (BRASSICACEAE)

The members of the Mustard Family can usually be recognized by the flowers and fruits. The flowers usually have four sepals, four petals arranged in the form of a cross, six stamens, two of them shorter than the other four, and one pistil. The fruit is a pod, which may be long or short, round or flat, but at maturity, in most cases, the two sides fall away from a central partition. The seeds are attached on both sides of the partition. The family contains a number of valuable edible plants, such as cabbage, cauliflower, turnip, radish, and cress. It also contains a number of rather troublesome weeds. It is usually necessary to have mature fruits as well as flowers in order to distinguish the various members of the family. The members of the family found in the Park may be distinguished as follows:

1 Pods 2-seeded, roundish, notched at the apex; petals white, minute or sometimes lacking .... PEPPERWORT (*Lepidium*, p. 116)

   Pods with more than 2 seeds 2

2 Pods hairy 3

   Pods smooth 7

3 Pods less than twice as long as wide, deeply notched at apex .... GREGG'S KEELPOD (*Synthlipsis greggii*, p. 119)

   Pod 4 or more times as long as wide 4

4 Flowers deep yellow .... SAND-DUNE WALLFLOWER .... (*Erysimum capitatum*, p. 115)

   Flowers white or rose 5

5 Leaves basal or nearly so, the inflorescence long-stalked .... WEDGE-LEAF STONECRESS (*Tomostima cuneifolia*, p. 119)

   Leaves borne throughout the length of the stem 6

6 Pods widely spreading, tipped by the elongate style .... BICOLORED FAN-MUSTARD (*Nerisyrenia camporum*, p. 117)

   Pods erect, the style very short or wanting .... MOUNTAIN CROSS .... (*Pennellia micrantha*, p. 117)

7 Pods inflated or nearly spherical BLADDERPOD (*Physaria*, p. 117)

   Pods not inflated or spherical............................. 8

8 Flowers yellow 9

   Flowers white or purple 11

9 Plants stemless; flowers large .... TEXAS SELENIA .... (*Selenia dissecta*, p. 118)

   Plants with stems; flowers small 10

10 Leaves once-lobed; hairs few, unbranched.... ROCKET-MUSTARD .... (*Sisymbrium irio*, p. 118)

   Leaves twice or three times lobed; hairs numerous, minute, branched .... TANSY-MUSTARD (*Descurainia*, p. 115)

11 Stem leaves with broad, clasping bases.......... JEWELFLOWER .... (*Streptanthus*, p. 118)

   Stem leaves narrowed at base, not clasping 12

12 Stem leaves stalked, pinnately compound .... LARGE-SEED BITTERCRESS (*Cardamine macrocarpa*, p. 115)

   Stem leaves not stalked, entire or merely toothed or lobed 13

13 Flowers white; leaves green... THELYPODY (*Thelypodium*, p. 119)

   Flowers purple; flowers with a whitish, waxy covering .... SLIM-LEAF PLAINS-MUSTARD (*Hesperidanthus linearifolius*, p. 116)

SUE CARNAHAN

WESTERN TANSY-MUSTARD
(*Descurainia pinnata*)

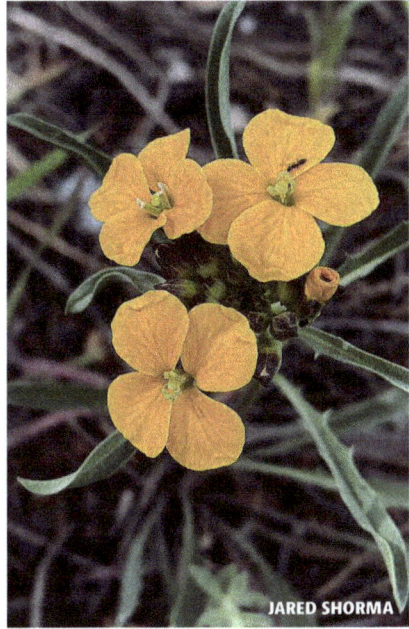

JARED SHORMA

SAND-DUNE WALLFLOWER
(*Erysimum capitatum*)

Large-Seed Bittercress (*Cardamine macrocarpa*)—An erect, leafy herb with pinnately compound leaves and whitish flowers. The pods are flattened but narrow and long and many-seeded, with one row of seeds on each side of the partition. This species has been found in the Chisos Mountains; it is not known to occur elsewhere in the United States, although it occurs farther south in Mexico.

■ **Tansy-Mustard** (*Descurainia*)—The tansy mustards are herbs that are more or less hairy with short, branched hairs. The leaves are usually very much lobed and the flowers are yellow or yellowish. **Cut-Leaf Tansy-Mustard** (*Descurainia incisa*) has ash-colored hairs and pinnately lobed leaves, the upper once and the lower twice pinnately lobed, most commonly found in the coniferous forest area of the Chisos Mountains. The pods have one row of seeds on each side of the partition. ⤳ **Western Tansy-Mustard** (*Descurainia pinnata*) is white-hairy and has twice pinnately lobed leaves. The pods have two rows of seeds on each side of the partition.

⤳ **Sand-Dune Wallflower** (*Erysimum capitatum*)—This is a low, stout plant with persistent basal leaves that are somewhat hairy with

ALINA MARTIN

STEVE MATSON

SLIM-LEAF PLAINS-MUSTARD	HAIRY-POD PEPPERWORT
(*Hesperidanthus linearifolius*)	(*Lepidium lasiocarpum*)

harsh, branched hairs attached at the middle, and yellow or orange flowers in long, terminal clusters. This plant has been found on somewhat moist, open slopes in the Chisos Mountains.

✔ Slim-Leaf Plains-Mustard (*Hesperidanthus linearifolius*)—A slender, smooth perennial with purple flowers and slender, cylindrical, short-stalked pods. The leaves are whitened by a waxy coating that can be rubbed off. Those on the stem are entire, while the basal ones are toothed. This species occurs in several places in the Chisos Mountains.

■ Pepperwort (*Lepidium*)—Low plants with toothed or pinnately lobed leaves. The flowers are small, usually white or greenish, and are borne in dense, many-flowered racemes; the pods are round or elliptic, flattened, and usually toothed or notched at the apex. Southern Pepperwort (*Lepidium austrinum*) is a small, annual plant that is finely hairy all over. The leaves are more or less spatulate and not much toothed or lobed. The petals of the flowers are small or sometimes lacking. ✔ Hairy-Pod Pepperwort (*Lepidium lasiocarpum*) is a much branched and spreading annual plant, very minutely hairy with very short, spreading hairs, and has very much cut and toothed leaves. Petals are usually lacking. Mesa Pepperwort (*Lepidium alyssoides*), a woody-

MICHELLE W.

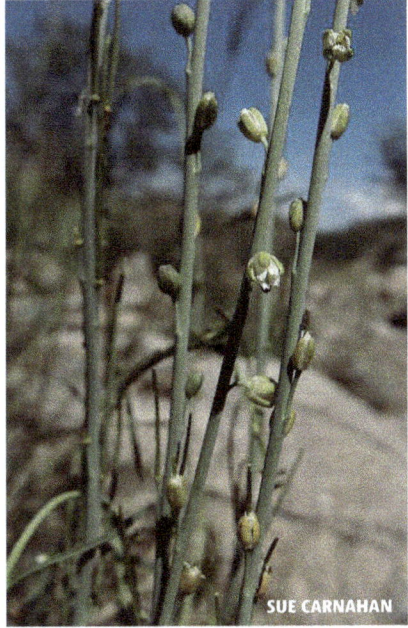
SUE CARNAHAN

BICOLORED FAN-MUSTARD	MOUNTAIN CROSS
(*Nerisyrenia camporum*)	(*Pennellia micrantha*)

based perennial, also occurs in the Park on the floodplain of the Rio Grande near Santa Elena Canyon.

➤ Bicolored Fan-Mustard (*Nerisyrenia camporum*)—A low, perennial plant, branching from the base and covered with star-shaped hairs. The flowers are rather large, white or purplish. The pods are linear, elongated, more or less curved, and tipped by a persistent style.

➤ Mountain Cross (*Pennellia micrantha*, synonym *Heterothrix micrantha*)—A slender, biennial herb with the basal leaves lance-shaped and toothed and the stem leaves narrower and entire. The small flowers are somewhat irregular because of the unequal size of the sepals and petals. The slender, cylindrical pods are about an inch long. Found in the upper part of the Basin near the Saddle.

■ Bladderpod (*Physaria*)—Low herbs covered with branched or star-shaped hairs. The leaves are entire or moderately toothed and the flowers are mostly yellow. The pods are inflated and spherical or football-shaped, and the seeds are flattened and sometimes winged. ➤ Fendler's Bladderpod (*Physaria fendleri*) usually grows erect and is densely white-hairy. The leaves are linear or narrowly lanceolate and

ANDY JORDAN

FENDLER'S BLADDERPOD
(*Physaria fendleri*)

CK KELLY

TEXAS SELENIA
(*Selenia dissecta*)

rather thick. The flowers are yellow. **Silver Bladderpod** (*Physaria argyraea*) usually grows more or less prostrate and is densely hairy with star-shaped hairs. The leaves are narrowly elliptic. The flowers are yellow but may become purplish with age. **Purple Bladderpod** (*Physaria purpurea*) differs from the other two in having white or rose-colored flowers.

⤷ **Texas Selenia** (*Selenia dissecta*)—A low annual herb with once or twice pinnately cut leaves, yellow flowers and large, oblong or elliptic, flat pods on rather long and spreading stalks. The seeds are in two rows in each half of the pod and are provided with broad wings.

⤷ **Rocket-Mustard** (*Sisymbrium irio*)—An annual, introduced herb of disturbed places, first forming a rosette of lobed basal leaves before developing its flowering stem. Stems are erect, mostly branched near the base, and may grow to 2 feet tall. Flowers are pale yellow, blooming in early spring to early summer. Fruits are thin tubular pods, 1 to 1½ inches long.

■ **Jewelflower** (*Streptanthus*)—Smooth herbs 1 to 3 feet high with rose-colored flowers and elongate pods, these flattened parallel to the partition. The lower leaves are sharply cut nearly to the midrib, but the

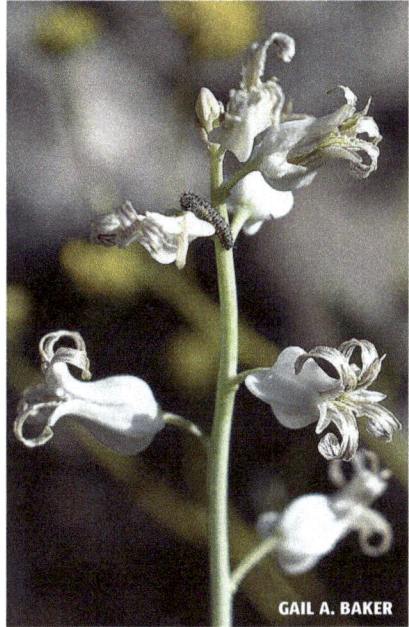

ROCKET-MUSTARD
(*Sisymbrium irio*)

BROAD-POD JEWELFLOWER
(*Streptanthus platycarpus*)

upper ones are entire with rounded basal lobes clasping the stem. The leaves are covered with a whitish wax. **Lyre-Leaf Jewelflower** (*Streptanthus carinatus*) has very narrow, somewhat twisted petals; ➤ **Broad-Pod Jewelflower** (*Streptanthus platycarpus*) has much broader, flatter petals.

Gregg's Keelpod (*Synthlipsis greggii*)—A much-branched, somewhat white-hairy herb with coarsely toothed or lobed leaves, rose-colored or white flowers, and oval pods which are about ½ inch long and narrowly winged.

■ **Thelypody** (*Thelypodium*)—Tall, branched, biennial herbs with white flowers. The upper leaves are entire, while the lower ones are pinnately cut. The slender, cylindrical pods are short-stalked. Two species occur in the Park area: ➤ **Wright's Thelypody** (*Thelypodium wrightii*) grows in the Chisos Mountains and **Texas Thelypody** (*Thelypodium texanum*) has been found in the Tornillo Creek bed near Hot Springs.

➤ **Wedge-Leaf Stonecress** (*Tomostima cuneifolia*, synonym *Draba cuneifolia*)—An annual herb with lance-shaped or ovate leaves that are entire or only sparingly toothed and all basal or on the lower parts of

DANIEL MCNAIR

WRIGHT'S THELYPODY
(*Thelypodium wrightii*)

SUE CARNAHAN

WEDGE-LEAF STONECRESS
(*Tomostima cuneifolia*)

the stems. They are somewhat hairy. The pods are flat but narrow and about ½ inch long. Found in Green Gulch and low places in the desert.

PINEAPPLE FAMILY (BROMELIACEAE)

A family of largely tropical plants many of which grow as epiphytes on other plants. The 6-cleft perianth, representing three sepals and three petals, is attached below the ovary of the flower and there are six stamens. The fruit is 3-celled and berrylike. The family is represented in the Big Bend flora by two very different species:

↗ **Texas False Agave** (*Hechtia texensis*)—A plant with a rosette of basal, rigid, spiny-toothed leaves often a foot long and a flowering stalk as much as 2 to 4 feet tall and bearing a large, branched panicle of flowers. The flowers are imperfect, and the staminate and pistillate flowers are on separate plants. The petals are white and the sepals brownish. This plant has been found in several places near Glen Springs, near Hot Springs, and in the Dead Horse Mountains but apparently nowhere else in the United States.

↗ **Bunchmoss** (*Tillandsia recurvata*)—This is a small plant with nearly cylindrical, ash-colored, scurfy leaves crowded in two rows near

TEXAS FALSE AGAVE
(*Hechtia texensis*)

BUNCHMOSS
(*Tillandsia recurvata*)

the base of the stem. The leaves are 1 to about 3 inches long and the stem is a little longer. The stem is naked above and bears one or two small, perfect flowers. The plant gets its specific name from the fact that the leaves are often recurved. This plant often grows as an epiphyte on the limbs of trees, but in the Chisos Mountains it is oftener found growing on damp, vertical rocks in canyons.

CACTUS FAMILY (CACTACEAE)

This is a large family, confined (apart from one species) to the Americas, with a great variety of unique and peculiar, mostly desert plants. The cacti may be recognized by the thick, fleshy, green, leafless stems, armed by spines that are produced within definite, spirally arranged structures called areoles. The flowers are usually conspicuous and beautiful. The parts of the flower are attached above the ovary, and there are numerous sepals, petals, and stamens, and one style with several stigmas. The fruit is a many-seeded, fleshy or dry berry, often spiny, and in many cases edible. About 50 species of cacti have been recognized in the Park and surrounding area, but this number varies depending on the source due

MATT BERGER
CHAUTLE LIVING ROCK CACTUS
(*Ariocarpus fissuratus*)

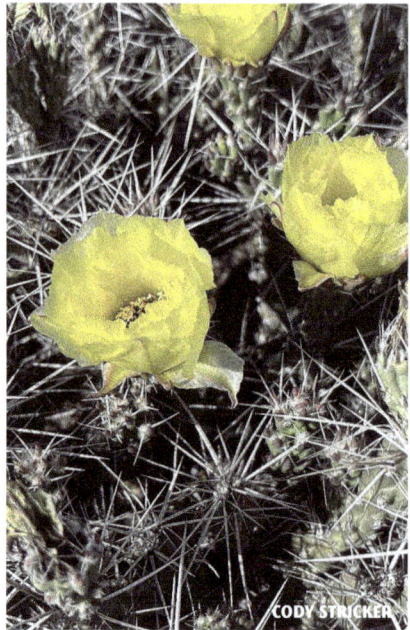
CODY STRICKER
BIG BEND CLUB-CHOLLA
(*Corynopuntia aggeria*)

to widely differing classifications of cactus genera and species. Descriptions for most of the Park's cactus species are given below.

↗ **Chautle Living Rock Cactus** (*Ariocarpus fissuratus*)—A flattened, spineless cacti growing to about 5 inches across, from a thick taproot. Stems are clustered in a rosette of wrinkled, triangular tubercles, brown, gray or green in color. In dry periods, the stems further wrinkle. Flowers emerge from a woolly mass at the top of the plant in fall or early winter, are pale pink to purple with an orange center. In the Park, uncommon on limestone at elevations less than 4,000 feet. Flowering time provides the best opportunity to find these diminutive plants.

↗ **Big Bend Club-Cholla** (*Corynopuntia aggeria*, synonyms *Grusonia aggeria, Opuntia aggeria*)—A low-growing cactus (to about 4 inches tall) with cylindric or club-shaped stems. The spines are 1 to 2 inches long, brown, black or gray in color, grouped 5 to 15 per areole. Spine lengths range from. Flowers are bright yellow, appearing between March and May. Fruits are pale yellow.

Graham's Club-Cholla (*Corynopuntia grahamii*, synonyms *Grusonia grahamii, Opuntia grahamii*)—A low-growing cactus, only several inches high, often forming a prickly mat to about 2 feet wide. The stems

SCHOTT'S CLUB-CHOLLA
(*Corynopuntia schottii*)

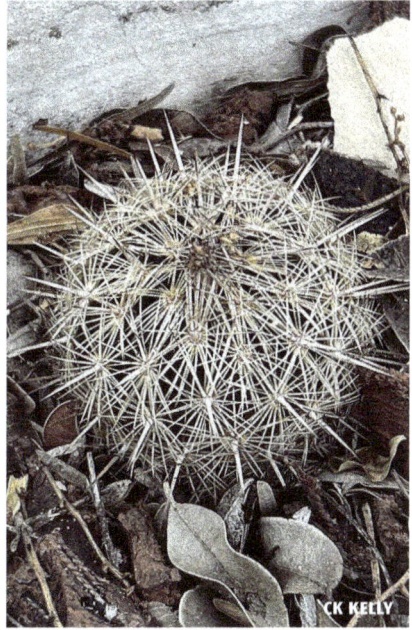

SEA-URCHIN CACTUS
(*Coryphantha echinus*)

are cylindrical, and obscured by the thick, gray-white spines, 1 to 1½ inches long, in a cluster of 8 to 15 per areole. Flowers are yellow with pink margins, appearing in May and June. Fruits are yellow and spineless.

➢ Schott's Club-Cholla (*Corynopuntia schottii*, synonyms *Grusonia schottii, Opuntia schottii*)—Low-growing clusters of stems forming a mat to 10 feet in diameter but the stems to only about 4 inches high. Stem segments easily broken off if disturbed, and can root to form new plants. Spines sharp, 2 to 3 inches long, with a definite central spine. Flowers bright yellow, blooming in June and July. Fruits yellow, fleshy, persistent. Found in the Park at elevations below about 5,000 feet.

➢ Sea-Urchin Cactus (*Coryphantha echinus*)—The common name refers to this cactus's similarity to a sea-urchin, as single stems of the plant form a sphere, covered in a mix of both appressed and projecting spines. When mature, the stems become cylindrical and up to 5 inches long, and can form sizable clumps of up to 50 stems, 2 feet or more across may form, with the stems largely hidden by the spines. The radial spines are between 15 and 25 per areole; central spines are usually one to four; both types are pale gray or pale brown, darker at tip, similar in

NIPPLE BEEHIVE CACTUS
(*Coryphantha macromeris*)

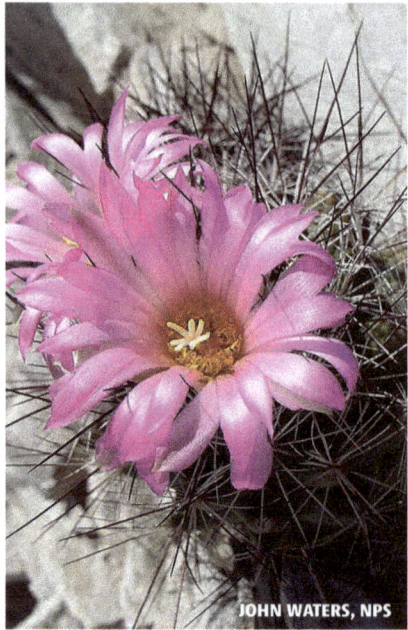

BIG BEND CORY CACTUS
(*Coryphantha ramillosa*)

length and up to 1 inch long. Flowers are pale yellow, red- or orange-tinged at the base, about 2 inches wide, and are visible from April and July, but opening fully only during bright sunshine and sometimes wilting after just several hours. The fruit is an oily green pod, up to 1 inch long. Found on limestone soils at lower elevations.

➤ Nipple Beehive Cactus (*Coryphantha macromeris*)—A small cactus, not exceeding 6 inches in height, characterized by elongated, upward-pointing tubercles. The 2 to 8 brown central spines are oriented in different directions, and are surrounded by 9 to 15 shorter, white, radial spines. The green stems are still clearly visible. Stems are solitary for several years then start to form clusters. Flowers are pink to purple, blooming in late-summer. The fruits are green. Found on gravelly or clayey soils below 4,000 feet.

➤ Big Bend Cory Cactus (*Coryphantha ramillosa*)—This uncommon cactus is spherical or cylindrical in shape, and grows to about 4 inches long. The areoles support curved spines, the central spine thick, dark, and to about 1½ inches long. The smaller spines are whitish in color. Flowers are pink, becoming paler toward their base, and some-

TREE CHOLLA
(*Cylindropuntia imbricata*)

CANDLE CHOLLA
(*Cylindropuntia kleiniae*)

times with darker mid-stripes. The fruits are green, fleshy and juicy and less than 1 inch long. The plant blooms in the summer, and may bloom for a longer time if rains occur. Due to its rarity (it is only known from the Big Bend region in the United States and in Coahuila in Mexico) this cactus is Federally listed as Threatened.

 Tree Cholla, Big Bend Cane-Cholla (*Cylindropuntia imbricata*, synonym *Opuntia imbricata*)—Large cactus to 15 feet tall, with a central trunk and most stems arranged quite high above the ground. Stem segments to 15 inches long and 2 inches wide. Spines white or pale yellow, 8 to 20 per areole, sparse enough so that the green stem is clearly visible. Flowers violet-pink. Fruit bumpy, spineless, yellow-green. Common throughout the Park, especially at elevations between 4,000 and 6,000 feet.

 Candle Cholla (*Cylindropuntia kleiniae*, synonym *Opuntia kleiniae*)—Cholla cactus with thin branches, to 6 inches long and less than one inch wide. The thick, white spines are relatively sparse, only one or two per areole (sometimes absent). Flowers are a distinctive pale reddish brown, with purplish tints. Fruit spineless, to one inch

CHRISTMAS CHOLLA
(*Cylindropuntia leptocaulis*)

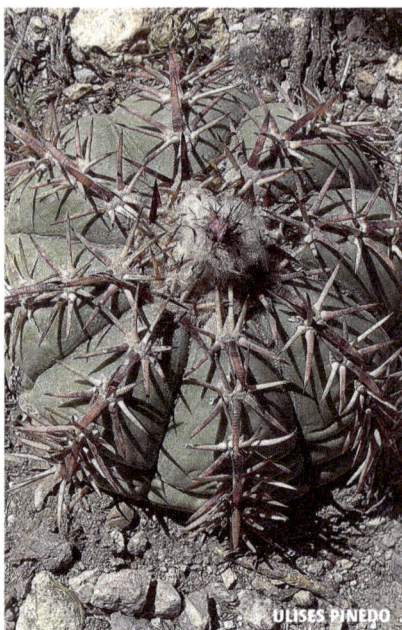

DEVIL'S-HEAD
(*Echinocactus horizonthalonius*)

long, green, maturing to a dull red, unlike the related Christmas Cholla (below) with bright red fruit. Mostly found at low elevations near the Rio Grande.

❧ **Christmas Cholla, Tasajillo** (*Cylindropuntia leptocaulis*, synonym *Opuntia leptocaulis*)—This cholla grows to about 5 feet tall, and is often found sheltered within a larger shrub. Notable for its long, very thin, smooth stems (usually about ¼ inch in diameter). The spines, however, are sharp and thick, often more than 2 inches long, and are easily detached if touched. Spines typically single per areole, white or golden brown in color, and angled slightly downwards. Some plants may be nearly spineless. Flowers are greenish yellow, opening in late afternoons of the spring and summer months. The egg-shaped fruits are small (around ½ inch long), spineless, bright red and remain on the plant through much of the winter, hence the common name. Often found in washes and flats and at elevations below 5,000 feet.

❧ **Devil's-Head, Eagle-Claws** (*Echinocactus horizonthalonius*)—A low-growing, greenish gray cactus, to about six inches tall, with broad ribs. Radial spines are in clusters of 5 to 8, and a curved downward-

HORSE-CRIPPLER
(*Echinocactus texensis*)

CHISOS MTN HEDGEHOG CACTUS
(*Echinocereus chisoensis*)

pointing central spine. The spines do not obscure the surface of the plant The greenish-gray surface is not obscured by the spines. Flowers are bright pink, develop in early summer, and grow out of a dense mat of woolly hairs at the top of the plant. Common in the Park at elevations up to 5,500 feet.

➤ **Horse-Crippler** (*Echinocactus texensis*)—This cactus is usually two times or more wider than tall, and can grow to a diameter of 12 inches. The ribs are wide and prominent. Radial spines are in clusters of 5 to 7, with a central downward-pointing spine up to 3 inches long. Flowers are a salmon pink color, with feathery margins and a reddish base. Fruits are bright red. In the Park, uncommon on sandy soils below about 3,500 feet. The common name refers to the plant's rigid, flattened stems with strong spines, a danger to any animal that may step on it.

➤ **Chisos Mountain Hedgehog Cactus** (*Echinocereus chisoensis*)— Stems grow up to 8 inches long by 3 inches wide, with 13 to 16 ribs. Spines number 11 to 20 per areole, with usually two being central. The spines are white, pale gray or pinkish, and darker at their tips. The flowers, up to 3 inches wide, typically are three-colored: pink in the upper

SCARLET HEDGEHOG CACTUS
(*Echinocereus coccineus*)

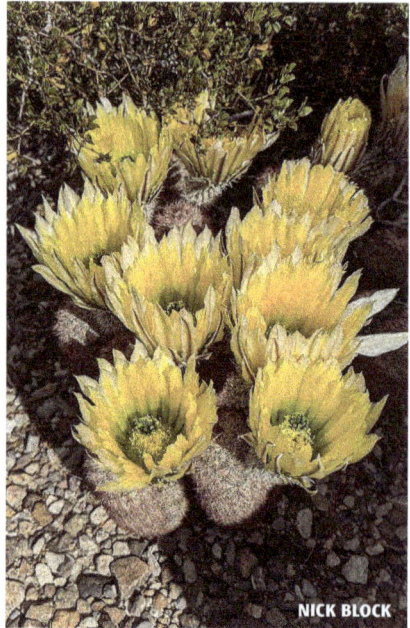

TEXAS RAINBOW CACTUS
(*Echinocereus dasyacanthus*)

portion, whitish in the middle, and red near the base. Flowers appear in March and April. Fruits are greenish red, 1 to 1½ inches long, spiny and woolly. This uncommon cactus is restricted to a narrow strip of land on the southeastern slopes of the Chisos Mountains, entirely within the Park, where it is found on gravelly soils at elevations below 2,400 feet.

❧ Scarlet Hedgehog Cactus, Claret-Cup Cactus (*Echinocereus coccineus*)—A clustered cactus, eventually covering several square feet, with stems branched several times or more. The branches may be up to 10 inches long and 4 inches wide. Spines sparsely cover the shiny green body of the stem, and are tan or grayish in color. Flowers are bright red to orange, blooming in April and May. Fruits are cylinder-shaped, red, and about 1 inch long. In Big Bend, this cactus is most common above 4,000 feet, especially on soils of volcanic origin.

❧ Texas Rainbow Cactus, Spiny Hedgehog Cactus (*Echinocereus dasyacanthus*)—Stems usually single or branched several times from the base of the plant, to 10 inches long and to 3 inches wide. The tan or yellowish spines cover the stem surface. Flowers are bright yellow with a green throat and form near the top of the stem, blooming in April and

PITAYA
(*Echinocereus enneacanthus*)

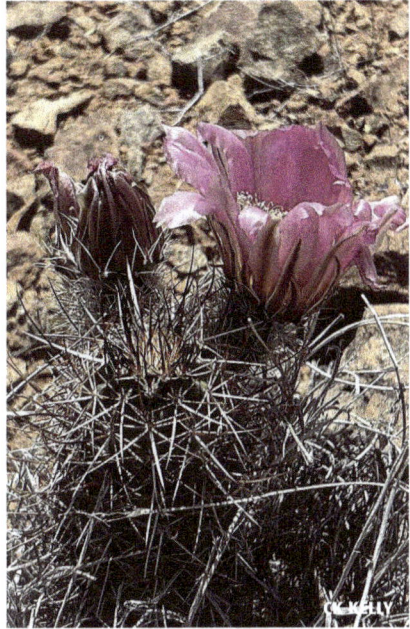

PINK-FLOWER HEDGEHOG CACTUS
(*Echinocereus fendleri*)

May. Fruits are green, often with a purplish tinge, and up to 2½ inches long. This locally common cactus is found on limestone hillsides at elevations to about 5,000 feet.

⚐ **Pitaya, Strawberry-Cactus** (*Echinocereus enneacanthus*)—Stems in groups of 100 or more, forming loosely clustered mounds to about 2 feet across. Stems may reach 12 inches long by about 4 inches in diameter. The spines vary from dense to sparse, and are yellowish to gray in color. One or several central spines are present and to about 3 inches long. The magenta flowers bloom from March through May. Fruits are greenish brown, to about 2 inches long, lightly spined (these easily removed), and taste similar to strawberries, so are often eaten, especially in Mexico, where they are known as pitaya. This cactus is found at low to mid-elevations in the Park.

⚐ **Pink-Flower Hedgehog Cactus** (*Echinocereus fendleri*)—Stems are single or in close clusters of up to about 20, each stem to about 6 inches tall and 3 inches wide. Areoles have one long, brownish central spine, and 4 to 10 shorter, white, radial spines. Flowers are pink and bloom in April and May. Fruits are red and spiny, one inch or more wide.

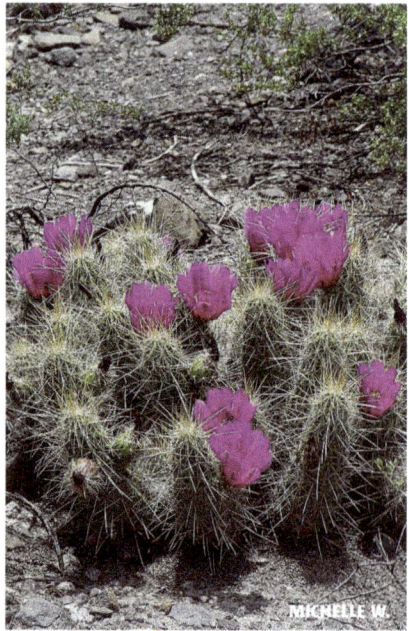

ULISES PINEDO

MICHELLE W.

RAINBOW CACTUS
(*Echinocereus pectinatus*)

STRAWBERRY HEDGEHOG CACTUS
(*Echinocereus stramineus*)

➔ **Rainbow Cactus** (*Echinocereus pectinatus*)—Stems usually single, growing to about 12 inches long and 2 to 4 inches wide. The 12 to 30 radial spines are short (to about ½ inch long), whitish to pinkish, and intertwine with those of the other areoles. The banded colors of spines explain the name Rainbow Cactus. Flowers are a rich pink color and bloom in spring and summer. Central spines vary from 1 to 5 and are ½ to 1 inch long. The purple spiny fruits are round to elliptic, and said to have a pleasant taste.

➔ **Strawberry Hedgehog Cactus** (*Echinocereus stramineus*)—This cactus forms large, rounded clusters, to about 3 feet across and to nearly 3 feet tall. Spines are straw-colored and largely hide the stem surface. Flowers are bright magenta and nearly 4 inches wide. Fruits are purple-red, to 2 inches long, edible with a taste similar to strawberries. Common in Big Bend at elevations to about 5,000 feet.

➔ **Brown-Flower Hedgehog Cactus** (*Echinocereus viridiflorus*, synonym *Echinocereus chloranthus*)—The cylindrical stems are single or sometimes once- or twice-branched, growing to 10 inches long and 3 inches wide. Spines are dense, covering the stem surface, and are reddish-brown in color. Flowers are also reddish-brown and about 1 inch

ANDERS HASTINGS

BROWN-FLOWER HEDGEHOG CACTUS
(*Echinocereus viridiflorus*)

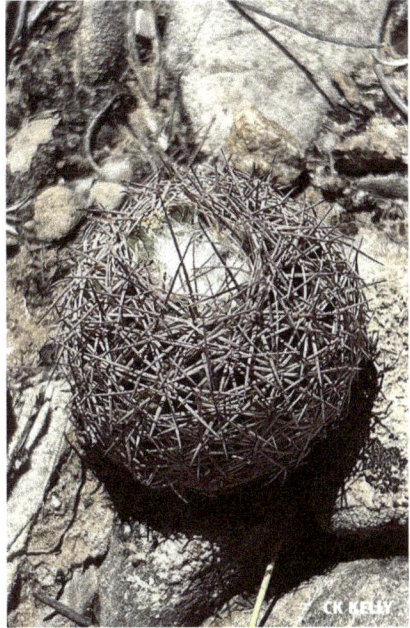

CK KELLY

WHITE FISH-HOOK CACTUS
(*Echinomastus intertextus*)

long, developing along the sides of the stem. Flowers bloom from February to May, making this one of the earliest species to flower in the Park. Fruits are dark red, round, and less than ½ inch in diameter. Present in Big Bend at all but the highest elevations.

❧ White Fish-Hook Cactus (*Echinomastus intertextus*)—Stems single, dull green, to 8 inches tall and 4 inches wide, often elevated above the ground atop its taproot. The spines largely cover the stem surface, and are gray, pinkish or pale brown, pink or reddish at the tip. Flowers are white to pale pink, to about 1¼ inches wide, with a distinctive red stigma, and appear early in the season (February and March). Fruits are a dry pod, green aging to tan or brown. In Big Bend, found in grasslands at mid-elevations of 3,000 to 4,000 feet.

❧ Mariposa Fish-Hook Cactus (*Echinomastus mariposensis*)—Stems egg-shaped, and similar in size to a golf ball or somewhat larger with age. Radial spines whitish, completely covering the stem surface. A single darker central spine is present. Flowers pink to white with a darker midvein. Fruits globe-shaped, yellowish, and about ½ inch across. Found on limestone soils below 3,500 feet elevation. This cactus was named for the Mariposa Mine located near Terlingua, Texas.

MATT BERGER

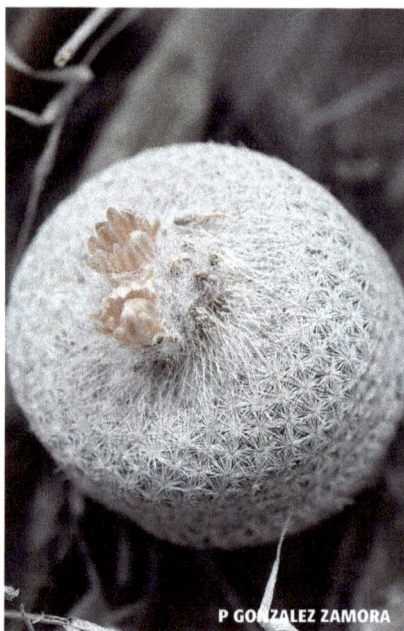

P GONZALEZ ZAMORA

MARIPOSA FISH-HOOK CACTUS
(*Echinomastus mariposensis*)

BOKE'S BUTTON CACTUS
(*Epithelantha bokei*)

Warnock's Fish-Hook Cactus (*Echinomastus warnockii*)—Stems are always single, blue-green in color, and 4 to 6 inches tall. Spines are thick, nearly covering the stem surface; central spines are tan with darker tips. Flowers are white, cream-colored, or pinkish, and about 1 inch wide, borne at the stem tip. Flowering begins in February. Fruits are round and less than ½ inch wide, green at first and becoming brown with age. Found in much of the Park at elevations below 4,000 feet.

↗ Boke's Button Cactus (*Epithelantha bokei*)—Similar to the more widespread Common Button Cactus (below), but plants appear smoother. Spines are small, and appressed to the stem surface, giving plants a satiny look. Flowers small, to only ¼ inch wide, and pinkish. Fruit bright red, narrowly cylindric, atop the stem. The Park's button cactuses are found on limestone at lower elevations.

Common Button Cactus (*Epithelantha micromeris*)—More widespread than Boke's Button Cactus, this species is round in cross-section, sometimes slightly flatter on top, and only between 1 and 2 inches in diameter. Radial spines, white or pale gray in color, number 20 to 35 per areole, are densely overlapping and appressed to the stem. Central spines are absent. The uppermost spines point upwards and surround

BIG BEND FOXTAIL CACTUS
(*Escobaria dasyacantha*)

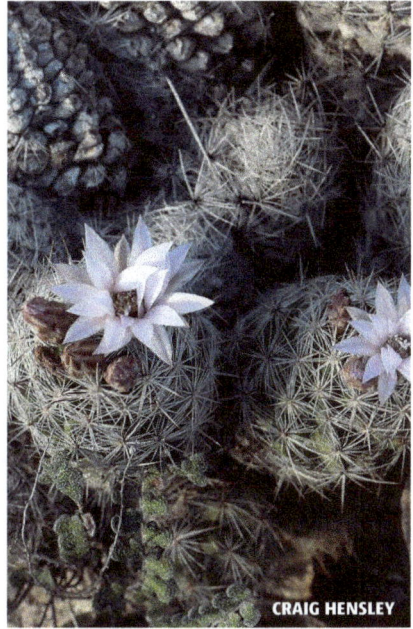

WHITE COLUMN FOXTAIL CACTUS
(*Escobaria tuberculosa*)

a woolly patch. From this patch, a few tiny pink flowers appear in spring. Fruits are bright red and narrowly cylindric.

⤳ Big Bend Foxtail Cactus (*Escobaria dasyacantha*, synonym *Coryphantha dasyacantha*)—Stems solitary, globe-shaped when young but elongating with age to about 6 inches long. Spines ¼ to ½ inch long; lower spines shed giving stems a corncob appearance due to the exposed tubercles. Fllowers white to pale pink, about 1 inch wide, and blooming from May until August. Fruits red, about ½ inch long. In the Park, this cactus is uncommon in the Chisos Mountain foothills.

Duncan's Snowball Cactus (*Escobaria duncanii*, synonym *Coryphantha duncanii*)—Stems solitary, sphere-shaped, and only to 1½ inches in diameter. The white spines densely cover and mostly hide the surface of the stem. Flowers white to pale pink, opening to about ½ inch wide at their tip. Blooming is in February and March. Fruits about ½ inch long, bright red when mature. This cactus is uncommon, and in Big Bend mostly known from limestone crevices near the Rio Grande.

⤳ White-Column Foxtail Cactus (*Escobaria tuberculosa*, synonym *Coryphantha tuberculosa*)—This cactus forms small spherical or cylin-

SUE CARNAHAN

SPINYSTAR
(*Escobaria vivipara*)

drical stems, growing to about 2 to 3 inches tall and 1 inch wide, the stems branching to create groups of 50 stems or more. Spines are short, white or gray, and largely covering the stem surface. The flowers, 1 and 2 inches wide, are white to pale pink, darker at their center, and fringed along their margin. Blooming time is late-spring and summer. Fruits egg-shaped, bright red in color.

❧ Spinystar (*Escobaria vivipara*, synonyms *Coryphantha vivipara*, *Pelecyphora vivipara*)—A small, round cactus growing to about 6 inches high; sometimes solitary but usually found in clusters of 20 or more stems. Radial spines dense, white, 10 to 40 in number; central spines darker, 3 to 12 (or absent in young stems). Flowers pink, blooming June through August. Fruits green, to 1 inch long. In the Park, Spinystar is found in grasslands and juniper woodlands below 6,000 feet elevation.

❧ Texas Barrel Cactus (*Ferocactus hamatacanthus*)—The stems of this cactus grow to 12 inches long and to 6 inches wide, and are usually green but may turn purple under full sunlight. Stems may be solitary or in clusters. The central spines are yellow, red or brown, may grow to 4 inches long, with the tip curving back on itself. The spines twist in

TEXAS BARREL CACTUS
(*Ferocactus hamatacanthus*)

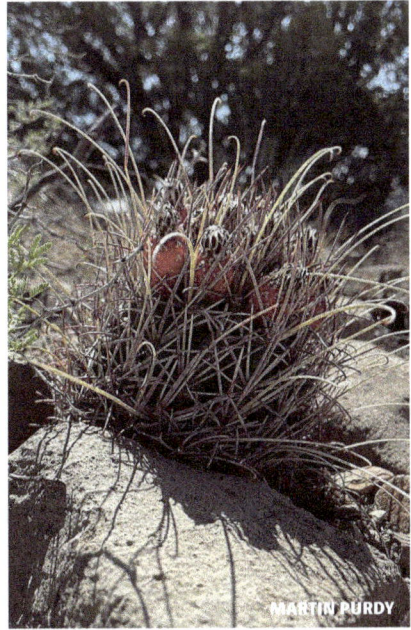

CHIHUAHUAN HOOK-SPINE CACTUS
(*Glandulicactus uncinatus*)

many directions. The flowers are yellow with a reddish base, up to 3 inches wide, and bloom in late-spring and summer. The fleshy fruits are about 1 inch long, and ripen to a brownish red color. In the Park, this cactus is found on rocky hillsides and cliffs to about 5,000 feet elevation.

⊰ **Chihuahuan Hook Spine Cactus** (*Glandulicactus uncinatus*)— Stems solitary, unbranched, barrel-like, growing to 5 inches tall and 3 inches across. The gray-green stem is clearly visible below the spines. Radial spines 5 to 10, reddish, with the 3 lower spines hooked at tip. Central spines 1 to 4, to 4 inches long, pale yellow, with the main central spine strongly hooked (usually upward) at tip. From a distance, this feature of the spines gives this cactus an appearance similar to a clump of grass. Flowers are brownish red, about 1 inch wide, and are found from March through June. the reddish fruits are egg-shaped and about 1 inch long. In the Park, Hook Spine Cactus is found at elevations below 4,000 feet.

⊰ **Pancake Nipple Cactus** (*Mammillaria heyderi*)—Plants grow close to the ground, forming a flattened hemisphere to about 6 inches

PANCAKE NIPPLE CACTUS
(*Mammillaria heyderi*)

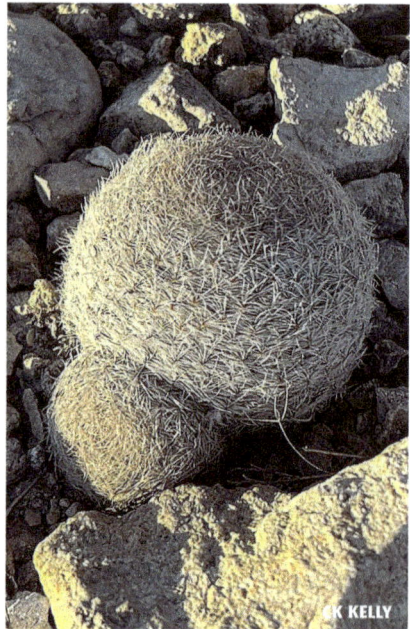

LACE-SPINE NIPPLE CACTUS
(*Mammillaria lasiacantha*)

in diameter. The whitish spines are all radial apart from a single slightly longer central spine; the spines do not obscure the stem's green surface. The cream-colored flowers grow in a neat ring around the top of the stem, and bloom from March through June. Fruits vary from ½ to 1 inch long. This is the largest of the four species of *Mammillaria* known from the Park, and it is fairly common at elevations below 5,500 feet.

⤷ **Lace-Spine Nipple Cactus** (*Mammillaria lasiacantha*)—The stems, usually single or less often in small clusters, are globe-shaped, to 1½ inches in diameter, and similar in size to a golf ball. The white radial spines are many per tubercle, and completely obscure the stem surface. The very tips of the spines are often darker in color. Central spines are absent. Flowers are cream or white, marked with reddish brown midstripes, growing to about ½ wide, and blooming from March through May. Fruits are bright red, club-shaped or cylindrical in shape, and about ½ inch long. In the Park, this cactus is found on limestone at lower elevations.

⤷ **Little Nipple Cactus** (*Mammillaria meiacantha*)—A low-growing, flattened disk cactus, up to 6 inches or more in diameter but only several

LITTLE NIPPLE CACTUS
(*Mammillaria meiacantha*)

RAT-TAIL NIPPLE CACTUS
(*Mammillaria pottsii*)

inches tall. The clusters of spines are borne on closely spaced tubercles, with usually 6 or 7 radial spines and a single central spine which is angled upwards. The spines are all similar in length (up to ½ inch long). The white or pale pink flowers have darker midstripes, and grow in several rings near the top of the plant, opening in stages from March to May. Fruits are purple or pink.

⚲ Rat-Tail Nipple Cactus (*Mammillaria pottsii*)—Plants form clusters, branching both from the base and along the stems. Stems are slender, growing to 8 inches long by 1 inches wide. The white radial spines are very short and thin, and very dense, hiding the stem surface. Central spines are brownish or dark purplish, one of which is curved upward. The maroon flowers are bell-shaped and about ½ inch wide. They form a ring below the top of the stem, and bloom from March through May. Fruits are red, fleshy, and about ½ inch long. In the Park, this cactus grows on limestone at lower elevations. In the United States, it is known only from the Big Bend region, but is more widespread in Mexico.

⚲ Chihuahuan-Beehive (*Neolloydia conoidea,* synonym *Cochemiea conoidea*)—Stems cylindrical, to about 4 inches long, usually in clusters

CHIHUAHUAN-BEEHIVE
(*Neolloydia conoidea*)

to 12 inches across. Spines fairly dense, but not hiding the stem surface. Radial spines white, central spines black when young, turning gray with age. The flowers are magenta to purple, up to 2 inches wide, and bloom in May and June. Fruits are small, round, and yellowish when young, becoming brown. This cactus is found on limestone at elevations below 4,000 feet.

Golden-Spine Prickly-Pear (*Opuntia aureispina*, synonym *Opuntia azurea* var. *aureispina*)—Stems upright, branching from a spiny trunk rather than growing along the ground, growing 3 to 5 feet high, with many stem segments. Pads are blue-green to yellow-green in color, circular or oval in shape and about 4 inches long and wide. Areoles have a narrow ring of glochids, 3 to 5 major spines, up to 2 inches long; and 1 to 7 thinner, lighter-colored spines, less than 1 inch long. Spines are generally bright yellow to orange (or gold) in color, hence the species name aureispina. Flowers yellow with reddish centers, to about 2½ inches in diameter; blooming in March and april. Uncommon in the Park on low-elevation limestone soils.

⤳ **Purple Prickly-Pear** (*Opuntia azurea*)—Stems in sprawling clumps, 2 to 3 feet high, bluish, reddish or purplish-green, with usually

MICHELLE W.

ERIC KNIGHT

PURPLE PRICKLY-PEAR
(*Opuntia azurea*)

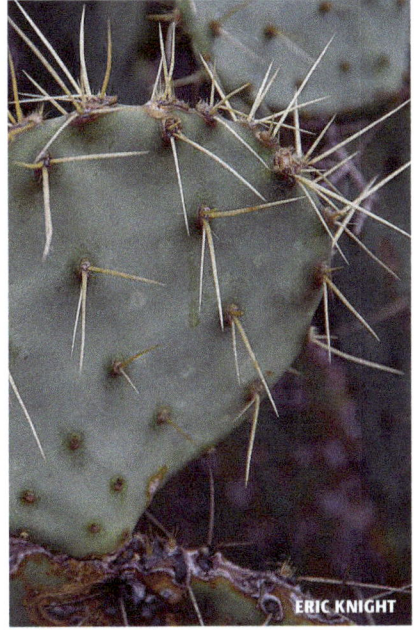

CHISOS MOUNTAIN PRICKLY-PEAR
(*Opuntia chisosensis*)

a single long red spine along the margin and upper part of each pad. Flowers orange or yellow-orange, with red centers, blooming in early summer. Fruits red-purple.

➤ **Chisos Mountain Prickly-Pear** (*Opuntia chisosensis*)—Stems single or in large clumps, sprawling or upright, growing to about 5 feet tall. Pads green, about 10 inches long by 8 inches wide and often nearly 1 inch thick. Areoles with 1 to 6 yellow spines which turn brown with age. Flowers usually waxy yellow (less often red), blooming in May and June. Fruits purple, to about 2 ½ inches long, and falling from the stem when it matures. Found on gravelly or sandy soils at elevations to about 5,500 feet.

➤ **Engelmann Prickly-Pear** (*Opuntia engelmannii*)—Large sprawling plants, growing to about 5 feet tall and forming sizable colonies. Plants spread at ground level, and the lateral pads readily root, enabling the plant to colonize areas up to 30 feet across. The bluish green pads are oblong or circular in outline, to 12 inches long and 7 to 10 inches wide. The white (less often yellow) spines, 1 to 5 in number, grow from widely spaced areoles, and always point downwards. Spines are short,

ENGELMANN PRICKLY-PEAR
(*Opuntia engelmannii*)

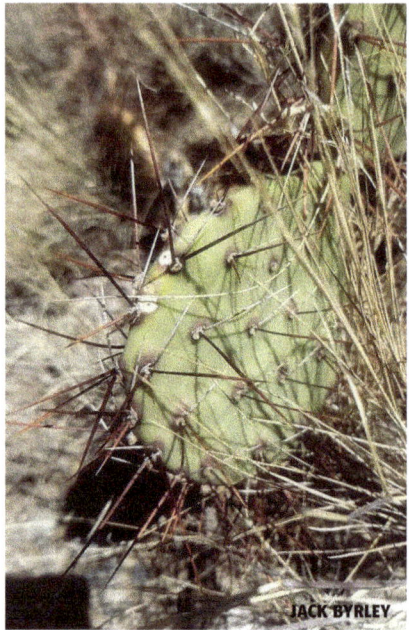

PURPLE-FRUIT PRICKLY-PEAR
(*Opuntia phaeacantha*)

1 to 2 inches long. Glochids are quite prominent. Flowers are yellow, 3 to 4 inches wide, and bloom in the spring. Fruits are purple-red, juicy and edible. These are called *tunas* in Mexico and used to make syrups and jellies. Common in Big Bend and throughout the southwest.

Texas Prickly-Pear (*Opuntia lindheimeri*, synonym *Opuntia engelmannii* var. *lindheimeri*)—Stems may sprawl to 5 feet, forming extensive clumps. Pads are large, to 12 inches long, with shiny yellowish spines up to 2 inches long, 1 to 6 per areole; this is one distinction from the similar Engelmann Prickly-Pear which has white or brownish spines. Flowers bright yellow, up to 3 inches in diameter.

➤ Purple-Fruit Prickly-Pear (*Opuntia phaeacantha*, synonym *Opuntia camanchica*)—Stems sprawling, forming clumps 2 to 3 feet high and to about 10 feet in diameter. Pads oval or nearly circular, to 12 inches long by 8 inches wide. Areoles towards the base of the pad often have no spines; sometimes spines are found only at the areoles on the uppermost portion of the pad. During dry periods the dark green pads may turn purplish at their tip. Flowers vary from yellow, to orange, salmon, or pink, appearing late-spring. The purple fruits are fleshy and edible, to almost 3 inches long, and remain on the plant until winter.

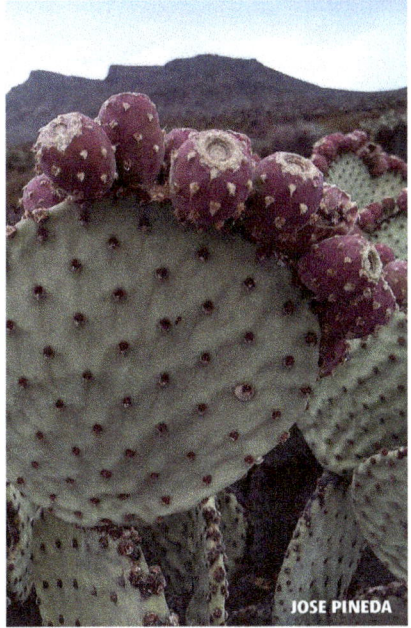

BRENDAN BOYD

JOSE PINEDA

BLIND PRICKLY-PEAR
(*Opuntia rufida*)

Pott's Prickly-Pear (*Opuntia pottsii*, synonym *Opuntia macrorhiza*)—Stems low and spreading, forming clumps and often partially hidden by neighboring grass plants. Pads blue-green, about 4 inches long by 2½ inches wide. Areoles with 1 to 6 whitish spines, with most spines on upper portion of the pad. Flowers yellow with reddish center. Fruits red-purple, persistent for several months. Found in gravelly soils of Big Bend at elevations to 7,000 feet.

✦ **Blind Prickly-Pear** (*Opuntia rufida*)—Stems grow into upright clumps about 5 feet high. The oval to round, gray-green pads are about 6 inches long. Spines are absent but the areoles have reddish glochids that are shed when plants are jarred. These glochids can enter the eyes of livestock, leading to infections and eventual blindness. Flowers are first yellow, maturing to an orange color, reddish at base, and bloom in April and May. Fruits are red, to 1 inch long, and soon drop from the stem. Found on sandy to gravelly soils in the Park at elevations mostly less than 4,000 feet.

✦ **Spiny-Fruit Prickly-Pear** (*Opuntia spinosibacca*)—Stems form clumps to 4 feet tall. The green pads are oval, 4 to 6 inches wide. Radial spines absent; central spines, up to 2½ inches long, are thick, reddish,

SPINY-FRUIT PRICKLY-PEAR
(*Opuntia spinosibacca*)

NIGHT-BLOOMING CEREUS
(*Peniocereus greggii*)

and 2 to 5 per areole. Flowers yellow-orange with red centers, about 2 inches across. Fruits spiny, yellow-green. Common at low elevations.

↗ **Night-Blooming Cereus** (*Peniocereus greggii*, synonym *Cereus greggii*)—Stems may have a few branches, but most branching occurs from the base. When in bloom is the best time to locate this cactus. The flowers are greenish-white, up to 1 inch in diameter, and have frilly margins. However, as the common name implies, flowering occurs at night, and the flowers remain only slightly open into the following morning. Fruits are bright red and remain on the stems for several months.

Although quite widespread across three Southwest states, it is uncommon and rarely seen since its thin, unremarkable stems are shriveled much of the year and resemble branches of the creosote bush and other shrubs with which the plant grows. This is the only species of genus *Peniocereus* found in the USA; more than a dozen are found in Mexico. This interesting cactus was once known from the Park but its current status is unknown.

↗ **Glory-of-Texas** (*Thelocactus bicolor*)—Stems single, egg-shaped, growing about 6-8 inches tall by about 3-4 inches wide. Spines densely cover the stems. Yellowish or reddish radial spines number 8 to 18,

GLORY-OF-TEXAS
(*Thelocactus bicolor*)

along with 3 to 4 yellowish or reddish central spines, these to 3 inches or more in length. Flowers are large and showy, magenta-colored with darker throats, and 3 to 4 inches across. Bloom period is from April through July. Fruits are green and dry, and about ½ inch long.

Named Glory-of-Texas because of its brilliant pink flowers, this cactus is uncommon in two small areas of Texas and reported for southeastern New Mexico, though it is much more widespread in Mexico. In Big Bend it is known from a few locations at lower elevations.

HEMP FAMILY (CANNABACEAE)

A family of trees and shrubs with alternate, deciduous, 2-ranked leaves, which are often somewhat unequal at the base. The flowers are small and inconspicuous.

■ Hackberry (*Celtis*)—The hackberries are trees or shrubs with mostly imperfect flowers but with staminate and pistillate flowers both on the same tree. Sometimes some of the flowers are perfect. The fruit is a small, berrylike drupe. Two species are found in the Park: Spiny Hackberry (*Celtis pallida*) is a somewhat spiny desert shrub with rather

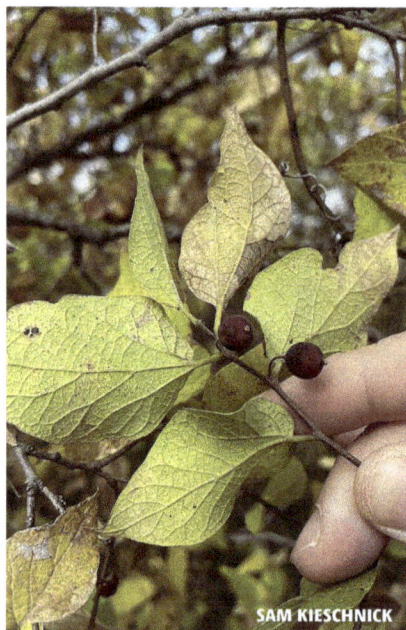

SAM KIESCHNICK

NET-LEAF HACKBERRY
(*Celtis reticulata*)

SHELBY LYN SANDERS

CARDINAL-FLOWER
(*Lobelia cardinalis*)

thick, stiff, oblong or ovate leaves, which are only about an inch long, and fruits that vary from yellow to red. ⇗ **Net-Leaf Hackberry** (*Celtis reticulata*) is a tree with mostly entire leaves 1½ to 3 inches long and about half as wide. They are very veiny and yellowish green below. The fruits vary from dark orange-red to yellow.

BLUEBELL FAMILY (CAMPANULACEAE)

A family of herbs with alternate, simple leaves and regular or irregular, usually showy flowers with the ovary below the other parts, five stamens usually free from the corolla, and a single style but sometimes two or more stigmas. The fruit is a many-seeded pod or capsule.

Represented in the Park only by two species of Lobelia, this genus is readily recognized by the fact that the corolla is irregular, 2-lipped, and split down one side clear to the base. **Berlandier's Lobelia** (*Lobelia berlandieri*) has lance-shaped, coarsely-toothed leaves and very numerous but relatively small, blue flowers. ⇗ **Cardinal-Flower** (*Lobelia cardinalis*) has narrowly lance-shaped leaves 3 to 5 inches long and large, bright-red flowers with corollas about 1¼ inches long.

ALEJANDRA PEÑA ESTRADA

INDIO BROWN

HONEYSUCKLE
(*Lonicera albiflora*)

SNOWBERRY
(*Symphoricarpos rotundifolius*)

HONEYSUCKLE FAMILY (CAPRIFOLIACEAE)

A rather large family consisting mostly of shrubs but containing some herbs. In all, the leaves are opposite, the flower parts are attached above the ovary, and the petals are grown together to form a tubular corolla. The family contains a large number of shrubs that are used for ornamental purposes.

➴ Honeysuckle (*Lonicera albiflora*)—A shrub with entire leaves broadly oval and 1 or 2 inches long, and fragrant, white, 2-lipped, funnel-shaped flowers that resemble the cultivated honeysuckle. The fruit is a blue berry about the size of a pea.

➴ Snowberry (*Symphoricarpos rotundifolius*)—A low, spreading shrub with elliptical or oval leaves that may be an inch long but often are less and may be entire or toothed along the margin with small teeth. The flowers are pink, about ¼ inch long, and the corolla tube is hairy in the throat. The fruit is a white, 2-seeded berry. The plant is very ornamental, especially when covered with berries.

PINK FAMILY (CARYOPHYLLACEAE)

The plants of this family have opposite leaves and often very brilliantly colored flowers. The flowers are regular and perfect and usually have 5 sepals, 5 petals, 10 stamens, and 1 pistil with 3 or 5 styles. Some members of the family, such as cockle, are very troublesome weeds, while others, such as carnations and pinks, are highly prized as ornamental plants. Members of this family found in the Park may be distinguished as follows:

1   Sepals united to form a tubular calyx .. CATCHFLY (*Silene*, p. 147)
    Sepals distinct or nearly so 2
2   Petals deeply notched or lobed at the end 3
    Petals entire or with a very shallow notch at the end 5
3   Styles 3 4
    Styles 5 . . . . CHICKWEED (*Cerastium*, p. 146)
4   Petals 2-lobed, longer than the sepals . . . . . MEXICAN STARWORT
    . . . . (*Stellaria cuspidata*, p. 148)
    Petals 4-lobed, shorter than the sepals . . . THICK-LEAF DRYMARY
    . . . . (*Drymaria pachyphylla*, p. 146)
5   Stipules lacking . . . . SANDWORT (*Arenaria benthami*, p. 146)
    Stipules present . . JAMES' NAILWORT (*Paronychia jamesii*, p. 147)

Sandwort (*Arenaria benthami*)—This is an inconspicuous little, annual herb growing 4 to 10 inches high with very slender, almost thread-like, repeatedly forked branches and small, oblong, entire, opposite leaves. The white flowers are very small, and the fruit is a capsule. Not common. Found in canyons of the Chisos Mountains.

■ Chickweed (*Cerastium*)—Hairy, often sticky, annual herbs with small, opposite, entire leaves and white flowers with 5 sepals, 5 petals, 10 stamens, and 1 pistil with 5 styles. Sticky Chickweed (*Cerastium fontanum*, synonym *Cerastium viscosum*) has small flowers on stalks that are no longer than the very sharp-pointed sepals, and petals that are shorter than the sepals. Short-Stalk Chickweed (*Cerastium brachypodum*) has flowers on stalks that are two or three times as long as the sepals. Neither species is common, but both are reported from the Chisos Mountains.

⚹ Thick-Leaf Drymary (*Drymaria pachyphylla*)—A smooth, annual plant with slender, usually tufted stems, thickish, ovate or elliptic leaves, and sessile or nearly sessile flowers in axillary clusters.

PATRICK ALEXANDER

ANDERS HASTINGS

THICK-LEAF DRYMARY
(*Drymaria pachyphylla*)

JAMES' NAILWORT
(*Paronychia jamesii*)

James' Nailwort (*Paronychia jamesii*)—This plant differs from most members of the family in having only 5 stamens instead of 10 in each flower. Also, there are no petals, or only small rudiments of petals. The plant is a low perennial, much branched from the somewhat woody base, and growing 4 inches or more high. The leaves are linear.

Catchfly (*Silene*)—Annual or perennial herbs with fairly conspicuous flowers. The flowers have a tubular calyx which is 5-toothed, 5 petals usually with 2 scales at the base of the blade, 10 stamens, and 1 pistil with 3 styles. The Sleepy Catchfly (*Silene antirrhina*) is a smooth annual herb that grows 1 or 2 feet high and has lance-shaped or linear leaves and pink flowers borne on long stalks in a. panicle. It is called sleepy because its flowers are usually closed while the sun is shining, and it is called catchfly because one or more portions of the upper part of the stem are covered with a sticky substance that prevents insects from creeping up the stem. Cardinal Catchfly (*Silene laciniata*), sometimes called Fire-Pink, has rather weak stems often partly supported by other vegetation. The leaves are narrowly lance-shaped or linear and the flowers are bright crimson with the petals deeply 4-cleft, and the scales at the bases of the blades erect and toothed.

CK KELLY

CARDINAL CATCHFLY
(*Silene laciniata*)

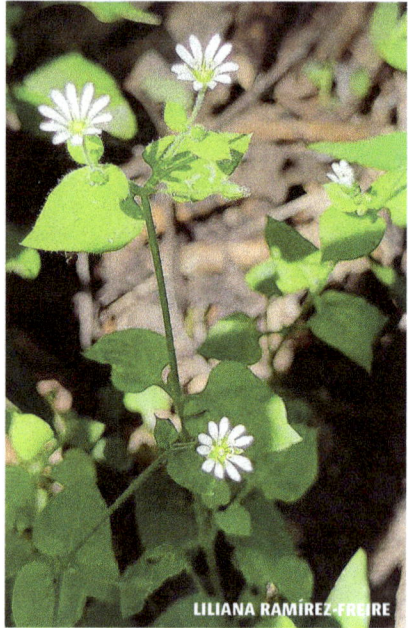

LILIANA RAMÍREZ-FREIRE

MEXICAN STARWORT
(*Stellaria cuspidata*)

🌱 **Mexican Starwort** (*Stellaria cuspidata*)—A low herb with stems forking and prostrate, smooth or nearly so. The leaves are ovate, on slender petioles, the lower ones often with heart-shaped bases. The deeply cleft petals are twice as long as the sepals.

BITTERSWEET FAMILY (CELASTRACEAE)

Shrubs with simple leaves, small, regular flowers, and, usually, conspicuous fruits. 🌱 **Desert-Yaupon** (*Schaefferia cuneifolia*) is a much-branched shrub, 2 to 4 feet high, with small, pale green, alternate, entire leaves, which are somewhat wedge-shaped and about ½ inch long. The flowers are small and inconspicuous, imperfect, and with the staminate and pistillate flowers on different plants; the fruits are about the size of somewhat flattened peas and are bright scarlet. Two additional genera (*Celastrus, Mortonia*) are reported from the Park.

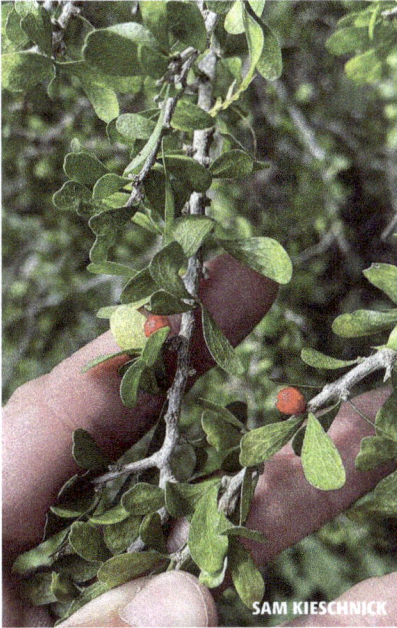

SAM KIESCHNICK

DESERT-YAUPON
(*Schaefferia cuneifolia*)

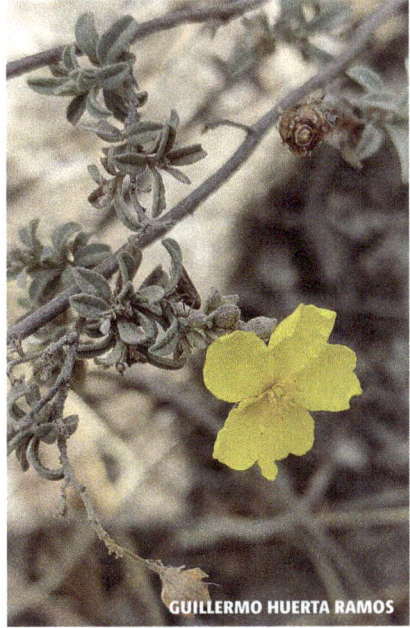

GUILLERMO HUERTA RAMOS

CLUSTERED FROSTWEED
(*Crocanthemum glomeratum*)

ROCK-ROSE FAMILY (CISTACEAE)

A small family of low shrubs or herbs with simple, entire leaves and regular flowers with five unequal sepals, three or five petals, an indefinite number of stamens, and one pistil.

■ Frostweed (*Crocanthemum*)—Low branching herbs often somewhat woody at the base. There are usually two kinds of flowers: early ones with yellow petals, which open only once in the sunshine and produce many-seeded pods, and later ones without petals, which produce smaller, few-seeded pods. ⚘ Clustered Frostweed (*Crocanthemum glomeratum*) has narrow, linear, or linear-oblong leaves. Flowers with petals are borne in terminal clusters and the yellow petals are about ¼ inch long. The flowers without petals are clustered in the leaf axils.

Chisos Mountain Pinweed (*Lechea mensalis*)—An uncommon herbaceous plant with densely clustered, erect, slender stems and very narrow leaves less than ½ inch long. The flowers have three red-purple petals, which are quite persistent, five unequal sepals, two small and bractlike and three concave or boat-shaped, and three feathery stigmas. The fruit is a slender, few-seeded pod.

CHIRICAHUA MTN. STINKWEED
(*Cleomella longipes*)

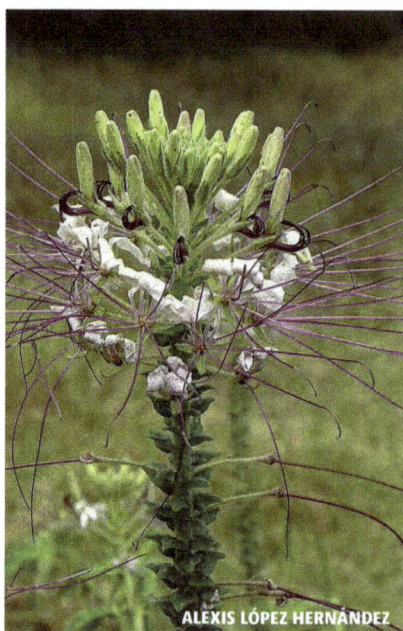

MEXICAN CLAMMYWEED
(*Polanisia uniglandulosa*)

SPIDER-FLOWER FAMILY (CLEOMACEAE)

A family of annual plants with watery juice usually having an unpleasant odor. The leaves are palmately compound with three leaflets, and the fairly large flowers are borne in terminal, crowded clusters. The flowers have four sepals, four petals, and six or more stamens, which are long and project from the flower conspicuously. The fruit is a one-celled pod. The following members of the family are found in the Park:

➢ **Chiricahua Mountain Stinkweed** (*Cleomella longipes*)—An erect annual 1 to 2 feet high with oblong or ovate leaflets and yellow flowers. The flowers have six stamens. Found in sandy ravines along the Rio Grande near Castolon but not common. A very odorous plant.

➢ **Mexican Clammyweed** (*Polanisia uniglandulosa*, synonym *Cleome uniglandulosa*)—A clammy, hairy herb growing 1 to 2 feet or more high with whitish or sulfur-yellow flowers in terminal crowded clusters. The stamens are often nearly 2 inches long. The leaflets are elliptic or ovate and the pods are sometimes as much as 4 inches long and contain numerous rather large, smooth seeds.

ROMI GALEOTA LENCINA

MATT BERGER

WHITE-MOUTH DAYFLOWER
(*Commelina erecta*)

BIRD-BILL DAYFLOWER
(*Commelina dianthifolia*)

SPIDERWORT FAMILY (COMMELINACEAE)

This is a small family of herbaceous plants with conspicuously jointed stems, parallel-veined leaves, and perfect flowers. The Wandering Jew, so common in greenhouses, is a member of this family. The base of each leaf forms a sheath about the stem.

■ Dayflower (*Commelina*)—The dayflowers produce flowers that are irregular, one of the three sepals and one of the three petals being smaller than the other two. There are six stamens and one pistil, but only three of the stamens are fertile, the others being sterile and smaller. The uppermost leaf has a heart-shaped, clasping base and is folded in such a way as to enclose the flowers. ⤳ White-Mouth Dayflower (*Commelina erecta*) has the two larger petals blue and the smaller one white. This species is fairly common in the open valleys and in the protection of shrubs in the desert scrub areas. ⤳ Bird-Bill Dayflower (*Commelina dianthifolia*), which has all three of the petals blue, grows in the more open canyons of the Chisos Mountains.

TRANS-PECOS SPIDERWORT
(*Tradescantia brevifolia*)

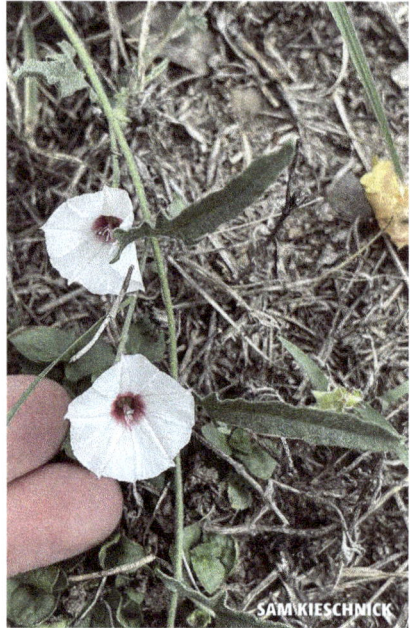

TEXAS BINDWEED
(*Convolvulus equitans*)

■ Spiderwort (*Tradescantia*)—The spiderwort differs from the dayflowers in having regular flowers. The three sepals are green, the three petals blue. The flowers are partly enclosed by two floral leaves that are very similar to the other leaves of the plant. The six stamens are all fertile. Canyon Spiderwort (*Tradescantia leiandra*) has a stout, often quite purplish stem with leaves 2 to 2½ inches long. The petals are broad at the base and distinct, and the filaments are not attached to the petals. ☙ Trans-Pecos Spiderwort (*Tradescantia brevifolia*) has broader, more ovate leaves. The petals are narrow at the base and are united into a tube, and the filaments are attached to the petals.

MORNING-GLORY FAMILY (CONVOLVULACEAE)

A family of annual or perennial herbs, mostly twining or trailing. The leaves, when present, are alternate. The flowers are complete, perfect, and regular. The five sepals are more or less united and remain on the fruit, while the five petals are completely united to form a bell-shaped or funnel-shaped corolla. The five stamens are attached to the corolla, and the fruit is a capsule containing a small number of relatively large seeds.

1 Leafless, twining parasites .... DODDER (*Cuscuta*, p. 153)
  Leafy, green plants 2
2 The 2 styles distinct; stems not twining 3
  The styles united up to the stigma; stems twining 4
3 Ovary deeply 2-lobed .... PONY'S-FOOT (*Dichondra*, p. 153)
  Ovary not deeply 2-lobed .... DWARF MORNING-GLORY
  .... (*Evolvulus*, p. 153)
4 Stigmas knob-shaped ...... MORNING-GLORY (*Ipomoea*, p. 153)
  Stigmas threadlike or cylindrical .... TEXAS BINDWEED
  .... (*Convolvulus equitans*, p. 153)

⤳ **Texas Bindweed** (*Convolvulus equitans*)—A twining or trailing plant with alternate, variously lobed or toothed or sometimes entire leaves and abundant flowers that resemble those of the morning-glory but are smaller. When the flowers first open they are white or pinkish but often becoming red-centered.

Large-Seed Dodder (*Cuscuta indecora*)—The dodder is a leafless parasite and is easily recognized by the twining, tangled mass of very slender, yellow stems growing on, and attached to, various other kinds of plants. It contains no chlorophyll and, therefore, has no green color.

■ **Pony's-Foot** (*Dichondra*)—Creeping but not twining herbs with alternate, entire, petioled leaves with kidney-shaped or nearly round blades. The flowers are shaped like those of a morning-glory but are very small and inconspicuous and yellowish or white in color. Two species occur in the Park: ⤳ **Silver Pony's-Foot** (*Dichondra argentea*) has silvery leaves and **New Mexico Pony's-Foot** (*Dichondra brachypoda*) green ones.

■ **Dwarf Morning-Glory** (*Evolvulus*)—Low, prostrate or somewhat erect herbs, often with woody base, with small, alternate, entire leaves and little, blue, morning-glory-like flowers usually less than a half inch across. **Shaggy Dwarf Morning-Glory** (*Evolvulus nuttallianus*) has leaves that are very hairy on both sides and flowers that are nearly ½ inch across. **Slender Dwarf Morning-Glory** (*Evolvulus alsinoides*) has the leaves nearly smooth above and flowers only about ¼ inch across.

■ **Morning-Glory** (*Ipomoea*)—The wild morning-glories are easily recognized because of their resemblance to cultivated morning-glories. **Lindheimer's Morning-Glory** (*Ipomoea lindheimeri*) has 3-lobed leaves and large pink or purple flowers as large or larger than those of cultivated varieties. ⤳ **Crest-Rib Morning-Glory** (*Ipomoea costellata*)

SILVER PONY'S-FOOT
(*Dichondra argentea*)

CREST-RIB MORNING-GLORY
(*Ipomoea costellata*)

has leaves that are cleft into five to seven narrow segments, and the flowers are only about an inch long and have smooth sepals. It is an annual. Cliff Morning-Glory (*Ipomoea rupicola*) is an uncommon species known from the Dead Horse Mountain area.

STONECROP FAMILY (CRASSULACEAE)

Usually smooth, mostly fleshy herbs with entire leaves and regular, perfect flowers, usually with a 4- or 5-parted calyx, four or five petals, stamens as many or twice as many as the petals, and pistils as many as the petals, the pistils distinct or united at the base. The fruit consists of four or five pods, which open along one side only.

➤ Desert-Savior (*Echeveria strictiflora*)—An herb with a basal cluster of fleshy, lance-shaped leaves, which may be 1 to 2 inches long, and an unbranched stem, 6 to 12 inches tall, bearing two or three small leaves and a spike of reddish flowers, the spike being 3 or 4 inches long. The petals are somewhat united at the base and there are 10 stamens.

ERIC KNIGHT

ERIC KNIGHT

DESERT-SAVIOR
(*Echeveria strictiflora*)

WRIGHT'S STONECROP
(*Sedum wrightii*)

■ **Stonecrop** (*Sedum*)—Small, fleshy or somewhat woody herbs with the usually oblong or ovate leaves, in our species, all less than an inch long, and the petals distinct nearly to the base. The 4 or 5 pistils are also distinct or nearly so, and there are usually 10 stamens. The flowers are borne in rather flat, terminal clusters and, in our species, are usually white or white tinged with pink. Three species have been recognized in the Park: Havard's Stonecrop (*Sedum havardii*), Robert's Stonecrop (*Sedum robertsianum*), and ➢ Wright's Stonecrop (*Sedum wrightii*). They are all rather similar and not readily distinguished from one another.

Rat's-Tail-Succulent (*Villadia squamulosa*)—A small, erect herb, partly prostrate at the base, with many linear leaves less than an inch long and spurred. The flowers are in a spikelike cluster. They are minute and have white petals tinged with pink and prominent, yellow nectar scales. Found in rock crevices and talus slopes in the Chisos Mountains, its only known location in the United States and its northernmost known locality.

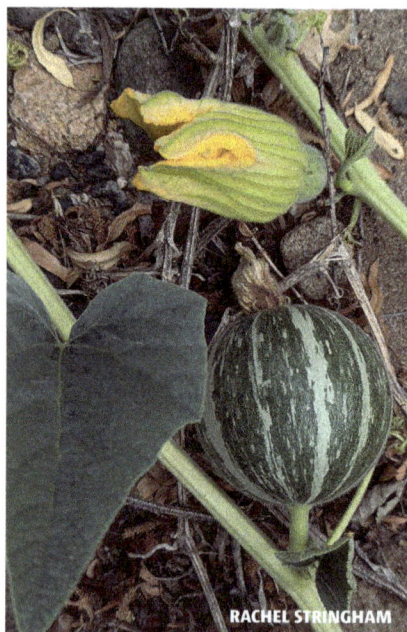

BUFFALO GOURD
(*Cucurbita foetidissima*)

DEER-APPLES
(*Ibervillea tenuisecta*)

GOURD FAMILY (CUCURBITACEAE)

This is the family to which all the gourds, melons, squashes, and cucumbers belong. Most of the members have rather fleshy stems and produce tendrils by which they climb over fences or over other plants. The flowers are imperfect, the stems and pistils being in separate flowers, sometimes on separate plants and sometimes on the same plant. The fruit may be like a melon, which is a modified berry, or it may be more berrylike, or, in some cases, dry and membranous.

➤ **Buffalo Gourd** (*Cucurbita foetidissima*)—A large, coarse, perennial plant with trailing stems. The leaf-blades are triangular-ovate, longer than wide, often nearly a foot long. The fruits are globose and gourdlike, about 2½ inches long.

➤ **Deer-Apples** (*Ibervillea tenuisecta*)—A slender-stemmed vine climbing by tendrils and often very diffusely branched. The leaves have rather thickish blades, ½ to 1½ inches in diameter and 3- to 5-parted, with the parts deeply cleft into narrow divisions. The flowers are yellow, and the fruits look like little scarlet melons about ½ inch in diameter.

SMOOTH BUR-CUCUMBER
(*Sicyos glaber*)

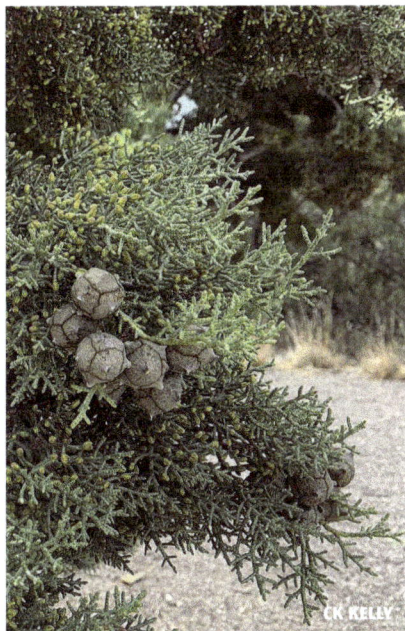

ARIZONA CYPRESS
(*Hesperocyparis arizonica*)

Little-Leaf Bur-Cucumber (*Sicyos microphyllus*, synonym *Sicyos parviflorus*)—A vine climbing by forked tendrils and bearing clusters of small, white flowers that are followed by bristly, egg-shaped berries, ¼ to ½ of an inch long. The alternate leaves are simple, with three to five triangular lobes, and are 2 to 6 inches long and about as broad. ❧ Smooth Bur-Cucumber (*Sicyos glaber*), a plant with much the same general appearance as the Little-Leaf Bur-Cucumber, but bearing smooth, nonbristly fruits, is found on moist, shaded slopes of the Chisos Mountains.

CYPRESS FAMILY (CUPRESSACEAE)

❧ Arizona Cypress (*Hesperocyparis arizonica*, synonym *Cupressus arizonica*)—This is a large tree that occurs only in the vicinity of Boot Spring in the Chisos Mountains. The leaves are similar to those of a juniper, but the cones are dry and they open at maturity to allow the seeds to drop out. The cones are from about ¾ inch to about 1¼ inches in diameter, and before maturity they look very much like berries.

ANDERS HASTINGS

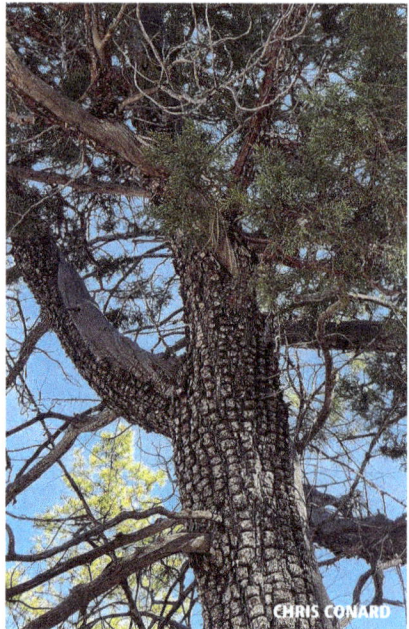

CHRIS CONARD

ONE-SEED JUNIPER
(*Juniperus monosperma*)

ALLIGATOR JUNIPER
(*Juniperus deppeana*)

■ Juniper (*Juniperus*)—The junipers, often called cedars, have scale-like leaves and fruits which are really little cones in which the scales have become so fleshy that they appear like berries. These fruits do not open at maturity as do those of the cypress and the pines. Three species of juniper found in the Park, all occurring at medium elevations in the Chisos Mountains, may be distinguished below. Notable is Drooping Juniper, reaching its northern limit in Big Bend, and found nowhere else in the United States.

1   Branches noticeably drooping . . . . Drooping Juniper
. . . . (*Juniperus flaccida*)
Branches not noticeably drooping 2
2   Bark of trunk separating into long, thin, persistent scales or fibers
. . . . ⇗ One-Seed Juniper (*Juniperus monosperma*)
Bark of trunk separated into thick, nearly square plates like the pattern on the skin of an alligator . . . . ⇗ Alligator Juniper
. . . . (*Juniperus deppeana*)

Red-Berry Juniper (*Juniperus coahuilensis*) and Pinchot's Juniper (*Juniperus pinchotii*) are also reported.

TEXAS PERSIMMON
(*Diospyros texana*)

WOODY CRINKLEMAT
(*Tiquilia canescens*)

EBONY FAMILY (EBENACEAE)

This is a small, chiefly tropical family of trees or shrubs with alternate, entire leaves and flowers which on some trees have, in our representative of the family, 20 to 40 stamens and no pistil, while on other trees they have a pistil and 10 or 12 imperfect stamens. The fruit is a several-celled berry. Our only representative of the family is the following:

 Texas Persimmon (*Diospyros texana*)—A shrub or small tree, which is widely branched and has heavy, white wood. The leaves are mostly oblong and nearly sessile. The leaves, small branches, and the outsides of the flowers are short-hairy. The calyx is 5- or 6-parted, and the fruit is black and edible when ripe. Frequent in arroyos and dry creek beds in the lower part of the Chisos Mountains and on the desert.

SCORPION-BUSH FAMILY (EHRETIACEAE)

 Crinklemat (*Tiquilia*, synonym *Coldenia*)—Small, very leafy shrubs with alternate leaves and sessile flowers variously arranged. Four species have been found in the Park. Woody Crinklemat (*Tiquilia*

HAIRY CRINKLEMAT
(*Tiquilia hispidissima*)

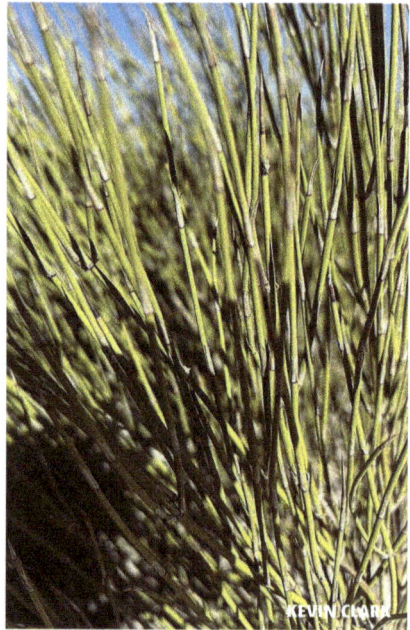

LONG-LEAF JOINT-FIR
(*Ephedra trifurca*)

canescens) has white or pink flowers and leaves about ¼ inch long and about half as wide. ⤳ Hairy Crinklemat (*Tiquilia hispidissima*) has pinkish flowers and very narrow leaves. Mexican Crinklemat (*Tiquilia mexicana*) has blue or purplish flowers and leaves that are about intermediate between the two preceding species. Plumed Crinklemat (*Tiquilia greggii*) is a low, much-branched shrub with small, ovate or oval leaves and pink to magenta flowers in headlike clusters. The calyx lobes are very narrow and the corolla is bell-shaped.

MORMON-TEA FAMILY (EPHEDRACEAE)

This is a family of peculiar shrubs called by various common names, including Desert Tea, Mormon-Tea, and Joint-Fir. They are loosely related to the Pine Family, but they cannot be said to produce cones since the fruits consist merely of one or more seeds enclosed by several or many scales. The stems are pointed and hollow, and the leaves are reduced to two or three scales at each joint of the stem. The stems of these plants are sometimes steeped as a substitute for tea. They were formerly much used for this purpose by the Mormons. All members of the family

ROUGH JOINT-FIR
(*Ephedra aspera*)

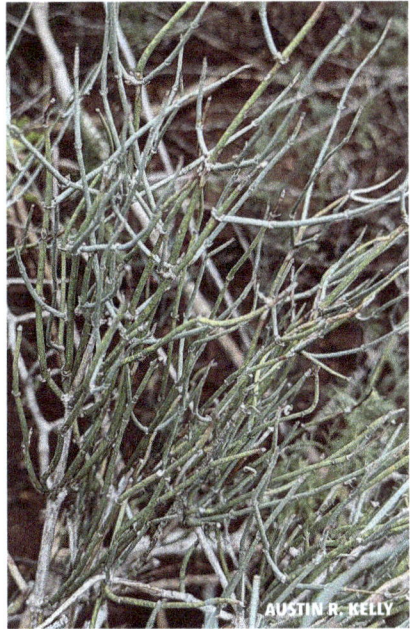

CLAPWEED
(*Ephedra antisyphilitica*)

found in the Park belong to the genus *Ephedra*.

Ephedra is a dioecious genus, that is, the staminate and pistillate flow-ers are produced on separate plants. ➹ Long-Leaf Joint-Fir (*Ephedra trifurca*) and ➹ Rough Joint-Fir (*Ephedra aspera*) are the two com-moner species in the Park area. *E. aspera* usually has two scale leaves at each joint; the fruit has five to seven pairs of greenish to red-brown scales with membranous margins and bears only one seed. *E. trifurca* usually has three scale leaves at each joint, and the fruit has six to nine whorls of nearly round, stalked, and somewhat transparent scales with entire margins. ➹ Clapweed (*Ephedra antisyphilitica*) is less common but has two scale leaves at each joint, and the fruit has four to six pairs of egg-shaped scales. The inner pairs of scales usually become fleshy, red, and somewhat juicy when ripe.

HEATH FAMILY (ERICACEAE)

A fairly large family containing such well-known plants as blueberries, rhododendron, and the mountain laurel of both the East and the West. The plants from which wintergreen essence is made also belong to this

NEPTALÍ MARCIAL

ALEXIS LÓPEZ HERNÁNDEZ

TEXAS MADRONE
(*Arbutus xalapensis*)

NEW MEXICO COPPERLEAF
(*Acalypha neomexicana*)

family. The members of the heath family are mostly shrubs with simple leaves and small or medium-sized flowers that are perfect and regular or nearly so. Only one representative of the family occurs in the Park:

🌱 Texas Madrone (*Arbutus xalapensis*, synonym *Arbutus texana*)— A shrub or small tree with red or reddish-brown branches. The outer bark peels off, exposing a very smooth, red or reddish-brown bark. The leaves are simple, alternate, oblong or ovate, and 1 to 3 inches long. The small flowers are white or flesh-color with a 5-toothed corolla and 10 stamens. The fruit is a reddish berry about the size of a currant.

SPURGE FAMILY (EUPHORBIACEAE)

Herbs or shrubs with acrid or often milky juice. The leaves are simple and the flowers are imperfect and in most cases inconspicuous, but in some cases very beautiful. In the African desert, many members of this family resemble American cacti in their growth habit. The ovary of the flower is usually 3-celled, but sometimes only 2 or more than 3; and the fruit is a 3-lobed and 3-celled capsule with one or two seeds in each cell. The members of the family found in the Park may be distinguished as follows:

1   Plants woody, branched from the base; usually with spatula-shaped, alternate leaves which appear after spring and summer rains. . . . . LEATHERSTEM (*Jatropha dioica*, p. 169)
Plants herbaceous or shrubby only at the base 2

2   Plants clothed with starlike or sometimes scalelike hairs; leaves entire or nearly so . . . . CROTON (*Croton*, p. 164)
Plants smooth or with simple hairs that may be attached at one end or in the middle 3

3   Flowers appearing to be perfect, the cluster of 1 pistillate and many to few staminate flowers surrounded by a persistent, somewhat united involucre, often bearing on the rim 1 to 5 glands with or without petallike appendages . . . . SPURGE (*Euphorbia*, p. 165)
Flowers plainly imperfect, not in an involucre 4

4   Petals present; filaments united into a column YUMA SILVERBUSH
. . . . (*Argythamnia serrata*, p. 164)
Petals none; filaments not united or united only at the base 5

5   Pistillate flowers subtended by leaflike bracts; styles divided into several hairlike segments . . . . COPPERLEAF (*Acalypha*, p. 163)
Pistillate flowers not subtended by leaflike bracts; styles undivided or divided into only 2 or 3 segments 6

6   Leaves with harsh, often stinging hairs; plants slender and often twining . . . . BRANCHED NOSEBURN (*Tragia ramosa*, p. 170)
Leaves without hairs as above; plants herbaceous or somewhat shrubby at the base, plants about 6 inches high . . . .
. . . . (see **Phyllanthaceae**, Leaf-Flower Family, p. 231)

■ Copperleaf (*Acalypha*)—Annual or perennial plants with simple, petioled, toothed leaves and imperfect flowers, the staminate and pistillate flowers sometimes on separate plants but more often on the same plant and often in the same spike. The staminate flowers have 4 sepals and 8 to 16 stamens, and the pistillate flowers have 3 to 5 sepals and one pistil with a cluster of hairlike stigmas and are subtended by leaflike bracts.

Three species are found in the Park: ⤳ New Mexico Copperleaf (*Acalypha neomexicana*) is an annual plant and has the spikes mostly axillary and the stigmas green and inconspicuous. Lindheimer's Copperleaf (*Acalypha phleoides*, synonym *Acalypha lindheimeri*) is perennial and has the spikes mostly terminal and the stigmas bright red and showy. The leaves are ovate to lanceolate and to 2 inches long.

ROUND COPPERLEAF
(*Acalypha monostachya*)

YUMA SILVERBUSH
(*Argythamnia serrata*)

➷ **Round Copperleaf** (*Acalypha monostachya*) is also perennial and has the spikes mostly terminal but the spikes are smaller, the stigmas are inconspicuous, and the leaves are nearly round and usually less than ½ inch in diameter.

➷ **Yuma Silverbush** (*Argythamnia serrata*, synonym *Ditaxis neomexicana*)—This is a low shrub usually less than a foot high with alternate, entire, lance-shaped leaves an inch or less in length. The inconspicuous, imperfect flowers are produced in small clusters. The staminate flowers have 10 stamens united into a central column and the pistillate flowers have one pistil with three styles, which are united below. The fruit is a small, 3-lobed pod.

■ **Croton** (*Croton*)—Annual or perennial, herbaceous or woody plants with simple, alternate, entire leaves and imperfect flowers, which are quire inconspicuous. The staminate flowers are above and the pistillate flowers are below in those species in which both kinds are on the same plant. The calyx is 4- or 5-lobed. Petals may be absent in staminate flowers and absent or rudimentary in pistillate flowers. The ovary is 3- or sometimes 2-celled, the ovules solitary, the styles 3 or sometimes 2 and 1- to 4-times forked. The capsules are 3- or sometimes 1-seeded.

BUSH CROTON
(*Croton fruticulosus*)

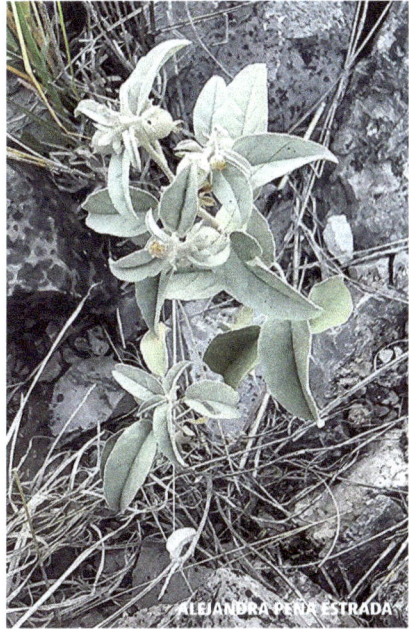

LEATHERWEED
(*Croton pottsii*)

Six species have been found in the Park; three are described as follows: ⌧ Bush Croton (*Croton fruticulosus*) is a slender-branched shrub, growing 3 to 6 feet high, with branches and the under surfaces of the leaves covered with gray or yellowish, velvety hairs. The leaf blades are narrowly ovate and 1 to 3 inches long, and the petioles are about half as long. ⌧ Leatherweed (*Croton pottsii*) is somewhat shrubby, especially at the base, and is silvery colored throughout from the velvety, silver-colored hairs. The leaves are oval or oblong and 1 to 2 inches long. Grassland Croton (*Croton dioicus*) is somewhat shrubby, especially at the base, and is silvery throughout except on the upper leaf surfaces. The leaf blades are narrowly oblong or lance-shaped and ½ to 2 inches long, and the petioles are very short.

■ Spurge (*Euphorbia*)—This is a large and variable genus with representatives on every continent. Some of the desert species are leafless or nearly so and have fleshy stems like cacti. Others grow in humid climates and are quite leafy. Many are entirely herbaceous, but some are shrubby. The most notable characteristic of the genus is the arrangement of the flowers. The flowers are imperfect, each staminate flower consisting of a single naked stamen and each pistillate flower of a single

pistil. However, the flowers are arranged with one pistillate flower surrounded by few to many staminate flowers and all within an involucre,
the five lobes of which alternate with fleshy glands, which may have
quite showy, petallike appendages. The whole cluster appears like a single flower with a pistil, several stamens, and a calyx or corolla.

   All the spurges have a milky juice that may contain some rubber,
sometimes in commercial quantities in foreign species. One species,
Euphorbia antisyphilitica, called Candelilla or Waxplant, produces a wax
that has been much used for the production of candles, phonograph
records, shoe polish, floor wax, and various other commercial articles.
This species has also been much used in Mexico as a remedy for vene-
real diseases. Some species are very ornamental. *Euphorbia marginata*,
called Snow-on-the-Mountain, is often cultivated as an ornamental
plant. The cultivated poinsettia, *Euphorbia pulcherrima*, with bright-red
floral bracts, is a favorite Christmas plant. Some of the species are very
readily recognized, while others are quite difficult to determine. The
following key will help in distinguishing some of the many *Euphorbia*
species found in the Park:

1   Stems mostly leafless ... ⫟ **Candelilla** (*Euphorbia antisyphilitica*)
    Stems leafy 2
2   Glands of the involucre without petallike appendages; leaf bases
    symmetrical or nearly so 3
    Glands of the involucre mostly with petallike appendages; leaves
    with unsymmetrical bases 6
3   Glands of the involucre either deeply cupped or concealed by the
    narrow segments of the margin which are bent in over the glands 4
    Glands of the involucre flat or convex and never concealed. . . . . . .
    . . . . ⫟ **Horned Spurge** (*Euphorbia brachycera*)
4   Capsules scarcely lobed and plainly longer than thick; glands con-
    cealed . . . . **Beetle Spurge** (*Euphorbia eriantha*)
    Capsules strongly lobed and plainly wider than long; glands naked
    5
5   Leaves mostly opposite throughout, mostly slightly to coarsely
    many-toothed; stems mostly hairy; introduced .. **David's Spurge**
    . . . . (*Euphorbia davidii*)
    Leaves on the middle portions of the stem alternate and entire or
    nearly so; stems not hairy; native . . . . . ⫟ **Fire-on-the-Mountain**
    . . . . (*Euphorbia cyathophora*)

CANDELILLA
(*Euphorbia antisyphilitica*)

6   Ovary and casule hairy. 7
    Ovary and capsule smooth. 11
7   Annuals 8
    Perennials 9
8   Involucres urn-shaped . . . . . . Yuma Sandmat (*Euphorbia setiloba*)
    Involucres obconical to bell-shaped . . . . Sonoran Sandmat
    . . . . (*Euphorbia micromera*)
9   Involucres borne in dense clusters; leaves often toothed . . . .
    . . . . Head Sandmat (*Euphorbia capitellata*)
    Involucres solitary at the nodes; leaves entire 10
10 Involucres urn-shaped . . Arizona Sandmat (*Euphorbia arizonica*)
    Involucres obconical to bell-shaped . . . . Ashy Sandmat
    . . . . (*Euphorbia cinerascens*)
11 Stipules united into a white, smooth, membranous scale 12
    Stipules otherwise 13
12 Annuals . . . . Matted Sandmat (*Euphorbia serpens*)
    Perennials . . Snow-on-the-Mountain (*Euphorbia albomarginata*)

HORNED SPURGE
(*Euphorbia brachycera*)

FIRE-ON-THE-MOUNTAIN
(*Euphorbia cyathophora*)

13 Glands of involucre without appendages 14
    Glands of involucre with appendages 16
14 Annuals 15
    Perennials .... Small-Seed Sandmat (*Euphorbia simulans*)
15 Staminate flowers 2 to 5 in an involucre ...... Sonoran Sandmat
    .... (*Euphorbia micromera*)
    Staminate flowers 31 to 36 in an involucre ... Terlingua Sandmat
    .... (*Euphorbia theriaca*)
16 Perennials... 17
    Annuals 18
17 Involucres borne in dense clusters; leaves often toothed ....
    .... ⮞ Head Sandmat (*Euphorbia capitellata*)
    Involucres solitary at the nodes; leaves entire . Fendler's Sandmat
    .... (*Euphorbia fendleri*)
18 Leaves mostly more than three-fifths of an inch long, toothed ...
    .... Hyssop-Leaf Sandmat (*Euphorbia hyssopifolia*)
    Leaves mostly more than 3/5 inches long, entire or toothed .. 19
19 Leaves more or less hairy................................ 20
    Leaves smooth 21

JARED SHORMA

JO ROBERTS

HEAD SANDMAT
(*Euphorbia capitellata*)

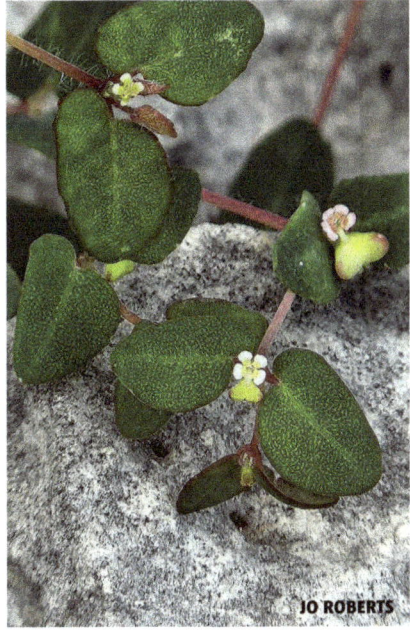

HAIRY SANDMAT
(*Euphorbia villifera*)

20 Capsules less than 1/16 inches long . . . . ❧ **Hairy Sandmat**
. . . . (*Euphorbia villifera*)
   Capsules more than 1/8 inches long . . . . **Sawtooth Sandmat**
. . . . (*Euphorbia serrula*)

21 Leaves entire . . . . **Boquillas Sandmat** (*Euphorbia golondrina*)
   Leaves toothed **22**

22 Staminate flowers 1 to 5 (mostly 4) in an involucre; seeds with defi-
   nite, transverse ridges . . . . **Rib-Seed Sandmat**
. . . . (*Euphorbia glyptosperma*)
   Staminate flowers 5 to 18 in an involucre; seeds smooth or slightly
   roughened, without regular ridges . . . . **Thyme-Leaf Sandmat**
. . . . (*Euphorbia serpillifolia*)

❧ **Leatherstem** (*Jatropha dioica*)—A shrub, usually 1 to 2 or more
feet high, sparingly branched, with ovate, heart-shaped, or spatulate
leaves, about 1 to 1 inches long, in clusters on short, lateral branches.
The staminate and pistillate flowers are on separate plants and have conspicuous corollas. Fairly common in the desert scrub throughout the
Park.

LEATHERSTEM
(*Jatropha dioica*)

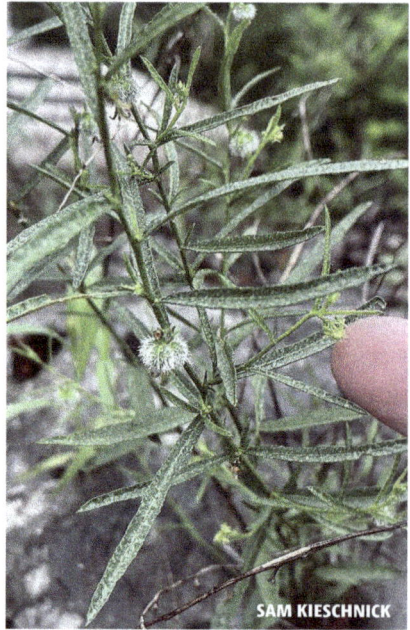

BRANCHED NOSEBURN
(*Tragia ramosa*)

↗ Branched Noseburn (*Tragia ramosa*)—A perennial herb with the stems erect or somewhat reclining. The leaves are narrowly lance-shaped or broadly linear, rather sharply toothed, and sparingly armed with stinging hairs. The small, imperfect flowers are produced in terminal or lateral racemes, the pistillate below the staminate. The calyx of the staminate flower is 4- or 5-parted, and there are four or five stamens. Found on some of the middle and lower slopes of the Chisos Mountains. Dog-Tooth Noseburn (*Tragia amblyodonta*) is also reported from the Park.

PEA FAMILY (FABACEAE)

The Pea Family is a large and important group. It contains not only all the different kinds of beans, peas, clovers, and peanuts, but many other herbaceous flowering plants and many trees and shrubs, some of which are very ornamental. The flowers are perfect, regular or irregular, usually with five petals, few or many stamens, and one pistil with the ovary superior. Leaves mostly compound. Most Fabaceae found in the Park can be keyed as follows:

1   Flowers regular, the petals not overlapping in the bud. 2
    Flowers usually more or less irregular, the petals overlapping in the
    bud 8
2   Stamens numerous, more than 10 3
    Stamens 10 or 5, distinct 4
3   Stamens distinct. . . . . ACACIA (former *Acacia*, p. 172)
    Stamens united . . . . TEXAS FAIRY-DUSTER
    . . . . (*Calliandra eriophylla*, p. 174)
4   Each anther bearing a gland. 5
    Anthers not gland bearing 6
5   Pods straight or merely curved . . . . . MESQUITE (*Prosopis*, p. 180)
    Pods spirally twisted. . . . . WESTERN HONEY MESQUITE
    . . . . (*Prosopis glandulosa* var. *torreyi*, p. 180)
6   Plants prickly from stipular spines . . . . MIMOSA (*Mimosa*, p. 179)
    Plants not prickly 7
7   Leaflets very small, linear, veinless . . . . VELVET BUNDLEFLOWER
    . . . . (*Desmanthus velutinus*, p. 177)
    Leaflets broadly oblong and veiny. . . . . . LITTLE-LEAF LEADTREE
    . . . . (*Leucaena retusa*, p. 178)
8   Uppermost petal enclosed in the bud by the other 4 9
    Uppermost petal enclosing the other 4 in the bud 12
9   Flowers pink or purple; leaves simple, entire 10
    Flowers yellow; leaves compound. 11
10 Low shrubs; leaves small, narrow . . . . *Krameria*
    . . . . (see **Ratany Family**, Krameriaceae, p. 193)
    Large shrub or small tree; leaves large, heart-shaped . . . . REDBUD
    . . . . (*Cercis canadensis*, p. 175)
11 Leaves once-pinnate. . SENNA, SENSITIVE PLANT (*Senna*, p. 181)
    Leaves twice-pinnate . . . . WAXY RUSH-PEA
    . . . . (*Hoffmannseggia*, *Pomaria*, p. 178)
12 Stamens 10, all distinct . . . . TEXAS MOUNTAIN LAUREL
    . . . . (*Dermatophyllum secundiflorum*, p. 177)
    Stamens 10, 9 united and 1 separate. 13
13 Stems climbing by leaf tendrils . . . . VETCH (*Vicia*, p. 181)
    Stems twining or trailing but without tendrils; leaflets 3 14
    Stems erect, not climbing or trailing 16
14 Flowers yellow. TEXAS SNOUT-BEAN (*Rhynchosia texana*, p. 180)
    Flowers not yellow. 15

15 Calyx 4-toothed; style not bearded .... LONG-LEAF COLOGANIA
.... (*Cologania angustifolia*, p. 175)
Calyx 5-toothed or cleft; style bearded . BEAN (*Phaseolus*, p. 179)
16 Leaves palmately compound .... BIG BEND BLUEBONNET
.... (*Lupinus havardii*, p. 178)
Leaves pinnately compound 17
17 Pods spirally twisted .... ALFALFA (*Medicago sativa*, p. 178)
Pods not spirally twisted 18
18 Flowers 1 or a few in the leaf axils 19
Flowers in spikes, racemes, or heads...................... 20
19 Herbs with somewhat woody base .... LONG-BRACT DEERWEED
.... (*Acmispon oroboides*, p. 173)
Shrubs LITTLE-LEAF GREENTWIG (*Brongniartia minutifolia*, p. 174)
20 Leaves dotted with glands 21
Leaves not dotted with glands 22
21 Corolla nearly regular, with 5 distinct and nearly equal petals ....
.... TEXAS KIDNEYWOOD (*Eysenhardtia texana*, p. 178)
One petal distinct and the other 4 borne on the middle of the cleft
stamen-tube .... PRAIRIE-CLOVER (*Dalea*, p. 175)
22 Pods transversely several-jointed with 1 seed in each joint ....
.... TICK-TREFOIL (*Desmodium*, p. 177)
Pods not transversely jointed ... MILKVETCH (*Astragalus*, p. 174)

■ Acacia (former *Acacia*)—Spiny or prickly shrubs with twice-pinnate leaves with small leaflets, and flowers with numerous, rather long stamens, borne in heads or cylindrical spikes in the axils of leaves. The nine species in the Park, formerly all considered genus *Acacia*, have been split into several new genera, and may be distinguished as follows:

1 Flowers in cylindrical spikes 2
Flowers in heads 3
2 Leaflets 2 to 4 pairs, ¼ to ½ inch long .... Blackbrush Acacia
.... (*Vachellia rigidula*, synonym *Acacia rigidula*)
Leaflets 4 to 6 pairs, much smaller .... ✈ Catclaw Acacia
.... (*Senegalia greggii*, synonym *Acacia greggii*)
3 Leaflets 20 to 40 pairs 4
Leaflets 6 to 10 pairs 5
Leaflets 2 to 6 pairs..................................... 6
4 Pods 8- to 10-seeded .... Guajillo
.... (*Senegalia berlandieri*, synonym *Acacia berlandieri*)

CATCLAW ACACIA
(*Senegalia greggii*)

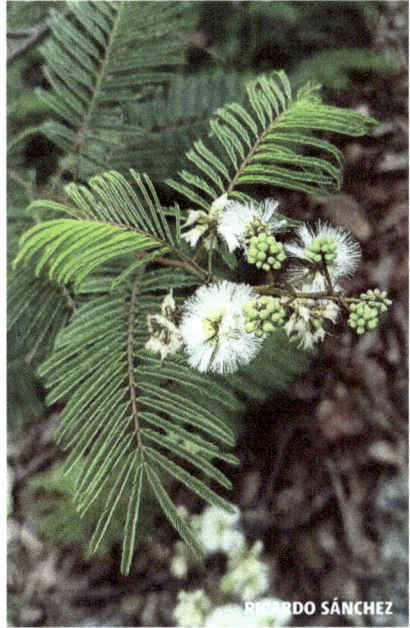

PRAIRIE ACACIA
(*Acaciella angustissima*)

Pods 3- to 7-seeded . . . . ➤ Prairie Acacia
. . . . (*Acaciella angustissima*, synonym *Acacia angustissima*)

5 Pods constricted between the seeds . . . . Mescat Acacia
. . . . (*Vachellia constricta*, synonym *Acacia constricta*)
Pods not constricted between the seeds . . . . Prairie Wattle
. . . . (*Acaciella angustissima* var. *hirta*, synonym *Acacia texensis*)

6 Spines ¼ to ½ inch long . . . . Viscid Acacia
. . . . (*Vachellia vernicosa*, synonym *Acacia vernicosa*)
Spines much shorter 7

7 Pods straight and large, 4 inches long and ½ inch wide; leaflets
broad . . . . Roemer Catclaw
. . . . (*Senegalia roemeriana*, synonym *Acacia roemeriana*)
Pods smaller and curved into a semicircle or nearly a complete cir-
cle; leaflets narrow, subcylindric . . . . Schott's Acacia
. . . . (*Vachellia schottii*, synonym *Acacia schottii*)

Long-Bract Deerweed (*Acmispon oroboides*, synonym *Lotus ple-
beius*)—An herbaceous plant, somewhat woody at the base, with compound leaves with about five oblong or linear leaflets and yellow flowers

SMALL-FLOWER MILKVETCH
(*Astragalus nuttallianus*)

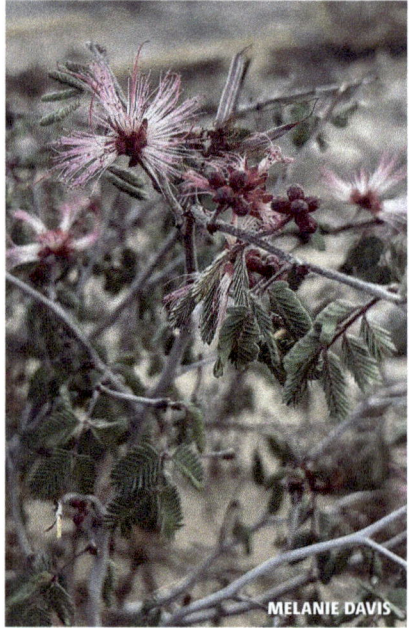

TEXAS FAIRY-DUSTER
(*Calliandra eriophylla*)

with corolla about an inch long on rather long stalks. The pods are 1 inch or more in length.

■ **Milkvetch** (*Astragalus*)—Herbs with odd-pinnate leaves and usually purple flowers in racemes or spikes. Some species are poisonous to stock and produce the disease known as loco. Four species are found in the Park, two are described below. ➤ **Small-Flower Milkvetch** (*Astragalus nuttallianus*, synonym *Astragalus davisianus*) grows only a few inches high and has very small leaflets, usually less than ¼ inch long. **Woolly Milkvetch** (*Astragalus mollissimus*) is a larger and stouter plant with leaflets about ¾ inch long and ¼ inch wide.

Little-Leaf Greentwig (*Brongniartia minutifolia*)—This is a low shrub, 1 to 3 or 4 feet high, with slender, smooth, green branches, feathery leaves 1 to 2 inches long with very small and very narrow leaflets, and solitary flesh-colored or yellowish flowers in the axils.

➤ **Texas Fairy-Duster** (*Calliandra eriophylla*)—A low, much-branched shrub 3 inches to a foot or more high with somewhat hairy branches and petioles. The leaves are twice-pinnate with 8 to 12 pairs of leaflets on each leaf branch, the leaflets only about one-sixth of an

REDBUD
(*Cercis canadensis*)

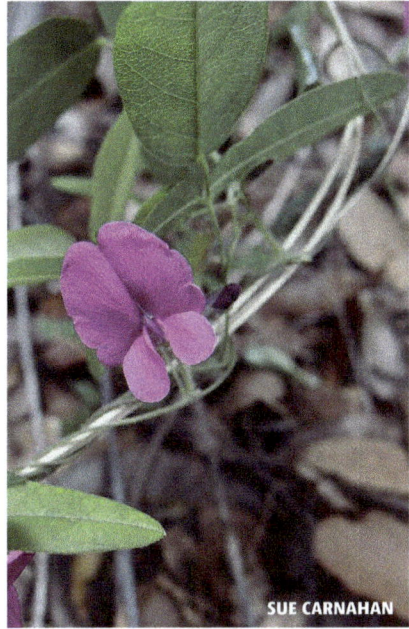

LONG-LEAF COLOGANIA
(*Cologania angustifolia*)

inch long. The flowers are in heads and the stamens extend far beyond the corolla. The pods are 1¼ inches long and ¼ inch broad. They are hairy with whitish, silky hairs except on the thickened margins, which are nearly smooth.

⤙ Redbud (*Cercis canadensis*)—A small tree with simple, heart-shaped or kidney-shaped leaves and clusters of pink flowers appearing before the leaves.

⤙ Long-Leaf Cologania (*Cologania angustifolia*)—Twining herbs with pinnate leaves with usually three narrowly linear leaflets 1 to 2 or more inches long and violet or red flowers, one or more in the axils of the leaves, with straight or curved pods that are 1 to 4 inches long.

■ Prairie-Clover (*Dalea*)—Herbs or shrubs with odd-pinnate leaves with small, entire leaflets dotted with glands and yellow or purple flowers in terminal spikes. The pods are small, flat, 1- or 2-seeded, and enclosed within the persistent calyx. Fourteen species have been identified in the Park; seven are keyed below:

1   Calyx not hairy, the teeth short; shrub ..... **Black Prairie-Clover**
 .... (*Dalea frutescens*)

FEATHERPLUME
(*Dalea formosa*)

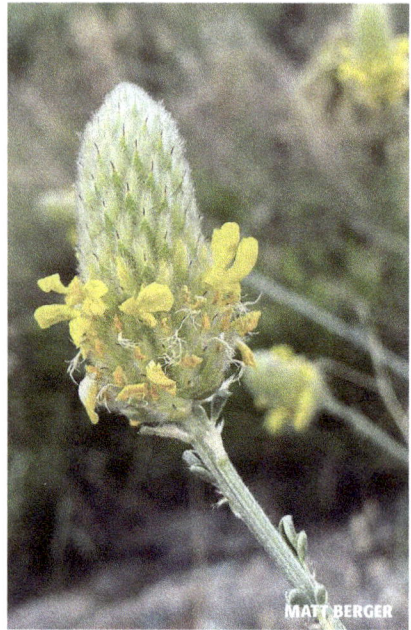

GOLDEN PRAIRIE-CLOVER
(*Dalea aurea*)

Calyx hairy, the teeth longer 2

2 Stems and leaves not hairy 3
   Stems and leaves hairy 4

3 Leaflets about 11 to 13 . . . . Bearded Prairie-Clover
   . . . . (*Dalea pogonanthera*)
   Leaflets 21 to 41 . . . . Fox-Tail Prairie-Clover (*Dalea leporina*)

4 Both stems and leaves beset with conspicuous, black glands . . . . . .
   . . . . Gland-Leaf Prairie-Clover (*Dalea lachnostachys*)
   Glands much less conspicuous 5

5 Plant spreading, densely white-hairy: leaflets about 11 to 15 . . . . .
   . . . . Downy Prairie-Clover (*Dalea neomexicana*)
   Plant erect, less densely hairy; leaflets 3 to 9, mostly 5 6

6 Plants shrubby; flowers purple ➷ Featherplume (*Dalea formosa*)
   Plants herbaceous; flowers yellow 7

7 Plant a foot or more high; spike about an inch long . . . .
   . . . . ➷ Golden Prairie-Clover (*Dalea aurea*)
   Plant 2 to 6 inches high; spike often 2 inches long . . . .
   . . . . Wright's Prairie-Clover (*Dalea wrightii*)

TEXAS MOUNTAIN-LAUREL
(*Dermatophyllum secundiflorum*)

VELVET BUNDLEFLOWER
(*Desmanthus velutinus*)

Texas Mountain Laurel (*Dermatophyllum secundiflorum*, synonym *Sophora secundiflora*)—A stout shrub with dark green leaves with nine oblong leaflets, and terminal racemes of showy, violet, fragrant flowers. The pods are woody, angular, 2 to 4 inches long, and contain three or four red beans as large as small marbles and very poisonous.

Velvet Bundleflower (*Desmanthus velutinus*)—An herbaceous or somewhat shrubby plant with twice-pinnate leaves and small heads of greenish-white flowers on axillary peduncles. The flowers have 10 stamens, which are not gland-bearing. The pods are slender and 1 to 3 inches long.

Tick-Trefoil (*Desmodium*)—Perennial herbs with simple or pinnate leaves with three leaflets, and white or purplish flowers in terminal racemes. The pods at maturity break up into flat, 1-seeded joints, which are scattered by clinging to clothes or the fur of animals. Two species occur in the Park. Simple-Leaf Tick-Trefoil (*Desmodium psilophyllum*, synonym *Desmodium wrightii*) has simple leaves and stalked pods, while Graham's Tick-Trefoil (*Desmodium grahamii*) has compound leaves with three leaflets and pods nearly if not quite sessile.

TEXAS KIDNEYWOOD
(*Eysenhardtia texana*)

LITTLE-LEAF LEADTREE
(*Leucaena retusa*)

🪶 **Texas Kidneywood** (*Eysenhardtia texana*)—A shrub with pinnate leaves, with about 25 to 33 leaflets, and small, white, nearly regular flowers in terminal spikes.

■ **Rush-Pea** (*Hoffmannseggia, Pomaria*)—Low herbs with twice-compound leaves, clusters of yellow flowers opposite the leaves or terminal, a 5-parted calyx, nearly equal petals, 10 distinct stamens, and a flat, oblong pod. **False Holdback** (*Pomaria jamesii*, synonym *Hoffmannseggia jamesii*) has the leaves dotted with back glands, while **Waxy Rush-Pea** (*Hoffmannseggia glauca*) is without such glands.

🪶 **Little-Leaf Leadtree** (*Leucaena retusa*)—A smooth shrub with twice-pinnate leaves and white flowers in spherical heads. The pods are large and flat, 6 to 10 inches long and about ½ inch wide.

🪶 **Big Bend Bluebonnet** (*Lupinus havardii*)—The only common member of the pea family in the Park having palmately compound leaves, usually with seven leaflets. The flowers are purple with a light spot on the uppermost petal and are borne in rather long racemes.

Alfalfa (*Medicago sativa*)—This is the common alfalfa escaped from cultivation and is not native to the region.

MATT BERGER

RODOLFO GUTIÉRREZ-SÁNCHEZ

BIG BEND BLUEBONNET
(*Lupinus havardii*)

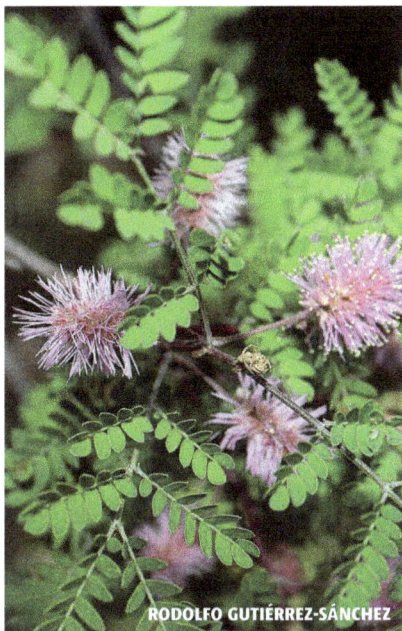

CAT-CLAW MIMOSA
(*Mimosa aculeaticarpa*)

■ Mimosa (*Mimosa*)—Shrubs with twice-pinnate leaves, which are often sensitive to the touch, stems armed with prickles, and yellowish or purple flowers in heads. Seven species occur in the Park; three are described below. ➷ Cat-Claw Mimosa (*Mimosa aculeaticarpa*) has yellowish flowers and about 10 to 15 pairs of leaflets on each leaf segment. The young branches are somewhat hairy. Fragrant Mimosa (*Mimosa borealis*) has purple flowers and pods that are much constricted and not spiny. Emory's Mimosa (*Mimosa emoryana*) has purple flowers and spiny pods that are not constricted.

■ Bean (*Phaseolus*)—Twining or prostrate herbs with pinnate leaves with three leaflets, and flowers clustered on rather long stalks. The purplish flowers are about ¼ inch long with strongly incurved keel (made up of the two lowest petals which are partly united) and bearded style. The pods are somewhat curved and several-seeded. Five species occur in the Park; two are described below. Narrow-Leaflet Bean (*Phaseolus angustissimus*) has narrowly lanceolate or linear leaflets, while Slimjim Bean (*Phaseolus filiformis*, synonym *Phaseolus wrightii*) has broadly lanceolate or triangular and often 3-angled or lobed leaflets.

HONEY-MESQUITE
(*Prosopis glandulosa*)

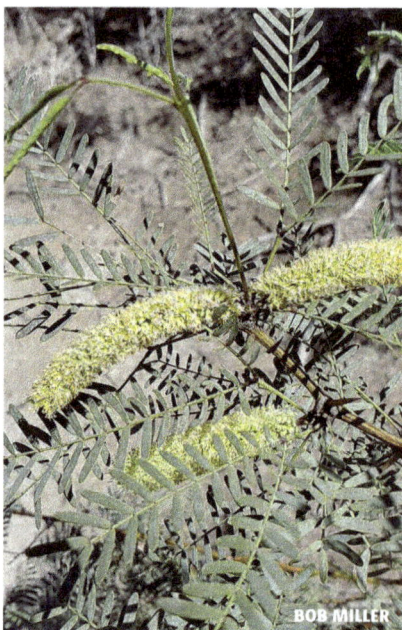

WESTERN HONEY-MESQUITE
(*Prosopis glandulosa* var. *torreyi*)

🗡 **Honey Mesquite** (*Prosopis glandulosa,* synonym *Neltuma glandulosa*)—A shrub or tree with compound leaves consisting of 2 divisions with 8 to 16 pairs of leaflets each, white or yellowish flowers in spikes, and pods 4 to 6 or more inches long containing oblong seeds. The stems are armed with sharp thorns. This is one of the most characteristic trees of Texas. The wood is valuable for cabinetwork as well as for fuel and the beans are nutritious and are eaten by many animals, including humans. The mesquite is also a valuable honey plant.

🗡 **Western Honey Mesquite** (*Prosopis glandulosa* var. *torreyi,* synonyms *Neltuma odorata, Strombocarpa odorata*)—A shrub or small tree with compound leaves with five to eight pairs of leaflets on each division, yellow flowers in crowded spikes, and pods that are tightly coiled into a narrow cylinder 1 to 2 inches long.

Texas Snout-Bean (*Rhynchosia texana,* synonym *Rhynchosia senna*)—A trailing but scarcely twining herb with pinnate leaves with three oval or ovate leaflets and yellow flowers, one to several on short stalks. The pods are oblong and hairy.

TWINLEAF SENNA
(*Senna bauhinioides*)

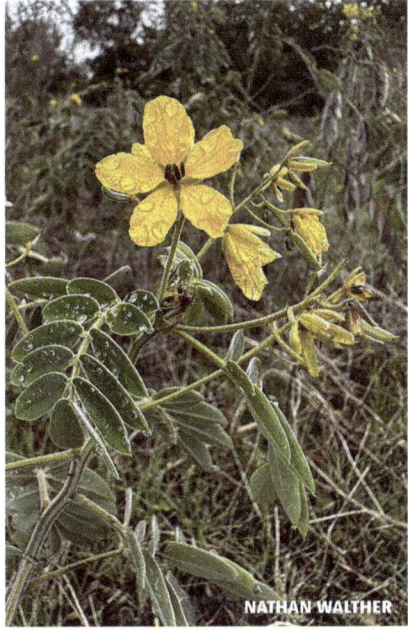

VELVET-LEAF SENNA
(*Senna lindheimeriana*)

■ **Wild Sensitive Plant** (*Senna*, synonym *Cassia*)—Herbs or shrubs with simply pinnate leaves, mostly yellow flowers with a 5-parted calyx and 5 to 10 stamens. Eight species occur in the Park, three are described below. ➢ **Twinleaf Senna** (*Senna bauhinioides*, synonym *Cassia bauhinioides*) and **Durango Senna** (*Senna durangensis*, synonym *Cassia durangensis*) are very much alike and difficult to distinguish in the field. Their leaves have only one pair of oblong leaflets with somewhat one-sided bases and rather small flowers with yellow petals with brown veins. ➢ **Velvet-Leaf Senna** (*Senna lindheimeriana*, synonym *Cassia lindheimeriana*) has leaves with six to eight pairs of leaflets and larger and more conspicuous, golden flowers.

Louisiana Vetch (*Vicia ludoviciana*)—An annual herb that climbs by means of tendrils at the ends of pinnate leaves. The leaves have three or four pairs of linear leaflets, and the flowers are usually solitary in the axils of leaves on slender stalks that are shorter than the leaves. The style is bearded with a tuft or ring of hairs at the tip; the pod is flat and 4- to 6-seeded.

EMORY'S OAK
(*Quercus emoryi*)

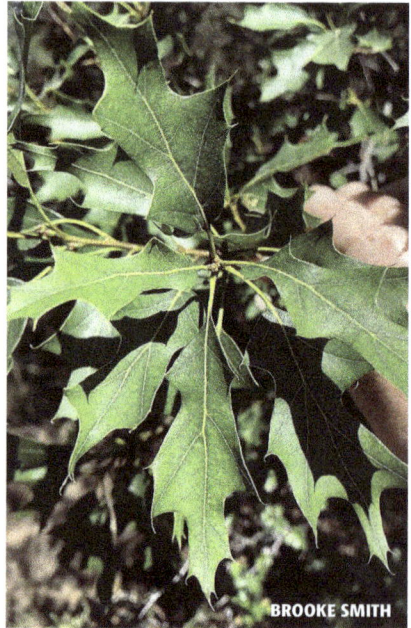

CHISOS RED OAK
(*Quercus gravesii*)

OAK FAMILY (FAGACEAE)

A family of trees and shrubs with simple, alternate leaves and imperfect flowers, the staminate in catkins and the pistillate on the same plant singly or in short spikes. The fruit is a 1-seeded nut or acorn partly enclosed in a cuplike structure, which is a modified and hardened involucre. The oaks are the representatives of this family in the Park. They belong to the genus *Quercus*, the species of which are very difficult to classify and name, partly because the various species hybridize so freely. There are about 16 different species of oak occurring in the Chisos Mountains, but they require a great deal of study before they can be distinguished with certainty. There are three species, however, that are quite frequent and readily recognized in the field by their leaves. These are:

⤳ **Emory's Oak** (*Quercus emoryi*)—The leaves are variable, but the typical leaf is lance-shaped or mostly oblong, 1 to 2½ inches long, and ½ to 1 inch wide. Sometimes the leaves are entire, but usually there are one to five sharp teeth on each side with a shallow but broad sinus above each tooth.

GRAY OAK
(*Quercus grisea*)

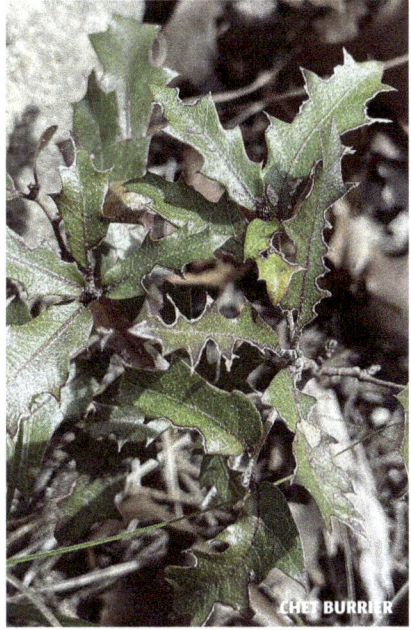

VASEY'S OAK
(*Quercus vaseyana*)

➤ **Chisos Red Oak** (*Quercus gravesii*)—Leaves 2 to 3½ inches long with three or four large teeth on each side, each tooth with a long, hairlike tip and a broad, deep sinus between.

➤ **Gray Oak** (*Quercus grisea*)—Leaves ½ to 1½ inches long and half as wide and entire.

Other less commonly observed oaks in the Chisos Mountains might be more easily identified by location: ➤ **Vasey's Oak** (*Quercus vaseyana*), for example, grows along Oak Creek and on the slopes of that general locality. **Gambel's Oak** (*Quercus gambelii*) grows on the upper slopes of the "crown" of Casa Grande. **Chinkapin Oak** (*Quercus muehlenbergii*) frequents Pulliam Canyon. **Chisos Mountains Oak** (*Quercus robusta*) has been named with the type tree growing near the Homer Wilson ranch house site in Lower Oak Creek Canyon. The hybrid formula is possibly *Q. emoryi* × *Q. gravesii*. **Chisos Oak** (*Quercus graciliformis*) is found in the Lower Blue Creek Canyon. **Dwarf Oak** (*Quercus intricata*) grows in the Laguna. **Late-Leaf Oak** (*Quercus tardifolia*) is described from above Boot Spring.

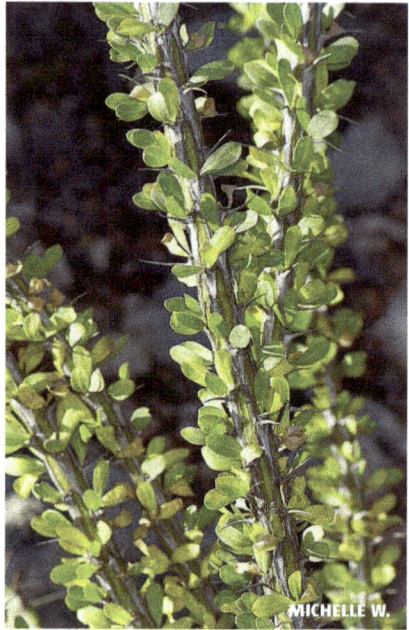

OCOTILLO
(*Fouquieria splendens*)

OCOTILLO FAMILY (FOUQUIERIACEAE)

A family of spiny shrubs with erect, wandlike stems. The blades of the primary leaves soon drop off, and the petioles develop into heavy thorns. Clusters of secondary leaves later appear in the axils of the thorns at each rainy season. The flowers are showy and are borne in long, terminal panicles. Each flower has 5 sepals, a 5-lobed, tubular corolla, about 10 stamens, which are attached to the corolla, and 1 pistil. Our only representative of the family is the following:

❧ Ocotillo (*Fouquieria splendens*)—A shrub with several or many spiny, unbranched stems 5 to 20 feet tall and leafless except during or immediately after a rainy season. The brilliant scarlet flowers are borne in terminal panicles 4 to 10 or more inches long. This plant is often mistaken for a cactus but it is not related to the cactus family. It is on the desert floor and the lower slopes of the Chisos Mountains.

EGG-LEAF SILKTASSEL
(*Garrya ovata*)

SILKTASSEL FAMILY (GARRYACEAE)

A small family of herbs, shrubs, and small trees with simple, entire leaves and clusters of relatively small flowers. The family is represented here only by the ❧ **Egg-Leaf Silktassel** (*Garrya ovata*), a shrub 2 to 8 feet high with leathery, oblong or oval leaves 1 to 3 inches long. The flowers are imperfect, with the staminate and pistillate flowers on separate plants. Both kinds of flowers are in catkins, but the pistillate catkins are shorter. The fruit is a small drupe.

GENTIAN FAMILY (GENTIANACEAE)

The Gentian Family is made up of smooth herbs with opposite or whorled leaves and perfect flowers, some of which are extremely beautiful. The calyx and corolla are both usually tubular and more or less toothed or lobed, and the stamens are on the tube of the corolla. There is one pistil with a single style and usually a 2-lobed stigma. Only two representatives of the family have been found in the Park:

ERIC KNIGHT

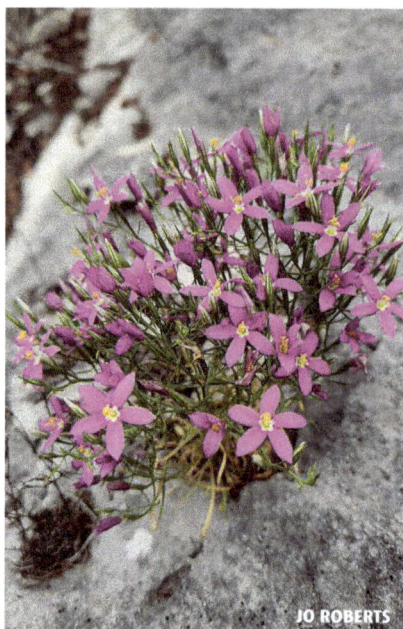

JO ROBERTS

PRAIRIE-GENTIAN
(*Eustoma exaltatum*)

MOUNTAIN-PINK
(*Zeltnera calycosa*)

🗡 Prairie-Gentian (*Eustoma exaltatum*)—A perennial herb growing 15 to 30 inches tall with broadly oblong leaves, which are sessile and have a tendency to clasp the stem with a somewhat heart-shaped base. The flowers are blue, lavender, or sometimes white, and quite large, the corolla nearly 2 inches long. The stamens are on the corolla tube and have very slender filaments. There are two stigmas, and the style is sometimes very short or lacking entirely. Found at several places along the Rio Grande and in the vicinity of certain springs.

🗡 Mountain-Pink (*Zeltnera calycosa*, synonym *Centaurium calycosum*)—An erect herb growing 4 to 10 inches high with opposite, simple, linear or oblong leaves to 1 inch long, and starlike, pink or rose-colored flowers about ½ inch across borne in the forks of the branches or in the axils of the upper leaves. Found at Gano Spring, west of the Chisos Mountain area, as well as along the Rio Grande.

GERANIUM FAMILY (GERANIACEAE)

Although a small group, this family contains some beautiful flowers including both the wild and cultivated geraniums and the stork's-bill.

RED-STEM STORK'S-BILL
(*Erodium texanum*)

PINEWOODS GERANIUM
(*Geranium caespitosum*)

🌂 Red-Stem Stork's-Bill (*Erodium texanum*)—This plant gets its common name from the fruits, which are 1 to 2 inches long and, in shape, resemble the bill of a stork. The plant grows 6 to 18 inches high and has long-stalked leaves, which have their blades cut into 3- to 5-toothed lobes. The purple or wine-colored flowers are about an inch across. They are beautiful if left alone, but the petals usually fall off if the flowers are picked. The fruits are interesting because of the method by which they plant themselves. The fruit is covered with stiff hairs that point upward, the lower end sharp-pointed. The tail, which is the developed style of the pistil, becomes spirally twisted. Whenever it becomes moist it untwists, and then when it dries it twists again. The twisting and untwisting gradually push the pointed fruit into the ground.

🌂 Pinewoods Geranium (*Geranium caespitosum*)—This geranium grows 8 to 20 inches high and has numerous basal leaves with long stalks and blades that are cleft into three to five lobes. The lobes, especially the lateral ones, are toothed and often again cleft. The stem leaves are similar but are reduced in size and have short stalks. The flowers are

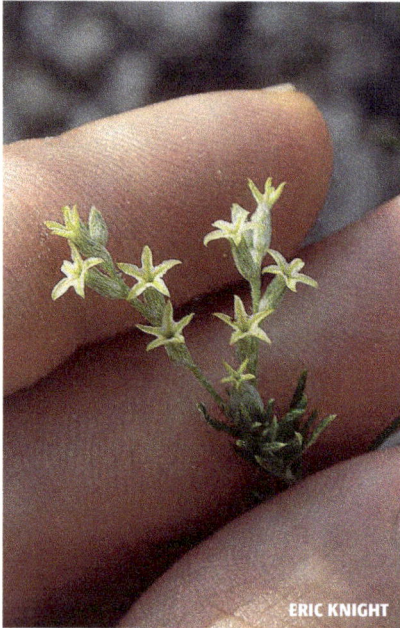

ERIC KNIGHT

TORREY'S EUPLOCA
(*Euploca torreyi*)

JOSÉ DÍAZ

LEAFY HELIOTROPE
(*Euploca confertifolia*)

white or sometimes with pink or purple veins. The pistil of the flower consists of five united parts, each part of the ovary containing one seed. At maturity the parts of the pistil separate at the base and curl upward so quickly that the seeds are thrown some distance.

HELIOTROPE FAMILY (HELIOTROPIACEAE)

■ Heliotrope (*Euploca, Heliotropium*)—Herbs or shrubs with usually alternate, entire leaves and flowers borne in spikes or spikelike clusters or sometimes along leafy stems between or opposite the leaves. The ovary of the flower may be unlobed or 2- or 4-lobed but not deeply lobed. In fruit, however, it usually splits up into four nutlets or sometimes only two. In some species the flowers are very fragrant.

⇗ Torrey's Euploca (*Euploca torreyi*, synonym *Heliotropium angustifolium*) is erect and densely branched from a woody base. The stems are stiff, very leafy, and more or less white-hairy. The leaves are ¼ to ½ inch long and very narrowly linear with rolled-in margins. The flowers are yellowish and are borne in few-flowered spikes, which are slender and nearly straight. ⇗ Leafy Heliotrope (*Euploca confertifolia*, syn-

SEASIDE HELIOTROPE
(*Heliotropium curassavicum*)

GREEN-EYE HELIOTROPE
(*Heliotropium glabriusculum*)

onym *Heliotropium confertifolium*) is very much branched and tufted from a woody base and is silvery-white with dense, silky hairs. The leaves are crowded, especially near the ends of the branches. They are narrowly oblong or linear, less than ¼ inch long, and white on both sides. The flowers are white or purplish and are mostly clustered among the leaves near the ends of branches. **Wide-Flower False Heliotrope** (*Euploca convolvulacea*, synonym *Heliotropium convolvulaceum*) is a loosely branched, hairy annual with narrowly lance-shaped or ovate leaves and white, fragrant flowers scattered along the stems, mostly opposite the leaves. ❧ Seaside Heliotrope (*Heliotropium curassavicum*) is smooth throughout and has narrowly lance-shaped, somewhat fleshy leaves. The flowers are borne in one-sided spikes, commonly in pairs or forked. **Four-Spike False Heliotrope** (*Euploca procumbens*, synonym *Heliotropium procumbens*) has partly trailing stems, oval, petioled leaves ½ to 1 inch long and small flowers in slender, one-sided spikes. ❧ Green-Eye Heliotrope (*Heliotropium glabriusculum*) is slightly hairy on the stems, but the leaves are green and smooth, narrowly lance-shaped, and about an inch long. The flowers are white with a green eye

MELANIE DAVIS

MARTIN PURDY

LITTLE-LEAF MOCKORANGE
(*Philadelphus microphyllus*)

FENDLERBUSH
(*Fendlera rupicola*)

and are borne in rather short, one-sided spikes, which are usually solitary but often forked. Soft Heliotrope (*Heliotropium molle*) is a low plant with fairly large, petioled leaves with blades 2 to 4 inches long and half as broad. The small flowers are crowded in several short, one-sided and coiled spikes, and the dry fruit is somewhat velvety. Fragrant False Heliotrope (*Euploca greggii*, synonym *Heliotropium greggii*) is a somewhat spreading plant with a more or less woody base. The leaves are narrowly linear, flat, and about an inch long. The showy, white flowers are very sweet-scented.

HYDRANGEA FAMILY (HYDRANGEACEAE)

Branching shrubs with small, opposite, entire leaves and showy white flowers with a 4-cleft calyx, large rounded petals, 20 or more stamens, and 1 pistil, which develops into a many-seeded capsule. Present are ✒ Little-Leaf Mockorange (*Philadelphus microphyllus*), which has the characters of the family, and two species of ✒ Fendlerbush (*Fendlera linearis, Fendlera rupicola*).

GYPSUM SCORPION-WEED
(*Phacelia integrifolia*)

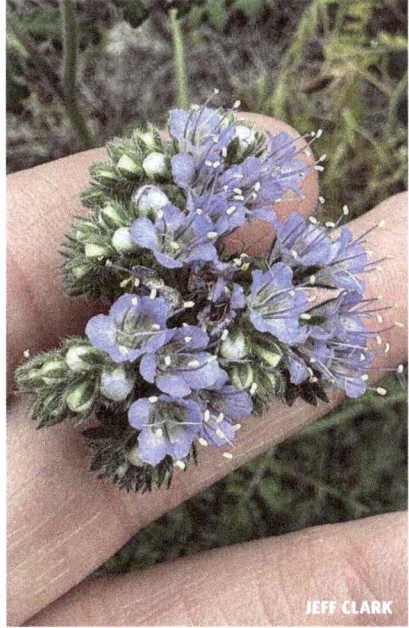

BLUE CURLS
(*Phacelia congesta*)

WATERLEAF FAMILY (HYDROPHYLLACEAE)

The Waterleaf Family is of little economic importance except for the ornamental flowering plants that it contains. Its members are mostly herbs with regular flowers having a numerical plan of five. Both the calyx and corolla are tubular and bell-shaped, and the five stamens are attached to the corolla tube. There are two styles, but in some cases they are completely united into one. The fruit is a dry capsule.

■ Scorpion-Weed (*Phacelia*)—*Phacelia* differs from Fiddleleaf (*Nama*, formerly placed in this family, now usually grouped in Fiddleleaf Family, Namaceae, p. 212) primarily in having the flowers arranged in a curved or partly coiled cluster. The four species that occur in the Park may be distinguished as follows:

1   Leaves not pinnately divided, though deeply lobed. 2
    Leaves pinnately divided 3
2   Plants large and stout, more than a foot high; stamens exserted from corolla . . . . ⤳ Gypsum Scorpion-Weed (*Phacelia integrifolia*)

POPE'S SCORPION-WEED
(*Phacelia popei*)

SKY-BLUE SCORPION-WEED
(*Phacelia caerulea*)

Plants smaller, less than a foot high; stamens included in corolla. .
. . . . Sky-Blue Scorpion-Weed (*Phacelia caerulea*)
3   Leaves with large, coarse lobes . ⤳ Blue Curls (*Phacelia congesta*)
    Leaves dissected into small lobes . . . . Pope's Scorpion-Weed
    . . . . (*Phacelia popei*)

WALNUT FAMILY (JUGLANDACEAE)

Trees or large shrubs with alternate, pinnately compound leaves and
small, imperfect flowers, the staminate flowers in catkins and the pistillate flowers solitary or in small clusters on the same plant. The family
is represented in the Park by Pecan (*Carya illinoinensis*) and two species
of walnut (*Juglans*): The ⤳ Texas Black Walnut (*Juglans microcarpa*)
is a small tree with 6 to 12 pairs of leaflets to each leaf, 20 to 30 stamens
in each staminate flower, and nuts that are about ½ inch in diameter.
The leaves and buds, when crushed, have a walnut odor. The fruit is the
familiar black walnut, a nut with a dry husk. Arizona Walnut (*Juglans
major*) is also reported.

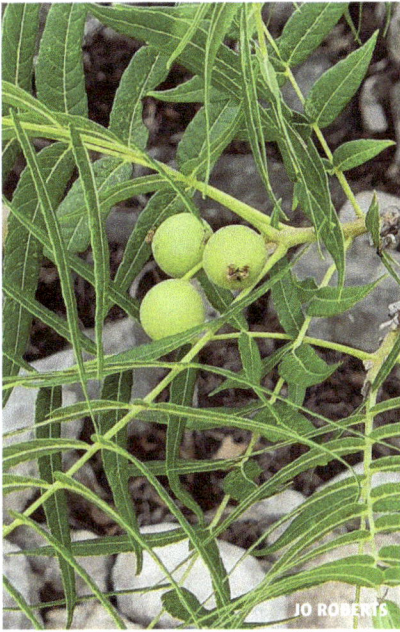

TEXAS BLACK WALNUT
(*Juglans microcarpa*)

CROWN-OF-THORNS
(*Koeberlinia spinosa*)

CROWN-OF-THORNS FAMILY (KOEBERLINIACEAE)

A small family represented in our flora only by the following species:

➤ **Crown-of-Thorns** (*Koeberlinia spinosa*)—This is a leafless shrub growing 1 to 4 or 5 feet high and usually seen as a tangle of green, sharp-pointed thorns. The flowers are small but quite conspicuous when the plant is in full bloom. They have four sepals, four greenish petals, eight stamens, and one pistil. The fruit is a spherical, black berry about ¼ inch in diameter. This shrub is frequent on the desert and is easily recognized because, as its common name implies, it is nearly all thorn.

RATANY FAMILY (KRAMERIACEAE)

■ **Ratany** (*Krameria*)—Shrubs with small, alternate, simple leaves and red-purple, showy, perfect flowers solitary in the axils of the leaves. The five sepals are petallike, and the lower one is broader than the other four. The five petals are smaller than the sepals, the two lower ones being reduced to short, fleshy scales. There are four stamens, and the fruit is a spherical, spiny pod. The two species found in the Park are

LITTLELEAF RATANY
(*Krameria erecta*)

very similar in general appearance, but in ⌇ Littleleaf Ratany (*Krameria erecta*, synonym *Krameria glandulosa*) there are weak barbs scattered along the upper half or third of each spine on the fruits, while in White Ratany (*Krameria bicolor*, synonym *Krameria grayi*) the barbs are clustered in an umbrellalike bunch at the tips of the spines on the fruits.

MINT FAMILY (LAMIACEAE)

The plants of this family have quite well marked family characteristics by which they are usually readily recognized. Most of them are aromatic, having a decided mint odor. The stems are usually square in cross-section, and the leaves are opposite. The corollas are usually decidedly irregular, having two lips, the upper of which may be either entire or 2-lobed and the lower 3-lobed, although some members of the family have nearly regular corollas. The ovary is 4-lobed, usually deeply so, and the fruit consists of four 1-seeded nutlets enclosed in the persistent calyx. Some members of the family are used in medicine, and others are used to flavor candy and chewing gum.

1   Ovary merely 4-lobed, the style arising from the apex . . . .
. . . . LACY GERMANDER (*Teucrium laciniatum*, p. 199)
Ovary deeply 4-cleft into 4 nearly distinct parts, the style arising
from between them 2

2   Corolla nearly regular; plants with mint odor and small flowers . .
. . . . MINT (*Mentha*, p. 196)
Corolla conspicuously 2-lipped 3

3   Calyx pouch-shaped and 2-lobed, the lobes entire 4
Calyx more than 2-lobed 5

4   Herbs; calyx split into 2 lobes, the upper lobe bearing a hump . . .
. . . . MEXICAN SKULLCAP (*Scutellaria potosina*, p. 198)
Shrubs; calyx bladderlike at maturity and without a hump on the
back . . . MEXICAN BLADDER-SAGE (*Scutellaria mexicana*, p. 198)

5   Calyx teeth 10 . . . . HOREHOUND (*Marrubium vulgare*, p. 196)
Calyx teeth 5 or fewer 6

6   Anther-bearing stamens 2 7
Anther-bearing stamens 4 8

7   Upper lip of corolla flat, not concave, the stamens usually extending
beyond it . . . . FALSE PENNYROYAL (*Hedeoma*, p. 195)
Upper lip of corolla concave, including the stamens under it in all
cases except in the species roemeriana in which the corolla is bright
red and an inch or more long . . . . SAGE (*Salvia*, p. 197)

8   Upper lip of corolla flat, not concave, the stamens usually extending
beyond it; flowers numerous in a whorl . . . . GIANT-HYSSOP
. . . . (*Agastache*, p. 195)
Upper lip of corolla concave, including the stamens under it; flowers
6 in each whorl . . . . HEDGE-NETTLE (*Stachys*, p. 198)

■ Giant-Hyssop (*Agastache*)—Tall perennial herbs with flowers in
dense or interrupted, terminal spikes. Two species occur in the Park:
White Giant-Hyssop (*Agastache micrantha*) has lanceolate leaves with
triangular, rather sharp teeth and small, white flowers. ❧ New Mexico
Giant-Hyssop (*Agastache pallidiflora*) has heart-shaped leaves with
rounded, blunt teeth and purple flowers.

■ False Pennyroyal (*Hedeoma*)—Annual or perennial herbs with
small, entire or toothed leaves and flowers in axillary clusters. There are
two stamens with anthers but often two sterile stamens as well. Six
species are found in the Park, three are described below. ❧ Drummond's False Pennyroyal (*Hedeoma drummondii*), the most common,

NEW MEXICO GIANT-HYSSOP
(*Agastache pallidiflora*)

DRUMMOND'S FALSE PENNYROYAL
(*Hedeoma drummondii*)

branches from the base and grows from a few inches to more than a foot high. It has entire leaves. Dwarf False Pennyroyal (*Hedeoma nana*) is a dwarf species growing only a few inches high. It also has entire leaves. Veiny False Pennyroyal (*Hedeoma plicata*) has sharply toothed leaves.

⚘ Horehound (*Marrubium vulgare*)—An introduced, white-woolly plant, usually about a foot high, with wrinkled, rounded-toothed leaves and dense, many-flowered, axillary whorls of flowers. The calyx has 10 curved teeth, the alternate ones shorter, and the small, white corolla has the upper lip erect and notched and the lower one spreading and 3-cleft.

◼ Mint (*Mentha*)—Strongly aromatic plants with petioled, toothed leaves and crowded, small flowers in axillary clusters or slender, terminal spikes. Two species occur in the Park: Wild Mint (*Mentha arvensis*) has stems about a foot high; they are somewhat short-hairy, especially on the angles. The leaves vary from ovate to lanceolate and are 1 to 2 inches long and toothed. The flowers are usually pink and all are in axillary clusters. Spearmint (*Mentha spicata*) is a European species that has been naturalized in this country and is now widely distributed. It

HOREHOUND
(*Marrubium vulgare*)

LANCE-LEAF SAGE
(*Salvia reflexa*)

is similar to *M. arvensis* but often grows a little taller, is not hairy, and the flowers are pale purple and are arranged in slender, terminal spikes.

■ Sage (*Salvia*)—Annuals or perennials, mostly with moderately large and showy flowers. The corolla is deeply 2-lipped with the upper lip straight or scythe-shaped and entire or barely notched and the lower 3-lobed with the middle lobe largest. The two stamens have short filaments, but at the end of the filament there is a transverse support bearing at one end a 1-celled anther and at the other an imperfect or deformed anther or none at all. Six species occur in the Park:

1 Flowers blue 2
   Flowers red 4
2 Leaves entire . . . . Canyon Sage (*Salvia lycioides*)
   Leaves toothed 3
3 Leaves triangular to broadly lance-shaped . . . . Arizona Sage
   . . . . (*Salvia arizonica*)
   Leaves narrowly oblong . . . . . ➢ Lance-Leaf Sage (*Salvia reflexa*)
4 Herbs; lower leaves with 3 to 5 leaflets . . . . Cedar Sage
   . . . . (*Salvia roemeriana*)

AUTUMN SAGE
(*Salvia greggii*)

MEXICAN SKULLCAP
(*Scutellaria potosina*)

Shrubs; leaves simple. 5
5   Leaves toothed, shaped like a poplar leaf; flowers nearly 2 inches
long . . . . **Mountain Sage** (*Salvia regla*)
Leaves entire, oval; flowers shorter ⚹ **Autumn Sage** (*Salvia greggii*)

Mexican Bladder-Sage (*Scutellaria mexicana*, synonym *Salazaria mexicana*)—A low, twiggy shrub with small, oval, entire leaves and violet or white flowers in short, terminal clusters. The stems are whitish with very short, white hairs but the leaves are nearly smooth and green. The calyx becomes much inflated and bladderlike after blooming.

⚹ **Mexican Skullcap** (*Scutellaria potosina*)—A much-branched plant, usually less than a foot high, with small entire leaves and blue flowers. Readily recognized by the peculiar hump on the calyx and by the fact that the plant lacks the odor characteristic of other mints.

■ **Hedge-Nettle** (*Stachys*)—Annual or perennial herbs with scarlet-red flowers in 2- to many-flowered whorls. The bell-shaped calyx is equally 5-toothed and the corolla is strongly 2-lipped. The four stamens are crowded together under the upper lip of the corolla. Two species

SUE CARNAHAN

CATHERINE GALLEY

COULTER'S WRINKLEFRUIT
(*Tetraclea coulteri*)

CUT-LEAF GERMANDER
(*Teucrium laciniatum*)

occur in the Park: **Scarlet Hedge-Nettle** (*Stachys coccinea*) has triangular to lance-shaped, toothed leaves with more or less heart-shaped base and flowers often nearly an inch long. **Rock Hedge-Nettle** (*Stachys bigelovii*) is similar, but the flowers are only about half as large and there are usually fewer in each cluster. In this species the stamens scarcely extend beyond the corolla tube, while in the preceding species they definitely do.

➣ **Coulter's Wrinklefruit** (*Tetraclea coulteri*)—An herb growing about a foot high with nearly entire, ovate leaves and cream-colored flowers borne in axillary, 3-flowered clusters; calyx deeply 5-cleft, corolla nearly regular. The four stamens extend beyond the corolla. (Note: not included in family key.)

➣ **Cut-Leaf Germander** (*Teucrium laciniatum*)—A herb with deeply cleft leaves and pale blue or white flowers borne singly in the axils. The calyx is 5-toothed and the corolla is 5-lobed, but the four upper lobes are turned forward so that there seems to be no upper lip and the lower lip is much longer.

BRUNSONM

CRICKET RASPET

PRAIRIE FLAX
(*Linum lewisii*)

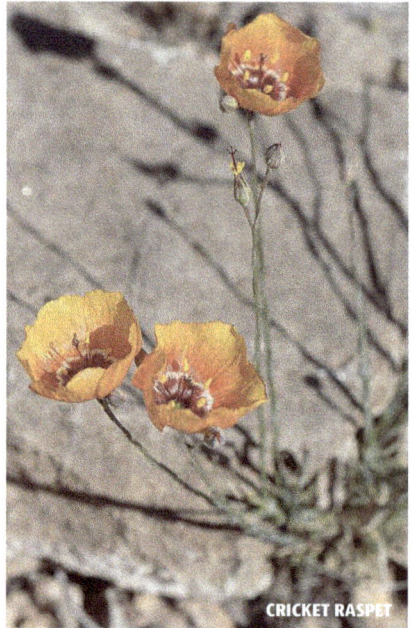

CHIHUAHUAN FLAX
(*Linum vernale*)

FLAX FAMILY (LINACEAE)

A small but very important family economically. It furnishes the fibers from which linen thread is made and also the seeds from which linseed oil is obtained. The family is represented in our flora by only one genus, *Linum* (Flax), comprised of slender, annual herbs with rather small leaves and regular, perfect flowers. The sepals are persistent, but the blue or yellow petals soon fall off. There are five perfect stamens, which are united at the base and sometimes bear five alternating rudimentary stamens. There is 1 pistil, but usually 5 styles; the fruit is a capsule completely or incompletely 10-celled. Several species of flax have been reported from the Park, most of which are included in the following key:

1 Flowers blue . . . . ⚘ **Prairie Flax** (*Linum lewisii*)
   Flowers yellow or whitish **2**
2 Leaves very narrow, linear **3**
   Leaves broader, oval or lance-shaped . . . . **Shied's Flax**
   . . . . (*Linum schiedeanum*)
3 Leaves numerous, overlapping on the stem . ⚘ **Chihuahuan Flax**
   . . . . (*Linum vernale*)

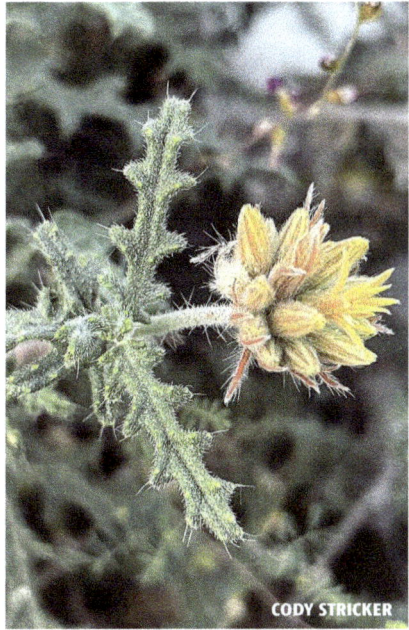

BERLANDIER'S YELLOW FLAX
(*Linum berlandieri*)

STINGING-SERPENT
(*Cevallia sinuata*)

Leaves scattered, not overlapping on the stem................. **4**
4 Petals less than ½ inch long..... **Southern Flax** (*Linum australe*)
Petals ½ inch or more long **5**
5 Leaves linear to lance-shaped, less than ½ inch long.............
.... **Bristle Flax** (*Linum aristatum*)
Leaves linear and sharp pointed, about ½ inch long ....
.... **Rock Flax** (*Linum rupestre*)
Leaves lance-shaped, usually more than an 1 inch long...........
.... 🡕 Berlandier's Yellow Flax (*Linum berlandieri*)

BLAZINGSTAR FAMILY (LOASACEAE)

Herbs with alternate leaves, either stinging or jointed and barbed hairs, and showy flowers with the ovary below the other parts, usually very numerous stamens, and a slender style.

🡕 **Stinging-Serpent** (*Cevallia sinuata*)—A stout herb with whitish stems, simple but pinnately lobed leaves with stinging hairs, and silky flowers clustered in hemispherical heads. The silky calyx tube is short and has five linear, erect lobes. The five petals are similar to the sepals,

CULLEN HANKS

ANNIKA LINDQVIST

YELLOW STINGBUSH
(*Eucnide bartonioides*)

STICK-LEAF
(*Mentzelia oligosperma*)

and there are only five stamens. The fruit is a 1-seeded structure crowned by the persistent, hairy calyx and corolla.

⚐ **Yellow Stingbush** (*Eucnide bartonioides*)—A tender, somewhat fleshy herb, branching and usually spreading on the ground, with ovate or heart-shaped leaves which are cut-toothed or slightly lobed and often 2 to 4 inches long and have slender petioles. The flowers have five ovate petals, and the very many slender stamens are fully an inch long. The stamens are attached to the base of the petals and fall with them. The style is 5-cleft and 5-angled, and the fruit is a many-seeded capsule. The flower stalks become very much elongated as the fruit develops.

■ **Blazingstar** (*Mentzelia*)—Herbs with usually whitish stems, which are rough with short, barbed but not stinging hairs, toothed or lobed, petioled leaves, and yellow or cream-colored flowers, with 5 or 10 petals and very numerous stamens attached with the petals to the throat of the calyx. The style is 3-cleft, and the fruit is a several-seeded capsule. The flowers open only in bright sunshine. ⚐ **Stick-Leaf** (*Mentzelia oligosperma*) has 5 petals to each flower, while ⚐ **Many-Flower Blazingstar** (*Mentzelia longiloba*) has 10. *Mentzelia asperula, Mentzelia lind-*

MELANIE DAVIS

MANY-FLOWER BLAZINGSTAR
(*Mentzelia longiloba*)

SUE CARNAHAN

CALIFORNIA LOOSESTRIFE
(*Lythrum californicum*)

heimeri, Mentzelia mexicana and *Mentzelia pachyrhiza* have also been reported from the Park.

LOOSESTRIFE FAMILY (LYTHRACEAE)

Mostly herbs with opposite, entire leaves and axillary or whorled flowers, mostly with 6 petals and 6 to 12 or 13 stamens borne on the throat of a tubular or bell-shaped calyx. The fruit is a many-seeded capsule enclosed within, but free from, the calyx.

Stalkflower (*Ammannia grayi*)—A much-branched and diffusely spreading plant that sprawls over neighboring vegetation like a vine. The leaves are opposite, linear, pointed, and have inrolled margins. Flowers pink, nearly ½ inch across, with bell-shaped calyx.

⟿ California Loosestrife (*Lythrum californicum*)—A slender herb 8 to 20 inches high with sessile, linear leaves less than an inch long and small, purple flowers with tubular calyx.

BARBADOS-CHERRY FAMILY (MALPIGHIACEAE)

A family of trees or shrubs, some with climbing stems. The leaves are opposite and usually entire and the flowers are perfect. There are 5 sepals, 5 petals, and 5, 6, or 10 stamens, some of which may be without anthers. The Park's only representative of the family is ➷ Slender Janusia (*Cottsia gracilis*, synonym *Janusia gracilis*), which is a twining or trailing shrub with very slender stems and lance-shaped or linear leaves about an inch long. The leaves as well as the stems are somewhat silky, and the leaves usually have two or three toothlike glands on the margin near the base. The flowers are yellow and of two sorts—normal flowers with a gland-bearing calyx, conspicuously clawed petals, six stamens, a 3-angled style, and three ovaries; and abnormal flowers with a calyx without glands, small or rudimentary petals, six stamens, some of which may be without anthers, no style, and two ovaries. In both sorts of flowers the ovaries develop into winged fruits, or samaras.

MALLOW FAMILY (MALVACEAE)

This family is extremely important because it is the one to which the cotton plant belongs. It also contains many plants with beautiful flowers, and many of these are used as ornamental plants. The well-known hollyhock, the Sharon-rose, and the hibiscus are familiar examples. The members of the family can usually be recognized by the flowers, which have a 5-parted calyx, five petals, and many stamens, which are united to form a column around the styles. The styles are united at the base but separate above. Many of the Park's genera are included in the following key:

1 Stamen column bearing anthers on a considerable portion of its length . . . . ROSE-MALLOW (*Hibiscus*, p. 207)
   Stamen column bearing anthers only at the summit 2
2 Sections of the pistil differentiated into a reticulated lower portion and a smooth upper portion, the two portions separated by a distinct notch . . . . GLOBE-MALLOW (*Sphaeralcea*, p. 208)
   Sections of pistil not differentiated into lower and upper portions or, if so, the portions not separated by a notch 3
3 Seeds only 1 in each cell of the fruit . . . . FANPETALS
   . . . . (*Sida* and former *Sida*, p. 207)
   Seeds 2 or more in each cell of the fruit 4

RACHEL STRINGHAM

ANDY JORDAN

SLENDER JANUSIA
(*Cottsia gracilis*)

VELVET-LEAF MALLOW
(*Allowissadula holosericea*)

4   Cells of the fruit with membraneous walls, rounded at the tip . . . .
. . . . BLADDER-MALLOW (*Herissantia crispa*, p. 206)
Cells of the fruit with leathery walls, pointed at the tip . . . .
. . . . INDIAN-MALLOW (*Abutilon, Allowissadula*, p. 205)

■ Indian-Mallow (*Abutilon, Allowissadula*)—The Indian-Mallows, sometimes called also Velvetleaf, are mostly herbs but are sometimes shrubby at the base. Both stems and leaves are usually somewhat velvety, and the leaves are mostly heart-shaped. The flowers vary from yellow to orange and pink. Common species in the Park may be distinguished as follows:

1   Stems and leaves densely velvety . . . . ➹ Velvet-Leaf Mallow
. . . . (*Allowissadula holosericea*)
Stems and leaves minutely velvety 2
2   Leaves large, 1½ to 4 inches long . . . . . . ➹ Yellow Indian-Mallow
. . . . (*Abutilon malacum*)
Leaves small, 1 inch or less in length . . . . . . Dwarf Indian-Mallow
. . . . (*Abutilon parvulum*)

LILIANA RAMÍREZ-FREIRE

SUE CARNAHAN

YELLOW INDIAN-MALLOW
(*Abutilon malacum*)

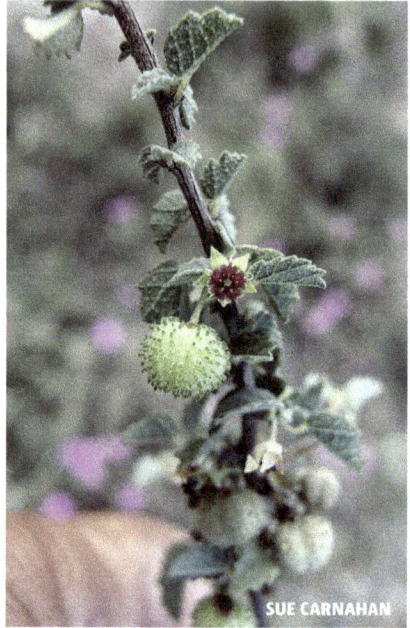

DENSE AYENIA
(*Ayenia microphylla*)

■ Ayenia (*Ayenia*). This genus was formerly placed in Cacao Family (Sterculiaceae), that family now incorporated into the Mallow Family. In Ayenia, the leaves are simple and alternate, and the flowers are perfect and have the five stamens more or less united. Two species are present in the Park: ➷ Dense Ayenia (*Ayenia microphylla*) is a low shrubby plant with stems that are very much branched and very small, roundish, heart-shaped, coarsely toothed leaves. The flowers are small, with dark red petals, and the five stamens are united into a 5-lobed cup with the anthers sessile in the sinuses. The fruit is a sessile, somewhat hairy and warty pod. Trans-Pecos Ayenia (*Ayenia filiformis*) is similar, but the stems are not much branched, the flowers are purple, and the pods are short-stalked. The former species is recorded from near Hot Springs and the latter in the Chisos Mountains. Neither is common.

Bladder-Mallow (*Herissantia crispa*, synonym *Gayoides crispa*)— This is a southern genus that occurs throughout the Tropics. The plants are perennial, diffusely branched, almost vinelike herbs. They are more or less velvety throughout. The leaves are heart-shaped, round-toothed, and ½ to 2 inches long. The flowers are yellow or yellowish. It grows mostly in sandy soil near springs or streams.

SUE CARNAHAN

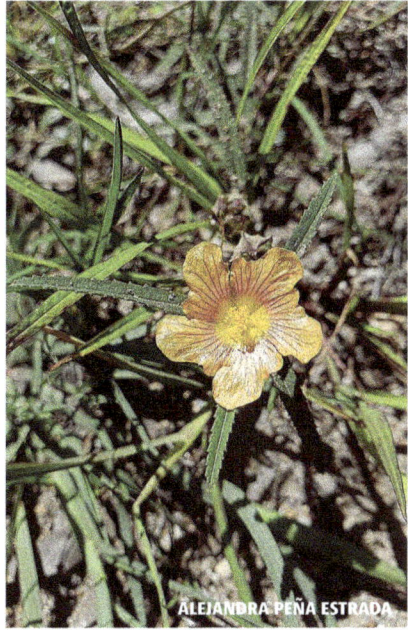
ALEJANDRA PEÑA ESTRADA

ROCK HIBISCUS
(*Hibiscus denudatus*)

NEW MEXICO FANPETALS
(*Sida neomexicana*)

■ Rose-Mallow (*Hibiscus*)—Low shrubby plants with large and showy flowers borne singly in the axils of the leaves. The calyx bears a circle of bracts; the stamen column bears anthers on most of its length but is naked at the top; there are five knoblike stigmas; and the fruit is a 5-celled, many-seeded capsule. Two species occur in the Park: Desert Rose-Mallow (*Hibiscus coulteri*) is usually 4 to 12 inches high and has deeply 3-lobed leaves and sulfur-yellow flowers. ⌇ Rock Hibiscus (*Hibiscus denudatus*) is usually 1 to 2 feet high and has nearly round, somewhat toothed leaves and light purple flowers.

■ Fanpetals (*Sida*, former *Sida*)—The sidas are herbaceous plants with mostly small, yellow flowers, and the calyx usually does not bear any bracts. The fruit is divided into 5 to 15 cells with 1 seed in each. Five species in this group occur in the Park. ⌇ New Mexico Fanpetals (*Sida neomexicana*) has linear or narrowly lance-shaped leaves and the calyx does not enlarge in fruit. ⌇ Beaked Sida (*Rhynchosida physocalyx*, synonym *Sida physocalyx*) has oblong or ovate leaves and the calyx becomes enlarged around or below the fruit. The stems and leaves of Scurfy-Mallow (*Malvella lepidota*, synonym *Sida lepidota*) are sparsely

BEAKED SIDA
(*Rhynchosida physocalyx*)

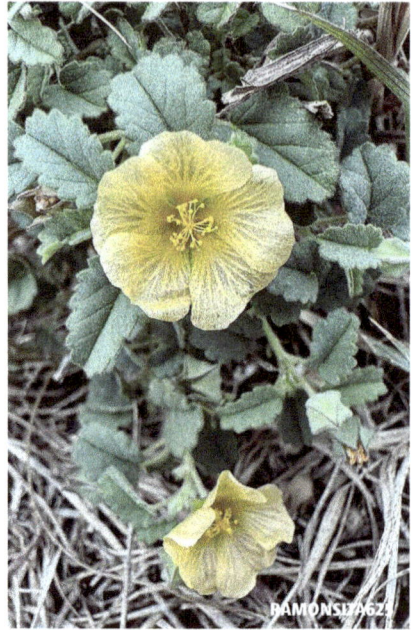

SPREADING FANPETALS
(*Sida abutilifolia*)

or densely silvery-hairy with scalelike hairs. The leaf blades are more or less triangular, longer than wide, and rather sharp-pointed at the tip. The petals of the flowers are white when fresh. ➤ **Spreading Fanpetals** (*Sida abutilifolia*) has prostrate or partly prostrate, somewhat hairy stems, and the flowers are solitary on long, slender stalks.

➤ **Narrow-Leaf Globe-Mallow** (*Sphaeralcea angustifolia*)—A perennial plant with a somewhat woody base, growing 1 to 5 feet high. The leaves are lance-shaped or narrowly oblong, sometimes with earlike lobes at the base. The leaf blades are 2 to 4½ inches long. The flowers are pink or red or sometimes almost white. Also present is **Spear Globe-Mallow** (*Sphaeralcea hastulata*) with somewhat spear-shaped, more or less lobed leaves. It is a perennial plant and is hairy with coarse, yellowish hairs.

NARROW-LEAF GLOBE-MALLOW
(*Sphaeralcea angustifolia*)

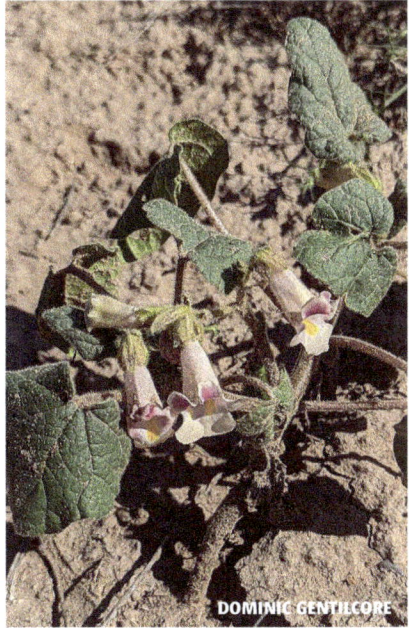

DOUBLECLAW
(*Proboscidea parviflora*)

UNICORN-PLANT FAMILY (MARTYNIACEAE)

Sticky-hairy herbs with opposite, large, simple leaves and a terminal cluster of showy flowers. The flowers are usually yellowish purple or reddish and slightly 2-lipped. There are four stamens, two long and two short, but sometimes the long ones are sterile. The fruit is a podlike capsule with a long, curved beak.

■ Unicorn-Plant (*Proboscidea*)—The characters are those given above for the family. Two species have been found in the Park: ↗ Doubleclaw (*Proboscidea parviflora*) has leaves that are shallowly lobed or angled and flowers that are usually not much over ½ inch long. Ram's-Horn (*Proboscidea louisianica*) has entire leaves and flowers often one inch long.

MOONSEED FAMILY (MENISPERMACEAE)

A family of woody plants that climb by twining. The name comes from the fact that the ovaries usually become curved as they ripen so that the seeds are more or less crescent-shaped. It is mostly a tropical family

CAROLINA SNAILSEED
(*Nephroia carolina*)

FALSE CARPETWEED
(*Hypertelis umbellata*)

and is represented in our flora only by the ⌇ Carolina Snailseed (*Nephroia carolina*, synonym *Cocculus carolinus*). This woody climber has alternate, simple leaves that vary from round or heart-shaped to distinctly three-lobed. The flowers are small and imperfect, with six sepals, six petals, and six stamens or three to six pistils. They are borne in small racemes or panicles in the axils of the leaves. The fruit is a one-seeded drupe. Found in the mountains, especially in the lightly wooded canyons.

CARPETWEED FAMILY (MOLLUGINACEAE)

This is a relatively small family of low herbs, represented in the Park by a single, introduced species. ⌇ False Carpetweed (*Hypertelis umbellata*, synonym *Mollugo cerviana*) is a low, smooth annual with very slender, much-branched stems, whorled, linear leaves, and axillary flowers on slender stalks. The flowers have five sepals, white on the inner side, but no petals. There are three or five stamens, and the fruit is a 3-celled capsule.

TEXAS MULBERRY
(*Morus microphylla*)

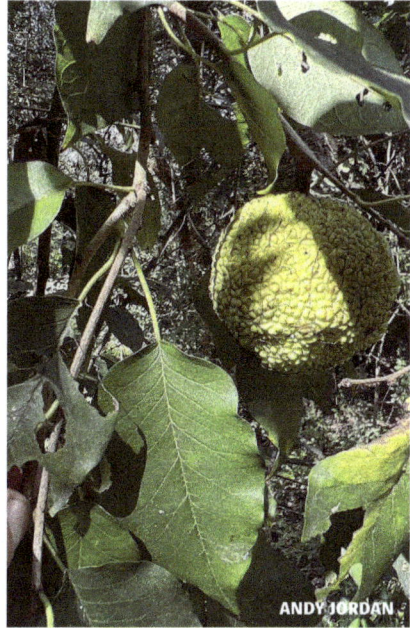

OSAGE-ORANGE
(*Maclura pomifera*)

MULBERRY FAMILY (MORACEAE)

A family of trees or shrubs with milky juice, alternate leaves and sometimes edible fruit. The flowers are imperfect, in spikes or headlike clusters. The fig is an important member of this family in which the flowers are on the inside of an enclosed receptacle, but in our representatives of the family the flowers are on the outside of the receptacle. The fruit consists of numerous one-seeded achenes each enclosed in the enlarged, fleshy calyx and all clustered very close together on the receptacle, forming a berrylike, aggregate fruit.

➷ Texas Mulberry (*Morus microphylla*)—A shrub or small tree with ovate or oval or somewhat heart-shaped leaves that are toothed along the margin and sometimes variously lobed. The fruits are small, only about ½ inch long, deep purple or nearly black, and edible.

➷ Osage-Orange (*Maclura pomifera*)—A shrub or small tree with ovate or oblong or lance-shaped leaves, which are entire, dark green and shining above, and dull and paler below. The fruit is spherical, as large as an orange, yellow-green in color, and not edible.

MATTED FIDDLELEAF
(*Nama havardii*)

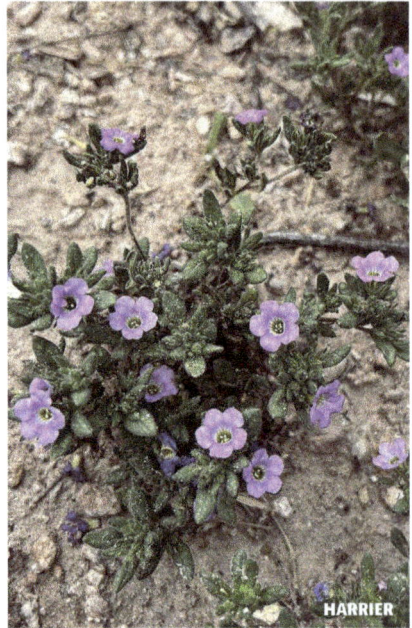

SANDBELLS
(*Nama hispida*)

FIDDLELEAF FAMILY (NAMACEAE)

■ Fiddleleaf (*Nama*)—Herbs or half shrubs with alternate, usually entire leaves and medium-sized flowers that vary from purplish to white but are most often purple. Placed in Borage Family (Boraginaceae) by some authorities. The following key distinguishes the species:

1   Plants prostrate; leaves less than ½ inch long; pedicels slender, to about ¾ inch long . . ➽ Matted Fiddleleaf (*Nama torynophyllum*)
    Plants more erect; leaves larger; pedicels rather stout, short or absent **2**
2   Stem leaves sessile, clasping stem, with undulate (wavy) margins .
    . . . . White-Whisker Fiddleleaf (*Nama undulata*)
    Stem leaves with petioles or sessile, but neither clasping nor undulate **3**
3   Calyx lobes covered with long, soft hairs. . . . . Havard's Fiddleleaf
    . . . . (*Nama havardii*)
    Calyx lobes covered with bristly hairs ➽ Sandbells (*Nama hispida*)

FOUR-O'CLOCK FAMILY (NYCTAGINACEAE)

This family contains many plants with beautiful flowers, and some of them are extensively cultivated as ornamental plants. The beauty of the flowers n this case, however, is due largely to the calyx, which is colored like a corolla, since the flowers have no corolla. It is sometimes due also to an involucre that surrounds the flowers. Some members of the family open their flowers late in the afternoon and close them the next morning, and the family gets its name from this habit. The flowers are perfect and regular, with stamens varying from one to many and a single pistil. The genera found in the Park may be distinguished as follows:

1   Involucre calyxlike with the parts united 2
    Involucre of one to many separate bract. 4
2   Involucre 3-parted . . . . FOUR-O'CLOCK (*Mirabilis*, p. 217)
    Involucre 5-parted 3
3   Fruit with 5 prominent ribs; involucre enlarged and membranous in fruit SPREADING FOUR-O'CLOCK (*Mirabilis oxybaphoides*, p. 218)
    Fruit smooth or slightly 5-angled, involucre not enlarged and membranous in fruit . . . . WINDMILLS (*Allionia*, p. 215)
4   Stigmas linear . . . . PURPLE SAND-VERBENA
    . . . . (*Abronia angustifolia*, p. 214)
    Stigmas spherical or hemispherical 5
5   Flowers in heads, each head surrounded by a many-bracted involucre . . . . DEVIL'S-BOUQUET (*Nyctaginia*, p. 218)
    Flowers not in heads, each flower with an involucre of 1 to 3 bracts 6
6   Fruit conspicuously winged . . . . MOONPOD (*Acleisanthes*, p. 214)
    Fruit not winged 7
7   Fruit unsymmetrical, swollen on one side. . . . . RED CYPHOMERIS
    . . . . (*Cyphomeris gypsophiloides*, p. 217)
    Fruit symmetrical, not swollen on one side 8
8   Calyx about 4 inches long, with a long and very slender tube . . . .
    . . . . ANGEL'S TRUMPETS (*Acleisanthes longiflora*, p. 214)
    Calyx less than an inch long with tube shorter and less conspicuous or wanting entirely 9
9   Fruit 10-ribbed; leaves thick and leathery, mostly basal . . . .
    . . . . RINGSTEM (*Anulocaulis*, p. 215)
    Fruit with 5 or fewer angles; leaves thin and scattered along the stems . . . . SPIDERLING (*Boerhavia*, p. 216)

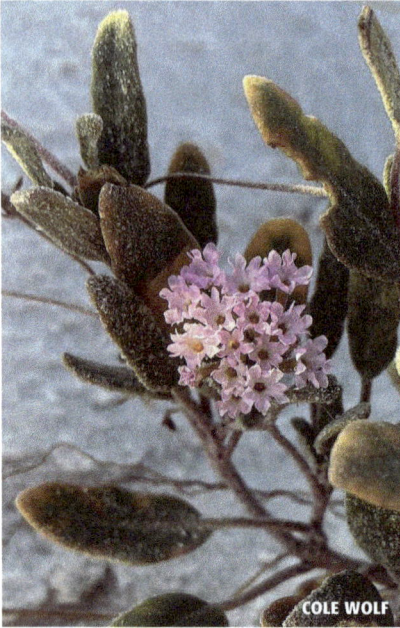

COLE WOLF

PURPLE SAND-VERBENA
(*Abronia angustifolia*)

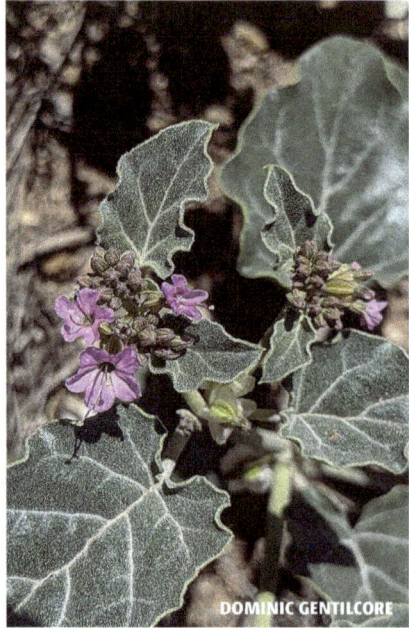

DOMINIC GENTILCORE

GOOSEFOOT MOONPOD
(*Acleisanthes chenopodioides*)

Purple Sand-Verbena (*Abronia angustifolia*)—This is an annual plant with somewhat prostrate stems, opposite leaves, and purplish-red flowers. It is one of the few plants that can grow on the gypsum sands at White Sands National Monument in New Mexico, and for many years it was believed that it grew nowhere else, but it has been found in the Park near Glen Spring, and elsewhere in Arizona, New Mexico, and Texas.

■ **Moonpod** (*Acleisanthes*, synonym *Selinocarpus*)—Perennial herbs, woody at the base, with small, opposite, short-petioled leaves and conspicuous flowers often with long tubes. The fruits have five wings. In addition to **Angel's Trumpets** (*Acleisanthes longiflora*), species found in the Park are distinguished as follows:

1   Flowers 1½ inches long or more . . . . **Little-Leaf Moonpod**
. . . . (*Acleisanthes parvifolia*)
    Flowers ½ inch long or less **2**
2   Stamens 5; flowers solitary or in pairs . . . **Narrow-Leaf Moonpod**
. . . . (*Acleisanthes angustifolia*)
    Stamens 2 or 3; flowers in umbels . . . . . . **Goosefoot Moonpod**
. . . . (*Acleisanthes chenopodioides*)

TRAILING WINDMILLS
(*Allionia incarnata*)

BIG BEND RINGSTEM
(*Anulocaulis eriosolenus*)

■ **Windmills** (*Allionia*)—Annual or perennial herbs with prostrate stems and opposite, petioled leaves. The purplish-red or rarely white flowers are borne three together in each involucre which consists of three oval, sepallike bracts and is solitary on an axillary stalk. The fruit is leathery and has a wing on each side. The inner side is smooth, and on the outer side there are two rows of glands, often concealed by the incurved wings. **Annual Windmills** (*Allionia choisyi*) is an annual and has smooth or only slightly hairy stems. The wings of the fruits have numerous slender teeth but are not incurved, and the leaves are oblong, waxy beneath, and somewhat crisped. It is reported from Brewster County but its presence in the Park has not been verified. ❧ **Trailing Windmills** (*Allionia incarnata*) is perennial and is very sticky, the wings of the fruit are incurved, and the leaves are usually ovate, not waxy beneath, and not crisped.

Southwestern Ringstem (*Anulocaulis leiosolenus*)—A stout, perennial herb with large, nearly round leaves mostly situated near the base. Some of the leaves are as much as 3 or 4 inches across. The stems are much branched and have sticky rings about the internodes. The flowers

SLIM-STALK SPIDERLING
(*Boerhavia gracillima*)

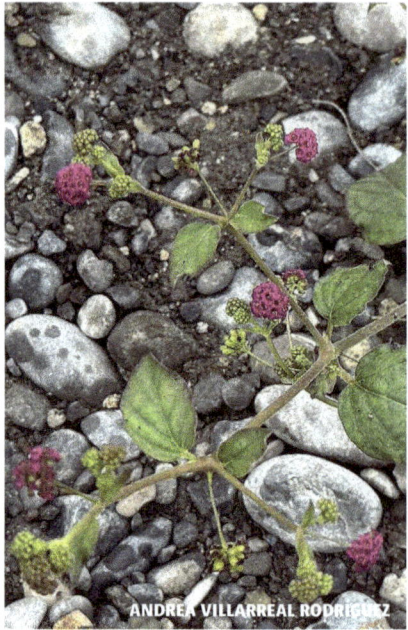

SCARLET SPIDERLING
(*Boerhavia coccinea*)

are arranged in short, spikelike clusters in the axils of scales at the nodes. Reported from Brewster County, its presence in the Park is unconfirmed. ⌁ **Big Bend Ringstem** (*Anulocaulis eriosolenus*) is similar but is more slender, with smaller leaves, and the flowers are solitary or only two or three in a cluster.

■ Spiderling (*Boerhavia*)—Annual or perennial herbs with opposite, unequal leaves and small flowers each subtended by one or two small bracts and having a 5-lobed calyx, variously arranged but often in panicles. Seven species have been found in the Park and they may be distinguished by the following key:

1 Fruits sticky-hairy. 2
   Fruits not sticky 3
2 Flowers solitary, long-stalked . . . . Slim-Stalk Spiderling
   . . . . (*Boerhavia gracillima*)
   Flowers clustered, nearly sessile . . . . ⌁ Scarlet Spiderling
   . . . . (*Boerhavia coccinea*)
3 Plants perennial. 4
   Plants annual 5

MICHELLE W.

MICHELLE W.

NARROW-LEAF SPIDERLING
(*Boerhavia linearifolia*)

RED CYPHOMERIS
(*Cyphomeris gypsophiloides*)

4   Leaves broad, ovate or oval . . **Wineflower** (*Boerhavia anisophylla*)
    Leaves narrow, linear to lanceolate . . . ➤ **Narrow-Leaf Spiderling**
    . . . . (*Boerhavia linearifolia*)
5   Flowers borne in few-flowered umbels . . . . **Slender Spiderling**
    . . . . (*Boerhavia triquetra*)
    Flowers borne in racemes. **6**
6   Fruits 4-angled . . . . . **Large-Bract Spiderling** (*Boerhavia wrightii*)
    Fruits 5-angled . . . . **Torrey's Spiderling** (*Boerhavia torreyana*)

➤ **Red Cyphomeris** (*Cyphomeris gypsophiloides*)—This is an erect, perennial herb with a somewhat woody base and thick, fleshy, ovate or triangular, entire leaves, the upper much narrower. The flowers are red and funnelform and are arranged in racemes. The fruit is 10-ribbed.

■ **Four-O'clock** (*Mirabilis*, synonym *Oxybaphus*)—Herbs with opposite leaves and usually three to five small but conspicuous flowers in each 5-lobed involucre. The calyx is rose or purple and bell-shaped with a very short tube at the base, and there are usually three stamens and a slender style with a knoblike stigma. **Marvel-of-Peru** (*Mirabilis aggregata*, synonym *Oxybaphus aggregatus*), a species of Mexico, is reported

JOSEPH AUBERT

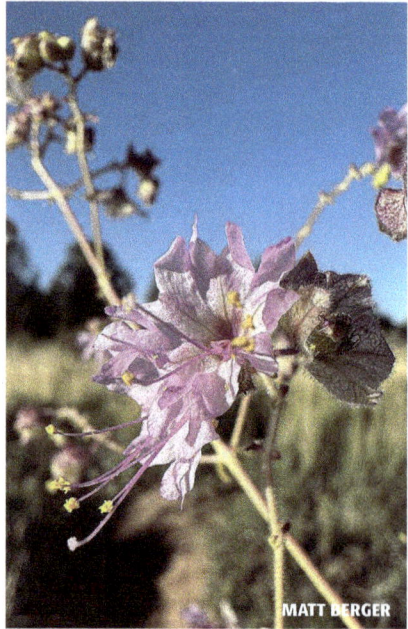

MATT BERGER

WHITE FOUR-O'CLOCK
(*Mirabilis albida*)

NARROW-LEAF FOUR-O'CLOCK
(*Mirabilis linearis*)

for the Park, and has smooth lance-shaped leaves, which are short-petioled. The fruits are also smooth. ≫ White Four-O'clock (*Mirabilis albida*, synonym *Oxybaphus albidus*) is nearly smooth except in the flower clusters and has oblong leaves, which are sessile or nearly so. The fruit is hairy. Hairy-Tuft Four-O'clock (*Mirabilis comata*, synonym *Oxybaphus comatus*) is hairy throughout and often sticky, and the leaves are rather thick, ovate, and petioled. The fruit is hairy, but the hairs are very short. ≫ Narrow-Leaf Four-O'clock (*Mirabilis linearis*, synonym *Oxybaphus linearis*) is smooth or somewhat hairy on the upper portions and has leaves that are linear, rather thick, 1 to 4 inches long, and sessile or nearly so. The fruit is hairy. Spreading Four-O'clock (*Mirabilis oxybaphoides*) is a low, much branched herb with more or less prostrate, sticky branches, opposite leaves, and loose panicles of flowers arranged three in each 5-lobed involucre and each having three stamens. Found on the upper slopes of Casa Grande Mountain.

≫ Devil's-Bouquet (*Nyctaginia capitata*)—A prostrate, hairy perennial with triangular pointed leaves and several red flowers in each 8- to 12-bracted involucre. The calyx is tubular and about 1 inch long. The

DEVIL'S-BOUQUET
(*Nyctaginia capitata*)

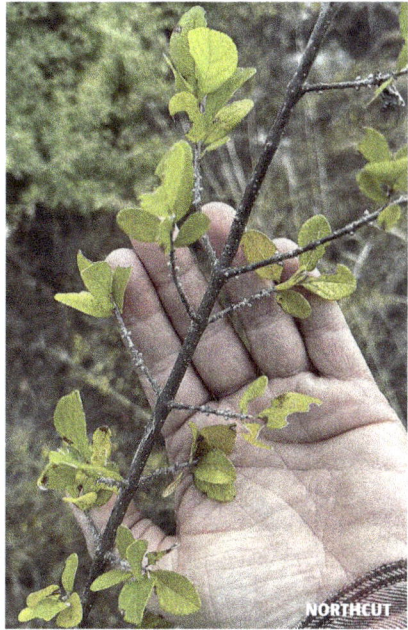

STRETCHBERRY
(*Forestiera pubescens*)

style with a headlike stigma and the five stamens extend well beyond the calyx tube.

OLIVE FAMILY (OLEACEAE)

A family of trees and shrubs with rather variable characters. The leaves are opposite and may be simple or pinnate. The flowers may be perfect or imperfect. The calyx usually is 4-cleft, but in one genus 5- to 15-lobed; the corolla may be 4-, 5-, or 6-lobed or cleft, or it may be lacking. There may be either two or four stamens. The fruit may be a drupe, capsule, or samara. Three genera are found in the Park:

■ Swamp-Privet (*Forestiera*)—Shrubs with simple, opposite leaves and inconspicuous flowers, which may be perfect or imperfect. The corolla is usually lacking, but there is a small calyx and two or four stamens. The fruit is a black drupe, edible but not very palatable. ➤ Stretchberry (*Forestiera pubescens*) has oblong leaves with very minutely toothed margins. Texas Swamp-Privet (*Forestiera angustifolia*) has narrow leaves with entire margins which are rolled inward. The leaves of both species are ½ to 1 inch long.

ERIC KNIGHT

MATT BERGER

FRAGRANT ASH
(*Fraxinus cuspidata*)

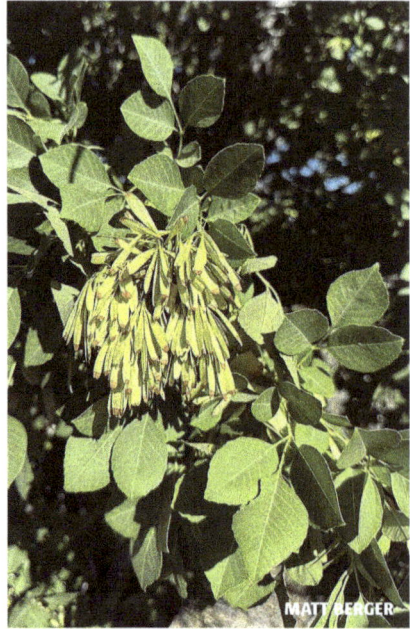

VELVET ASH
(*Fraxinus velutina*)

■ **Ash** (*Fraxinus*)—Trees or shrubs with opposite, pinnate leaves, small, greenish or white flowers, and winged, usually 1-seeded fruits (samaras). Four species have been found in the Park:

1   Flowers with corollas; leaflets 3 to 7 . . . . ⤷ **Fragrant Ash**
. . . . (*Fraxinus cuspidata*)
Flowers without corollas **2**

2   Leaflets usually not more than ¾ inch long; petiole and central axes of leaves narrowly winged . . . . **Gregg's Ash** (*Fraxinus greggii*)
Leaflets more than ¾ inch long; petioles and central axes of leaves not winged **3**

3   Wing of fruit terminal or only slightly extended on the body . . . . .
. . . . ⤷ **Velvet Ash** (*Fraxinus velutina*)
Wing of fruit extending to below the middle of the body . . . .
. . . . **Mexican Ash** (*Fraxinus berlandieriana*)

■ **Menodora** (*Menodora*)—Low plants that are partly herbaceous but woody at the base. The leaves are opposite, sessile or nearly so, and mostly entire. The flowers are yellow, perfect, with a 5- to 15-lobed calyx with narrow lobes, a 5- or 6-lobed corolla, 2 stamens, and 1 pistil. The

ROUGH MENODORA
(*Menodora scabra*)

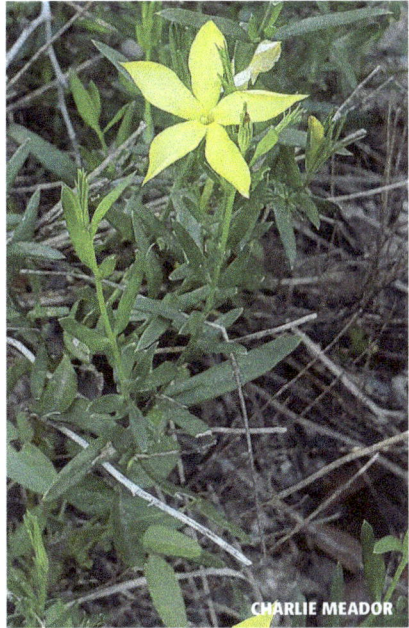

SHOWY MENODORA
(*Menodora longiflora*)

fruit is a 2-celled and usually 4-seeded capsule. ⭢ Rough Menodora (*Menodora scabra*) has narrowly linear leaves, usually less than an inch long, and rather large flowers with short tubes. ⭢ Showy Menodora (*Menodora longiflora*) has linear or lance-shaped leaves, and flowers with tubes 1 to 2 inches long.

EVENING-PRIMROSE FAMILY (ONAGRACEAE)

A rather large family containing many plants with showy flowers. The flowers are perfect and regular, and the parts are mostly in twos or fours. The ovary is below the other parts of the flower, and in many cases the calyx tube is prolonged beyond the ovary, the petals attached to its summit. The fruit is a capsule or, in some cases, dry and nutlike.

■ Evening-Primrose (*Eremothera, Oenothera*)—Plants with alternate or all basal leaves and conspicuous, yellow, white, purple, or rose-colored flowers with the calyx tube prolonged beyond the ovary and its four lobes turned hack, four petals, eight stamens, and a four-celled capsule containing many seeds. There are a dozen or more species in the Park.

AUSTIN R. KELLY

SUE CARNAHAN

HARTWEG'S SUNDROPS
(*Oenothera hartwegii*)

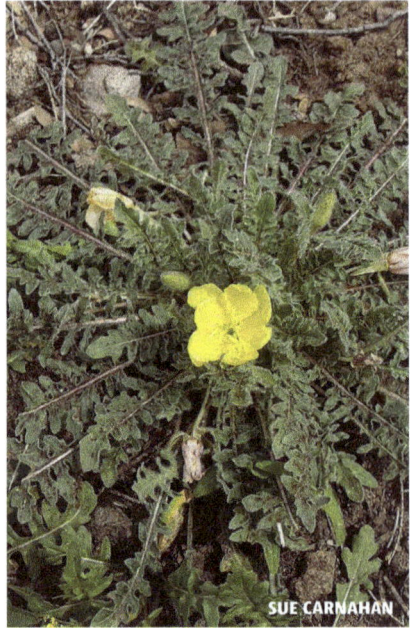

DESERT EVENING-PRIMROSE
(*Oenothera primiveris*)

1 Stigma knob-like, disk-like, or merely 4-toothed 2
   Stigma with 4 linear lobes 4
2 Stigma knob-like; petals less than one-sixth inch long, white . . . .
   . . . . **Long-Capsule Mooncup**
   (*Eremothera chamaenerioides*, synonym *Oenothera chamaenerioides*)
   Stigma disk-like; petals much larger, yellow 3
3 Calyx tube much less than 1 inch long, the lobes less than one-sixth
   inch long . . . . **Texas Sundrops** (*Oenothera tubicula*)
   Calyx tube over an inch long, the lobes ¼ inch long or more . . . . .
   . . . . ⚐ **Hartweg's Sundrops** (*Oenothera hartwegii*)
4 Flowers yellow or cream color (sometimes turning purple in age)
   5
   Flowers white or pink; plants with stems 8
5 Capsules winged on the angles at apex 6
   Capsules not winged; plants stemless . . . .
   . . . . ⚐ **Desert Evening-Primrose** (*Oenothera primiveris*)
6 Plants with elongate stems . . **South American Evening-Primrose**
   . . . . (*Oenothera pubescens*)

PINKLADIES
(*Oenothera speciosa*)

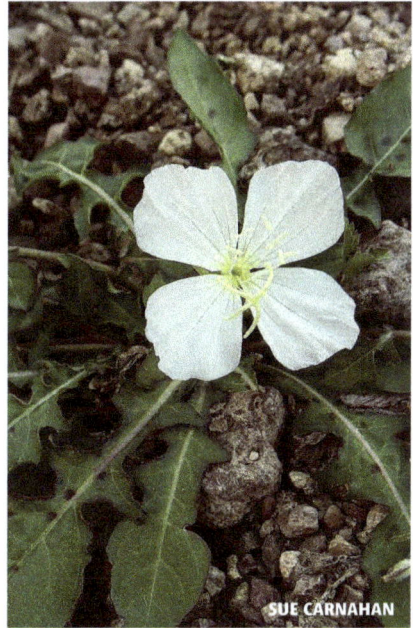

KUNTH'S EVENING-PRIMROSE
(*Oenothera kunthiana*)

Plants stemless or nearly so 7

7 Plants densely short-hairy. . . . . . . Short-Fruit Evening-Primrose
. . . . (*Oenothera brachycarpa*)
Plants smooth or inconspicuously hairy . . . .
. . . . Stemless Evening-Primrose (*Oenothera triloba*)

8 Flower buds drooping; petals mostly 1 inch long or more. . . . .
. . . . ⤳ Pinkladies (*Oenothera speciosa*)
Flower buds erect. 9

9 Calyx tube 1/3 inch long or less; petals less than 1/2 inch long . . .
. . . . Rose Evening-Primrose (*Oenothera rosea*)
Calyx tube 1/2 inch long or more; petals mostly 1/2 inch long or
more. . . . . . . ⤳ Kunth's Evening-Primrose (*Oenothera kunthiana*)

In addition, several former members of genus *Gaura* are now placed
in *Oenothera*. These are herbs, sometimes with woody base, with rather
crowded, sessile, alternate leaves, and white or rose-colored flowers in
spikes, with the calyx tube much prolonged beyond the ovary and with
its four lobes turned back, four petals, eight stamens, and a four-lobed
stigma. The fruit is hard and nutlike and contains one to four seeds. In

SCARLET EVENING-PRIMROSE
(*Oenothera suffrutescens*)

WATER-PRIMROSE
(*Ludwigia peploides*)

🗡 Scarlet Evening-Primrose (*Oenothera suffrutescens*, synonym *Gaura coccinea*) the fruit is sessile or nearly so, while in Trans-Pecos Evening-Primrose (*Oenothera arida*, synonym *Gaura macrocarpa*) it is slender-stalked.

🗡 Water-Primrose (*Ludwigia peploides*, synonym *Jussiaea diffusa*)—This plant grows in wet places or in streams, and the stem may be creeping or floating. The alternate leaves are oblong and taper into a slender petiole, and the flowers are fairly large and conspicuous. The calyx tube is not prolonged beyond the ovary. There are 5 calyx lobes, 5 yellow petals, and 10 stamens. The capsule is cylindrical with a tapering base.

ORCHID FAMILY (ORCHIDACEAE)

The orchid family produces some of the most beautiful and highly prized of all flowers. It is a rather recent family in point of origin and has developed some remarkable adaptations for cross pollination by insects, but it cannot be said to have evolved along lines of greatest efficiency. In the first place, the orchids have become so dependent upon insects that, in most cases, they cannot produce any seeds at all unless

SUE CARNAHAN

SAM KIESCHNICK

LARGE-FLOWER CRESTED-CORALROOT
(*Hexalectris grandiflora*)

TEXAS CRESTED-CORALROOT
(*Hexalectris warnockii*)

they are visited by certain of these small animals. In the second place, the seeds are extremely small and in most cases will not germinate unless they are stimulated by certain kinds of fungi or by some artificial means such as a sugar solution. The result is that many kinds of orchids are extremely rare, except as they are cultivated by humans.

The orchid flower consists of three sepals, three petals, one of which is very different from the others and is called the lip, and a central column made up of a single stamen and a style united together. The ovary is below the other parts of the flower. The pollen is in the form of two pear-shaped masses, which are attached by stalks to a sticky disk, and the whole structure usually adheres to the head or body of an insect when the flower is visited for nectar. Five genera are reported from the Park, all uncommon in the Park, and several are keyed below.

1 Plants leafless . . . . ❧ Large-Flower Crested-Coralroot
. . . . (*Hexalectris grandiflora*)
Plants with a single, grasslike leaf . . . .
. . . . ❧ Texas Crested-Coralroot (*Hexalectris warnockii*)
Plants with more than one leaf 2

GITTERGRAVEL

ALEXIS LÓPEZ HERNÁNDEZ

GIANT HELLEBORINE
(*Epipactis gigantea*)

SCARLET MOCK LADIES'-TRESSES
(*Dichromanthus cinnabarinus*)

2   Flowers greenish and strongly veined with purple . . . .
. . . . ❧ Giant Helleborine (*Epipactis gigantea*)
Flowers vermilion-red externally and bright yellow within . . . .
. . ❧ Scarlet Mock Ladies'-Tresses (*Dichromanthus cinnabarinus*)

BROOMRAPE FAMILY (OROBANCHACEAE)

Perennial, parasitic herbs, sometimes without green leaves, and attached underground to the roots of other plants. The portion above ground consists of an unbranched stalk bearing leaves or scales and numerous flowers with 2-lipped corollas. The fruits are capsules, and the seeds are very numerous and extremely small.

■ Indian-Paintbrush (*Castilleja*)—Herbs with alternate, usually narrow leaves and flowers arranged in spikes subtended by bracts that are colored and more showy than the flowers themselves. Five species occur in the Park; three are described here: ❧ Woolly Indian-Paintbrush (*Castilleja lanata*) is white-woolly all over. Wholeleaf Indian-Paintbrush (*Castilleja integra*) has short spikes and leaves that are linear and entire but not conspicuously hairy. Stiff Indian-Paintbrush

ALINA MARTIN

MARK POLLOCK

WOOLLY INDIAN-PAINTBRUSH
(*Castilleja lanata*)

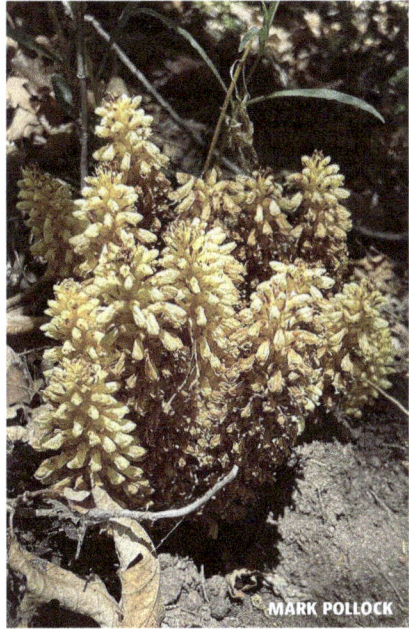

ALPINE CANCER-ROOT
(*Conopholis alpina*)

(*Castilleja rigida*) has longer spikes and broader leaves, and both the bracts and the leaves are prominently 3-nerved. This is the most common species in the Park.

➤ **Alpine Cancer-Root** (*Conopholis alpina*, synonym *Conopholis mexicana*)—Parasitic on the roots of oak trees. Plants usually about 8 inches high with a yellowish stem and flowers of about the same color in a dense, terminal spike. The corolla is curved and strongly 2-lipped. There are four stamens in two pairs. The calyx is split down the lower side.

Broomrape (*Orobanche ludoviciana*, synonym *Aphyllon multiflorum*)—Parasitic on the roots of mesquite and several other plants. The entire plant, including the flowers, is purplish or brownish and usually grows 4 to 15 inches high. The corolla is slightly curved, and the calyx is almost equally 5-lobed and is not split down the lower side.

Black-Senna (*Seymeria scabra*)—A low, much-branched herb with numerous small, opposite leaves, which are entire or sparingly parted into narrow lobes. The flowers are yellow with a deeply 5-cleft calyx, a corolla with a short tube and five nearly equal lobes, and four stamens.

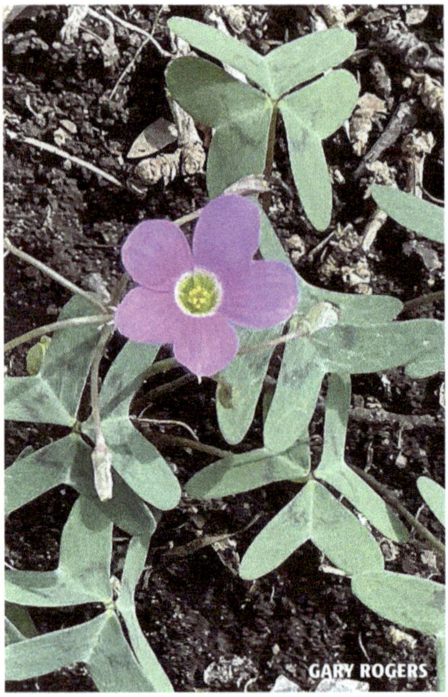

DRUMMOND'S WOOD-SORREL
(*Oxalis drummondii*)

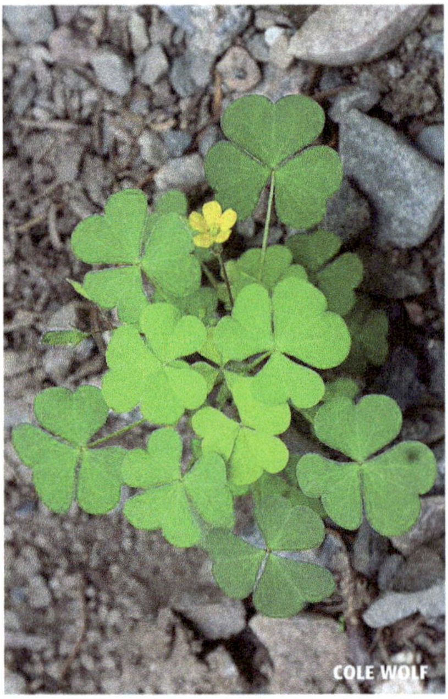

YELLOW WOOD-SORREL
(*Oxalis stricta*)

WOOD-SORREL FAMILY (OXALIDACEAE)

■ **Wood-Sorrel** (*Oxalis*)—Low perennial plants with compound leaves with usually three inverted heart-shaped leaflets. The flowers are rose-color or yellow and have 5 sepals, 5 petals, 10 stamens, and 1 pistil with 5 cells in the ovary. The fruit is a capsule. Three species are found in the Park:

1 Plants with leafy stems; flowers yellow........................ 2
Leaves all basal; flowers rose or violet ....
.... **Drummond's Wood-Sorrel** (*Oxalis drummondii*)

2 Leaves smooth or nearly so **Yellow Wood-Sorrel** (*Oxalis stricta*)
Leaves hairy on both sides................. **Hairy Wood-Sorrel**
.... (*Oxalis albicans*)

POPPY FAMILY (PAPAVERACEAE)

Herbs or shrubs with milky or colored juice and usually alternate leaves without stipules. The flowers are regular, complete, usually showy and

WHITE PRICKLY-POPPY
(*Argemone polyanthemos*)

GOLDEN CORYDALIS
(*Corydalis aurea*)

often a given plant has several in bloom at the same time. There are two or three sepals, twice as many petals, numerous stamens, and one pistil with a short style. The fruit is a capsule with many or few seeds. ❧ White Prickly-Poppy (*Argemone polyanthemos*) has such prickly stems and leaves that it reminds one of a thistle. The juice of this plant is orange colored, and the flowers are white and 2 to 4 inches across. Occasionally plants are found with pink flowers. There are usually three sepals and six petals, and the fruit, which is about an inch long, is very spiny. ❧ Golden Corydalis (*Corydalis aurea*) has numerous golden-yellow, spurred, tubular flowers about ½ inch long, resembling those of a pea. Its waxy leaves are up to 3 inches long, pinnately compound, with the leaflets deeply divided into narrowly elliptic, pointed segments.

PETIVERIA FAMILY (PETIVERIACEAE)

Petiveriaceae is a family of flowering plants formerly included as subfamily Rivinoideae in the Pokeweed Family (Phytolaccaceae). This family is represented in our flora only by the ❧ Pigeonberry (*Rivina*

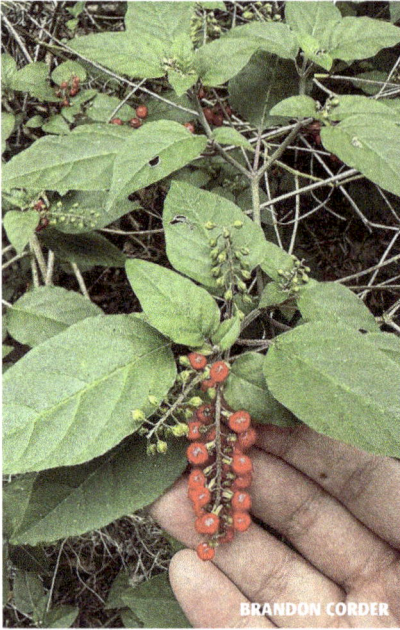

BRANDON CORDER

PIGEONBERRY
(*Rivina humilis*)

ALISON NORTHUP

TEXAS MONKEYFLOWER
(*Erythranthe inamoena*)

humilis), a dark green, bushy plant with slender spikes of pink or some-times white flowers and small, red berries. The alternate leaves are ovate with long points, the blades 1 to 6 inches long and the margins slightly wavy. The flowers are a little less than a ¼ inch across. They have no petals, but the four sepals are colored like petals, and there are four very small stamens. The fruit is really a one-seeded stone-fruit, like a plum rather than a berry. The flower clusters are 1 to 4 inches long, and often ripe fruits occur at the base of a cluster while flowers continue to bloom at the tip. The fruits were formerly a source of ink and dye before they were replaced by commercial products.

LOPSEED FAMILY (PHRYMACEAE)

⌇ Texas Monkeyflower (*Erythranthe inamoena*, synonym *Mimulus glabratus*)—A smooth herb with creeping stems, opposite, round-oval, toothed leaves and yellow, 2-lipped flowers. Growing in creek beds or other moist places.

SMARTWEED LEAF-FLOWER
(*Phyllanthus polygonoides*)

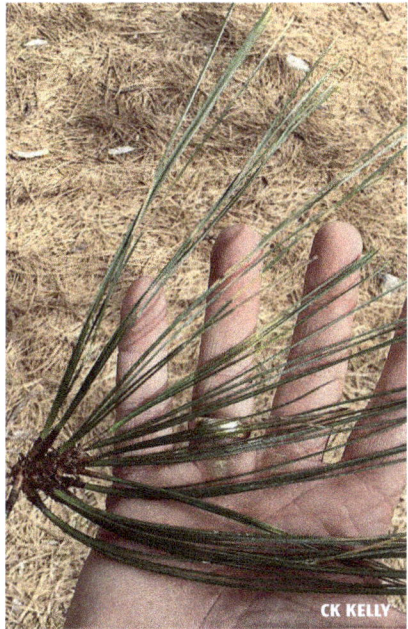

ARIZONA PINE
(*Pinus arizonica*)

LEAF-FLOWER FAMILY (PHYLLANTHACEAE)

Smartweed Leaf-Flower (*Phyllanthus polygonoides*)—A low, somewhat shrubby plant, usually not much over 6 inches high, with elliptical, smooth, short-petioled leaves and 2 or 3 small, imperfect flowers in the axils. The leaves, which are about ½ inch or less long, have white stipules, and the margins of the tiny calyx lobes are also white.

PINE FAMILY (PINACEAE)

This is the family of the cone-bearing trees and shrubs. It is the most important lumber-producing family. Three species are reported for the park.

Arizona Pine (*Pinus arizonica*)—This pine grows only at high altitudes in the Chisos Mountains and is one of only three species of large trees in the Park, the others being the Douglas-Fir and the Arizona Cypress. The Arizona Pine has its leaves mostly in clusters of 4 or 5, and occasionally in bundles of only 2 or 3. The leaves are 4 to 10 inches long. The tree is very easily recognized by these leaves because there is no

MEXICAN PINYON
(*Pinus cembroides*)

DOUGLAS-FIR
(*Pseudotsuga menziesii*)

other tree in the Park with needle leaves that are so long. The cones average about 2½ inches long. Arizona Pine is closely related to **Ponderosa Pine** (*Pinus ponderosa*) and the two species are thought to hybridize, but its presence in the Park has not been confirmed.

➤ **Mexican Pinyon** (*Pinus cembroides*)—Very common at medium elevations in the mountains, this tree usually grows 15 to 40 feet high. The needlelike leaves are 1 to 2 inches long and are produced in clusters of two or sometimes three. The cones are 1 to 2 inches in diameter and about as long. The seeds are large and edible. **Paper-Shell Pinyon** (*Pinus remota*) is also present in the Park, and can be distinguished from other pinyon species by its thin-walled seeds, which made it especially attractive as a food.

➤ **Douglas-Fir** (*Pseudotsuga menziesii*)—The Douglas-fir is one of the most valuable lumber trees in the world. The leaves are scattered, one in a place. They are needle-shaped but soft and flat and usually not much more than one inch long. The cones are pendulous and very distinctive: 3-toothed bracts project from between the scales and give the cone a shaggy or fringed appearance. The cones are 4 to 6 inches long and oval or oblong in shape.

CONWAY HAWN

VINE-SNAPDRAGON
(*Maurandella antirrhiniflora*)

BÁRBARA SALAS OSORIO

TEXAS TOADFLAX
(*Nuttallanthus texanus*)

PLANTAIN FAMILY (PLANTAGINACEAE)

Includes plants such as **Beardtongue** (*Penstemon*) formerly placed in Figwort Family (Scrophulariaceae).

⤷ Vine-Snapdragon (*Maurandella antirrhiniflora*)—A vine with small, triangular, or spear-shaped leaves and snapdragonlike, rose or purple flowers. Growing among low shrubs and other plants in protected places.

⤷ Texas Toadflax (*Nuttallanthus texanus*, synonym *Linaria texana*)—A slender plant growing to 2 feet high, with scattered, narrow leaves and a loose spike of fragrant, blue, 2-lipped, spurred flowers.

■ Beardtongue, Penstemon (*Penstemon*)—Shrubs or perennial herbs with opposite leaves and showy, red, blue, or purple flowers with four perfect stamens and one sterile one, which may be either naked or bearded. The stems and leaves in most species are very smooth. Seven species are reported for the Park; five are keyed below.

1   Flowers red. 2
    Flowers blue. 4

ROCK PENSTEMON
(*Penstemon baccharifolius*)

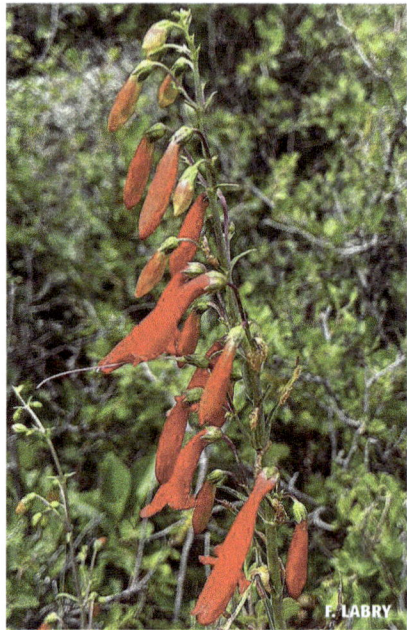

BEARD-LIP PENSTEMON
(*Penstemon barbatus*)

2 Plants shrubby... ➤ **Rock Penstemon** (*Penstemon baccharifolius*)
Plants herbaceous.. **3**
3 Leaves broad, ovate **Big Bend Beardtongue** (*Penstemon havardii*)
Leaves linear.... ➤ **Beard-Lip Penstemon** (*Penstemon barbatus*)
4 Leaves smooth.... ➤ **Fendler's Penstemon** (*Penstemon fendleri*)
Leaves covered with minute hairs........ **Cochise Beardtongue**
.... (*Penstemon dasyphyllus*)

■ **Plantain** (*Plantago*)—Herbs with the foliage leaves all basal. The flowers are small, perfect or imperfect, regular, and are borne in terminal, long-stalked spikes. Common species are keyed below:

1 Some flowers perfect and some imperfect; many of them permanently closed and others wide open......... **Red-Seed Plantain**
.... (*Plantago rhodosperma*)
Flowers all perfect and none of them permanently closed...... **2**
2 Bracts narrowly lance-shaped, their margins not conspicuously dry and whitish.......... ➤ **Woolly Plantain** (*Plantago patagonica*)
Bracts triangular to lance-shaped; their margins conspicuously dry and whitish........... **Wright's Plantain** (*Plantago wrightiana*)

FENDLER'S PENSTEMON
(*Penstemon fendleri*)

WOOLLY PLANTAIN
(*Plantago patagonica*)

PHLOX FAMILY (POLEMONIACEAE)

The Phlox Family consists of small or medium-sized herbs or low shrubs, often with very beautiful flowers. The flowers have a numerical plan of five, with a 5-lobed, persistent calyx, a 5-lobed, tubular corolla, five stamens, and one pistil with a 3-lobed style. The fruit is a dry pod or capsule.

■ **False Calico** (*Dayia, Loeselia*)—This genus has flowers somewhat intermediate between Phlox and former *Gilia*, and the leaves may be either opposite or alternate but usually are not entire. The uncommon **Chisos Mountain False Calico** (*Loeselia greggii*) produces long, wandlike branches with opposite, lance-shaped, toothed leaves about an inch long and small, pinkish flowers. ⤴ **Havard's Skyrocket** (*Dayia havardii*, synonym *Loeselia havardii*) is usually only 3 or 4 inches high and profusely branched. The leaves are alternate and each consists of a stalk and three or more very narrow leaflets.

■ **Gilia** (*Giliastrum, Ipomopsis*)—The flowers of the gilias have funnel-shaped corollas, and the leaves are usually alternate and not entire. The species below were formerly placed in genus Gilia. The most con-

ERIC KNIGHT

HAVARD'S SKYROCKET
(*Dayia havardii*)

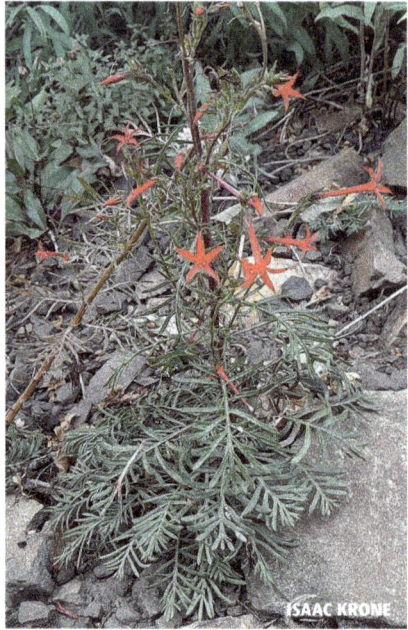

ISAAC KRONE

SCARLET GILIA
(*Ipomopsis aggregata*)

spicuous of these is ↘ Scarlet Gilia (*Ipomopsis aggregata*, synonym *Gilia aggregata*), which has bright scarlet flowers with corolla tubes about 1¼ inches long and pinnate leaves with very narrow lobes. It is found mostly on shady slopes in the mountains and grows 1 to 2 feet tall with few or no branches. The other species are much-branched and have much smaller flowers which are purplish in color. Iron Skyrocket (*Ipomopsis laxiflora*, synonym *Gilia laxiflora*) grows about 6 to 8 inches high and has flowers with very narrow tubes about an inch long. The leaves are similar to those of Ipomopsis aggregata but smaller. Bluebowls (*Giliastrum rigidulum*, synonym *Gilia rigidula*) has flowers that are very short funnel-shaped and leaves that are reduced to simple, very narrow blades 1 inch or less long. It is found on Dog Flats and in the Dog Canyon area. ↘ Splitleaf Gilia (*Giliastrum incisum*, synonym *Gilia incisa*) also has short, funnel-shaped flowers and is the only species with broad leaves. The leaves are 1 inch or less long and ½ inch or less broad, with conspicuously toothed margins.

↘ Santa Fe Phlox (*Phlox nana*)—A herbaceous plant growing 8 or more inches high with opposite, linear, sessile leaves 2 to 4 inches long, and conspicuous, pink, purplish, or sometimes white flowers. The

SPLITLEAF GILIA
(*Giliastrum incisum*)

SANTA FE PHLOX
(*Phlox nana*)

corollas have a long, narrow tube and broad flat lobes and are about an inch or less across.

MILKWORT FAMILY (POLYGALACEAE)

Herbaceous or somewhat shrubby plants with entire, alternate, opposite, or whorled leaves. The flowers are very irregular and remind one somewhat of the butterfly-shaped flowers of the pea family. The family is represented in the Park by eight species, all formerly placed in genus *Polygala* but now separated into several new entities; six species are keyed below.

■ Milkwort (*Hebecarpa, Polygala, Rhinotropis*)—The flowers are very irregular. There are five sepals, two of them, called the wings, much larger than the other three and colored like petals, and usually three petals, which are somewhat united to each other and to the stamen tube, the middle petal different from the other two. The six to eight stamens have their filaments united below into a split tube. There is one pistil which develops into a flat, 2-celled pod, each cell with a single seed.

BROOM MILKWORT
(*Polygala scoparioides*)

LINDHEIMER'S MILKWORT
(*Rhinotropis lindheimeri*)

1   Flowers white 2
    Flowers purple. 3
2   Flowers in spikelike racemes which are 1 to 4 inches long and many-
    flowered . . . . ➤ Broom Milkwort (*Polygala scoparioides*)
    Flowers in very short racemes with only 3 or 4 flowers . . . .
    . . . . ➤ Lindheimer's Milkwort
    . . . . (*Rhinotropis lindheimeri* var. *parvifolia*,
    . . . . synonym *Polygala lindheimeri* var. *parvifolia*)
3   Plants very low and shrubby, 2 to 4 inches high, very compact and
    very leafy; the leaves oblong, but only about ¼ inch long or less . .
    . . . . Gland-Leaf Milkwort
    . . . . (*Hebecarpa macradenia*, synonym *Polygala macradenia*)
    Plants 4 to 20 inches tall and shrubby only at the base, less compact
    and not densely leafy 4
4   Flowers in short, few-flowered racemes; leaves mostly oblong or el-
    liptic and about ¼ inch long; plant hairy with short spreading hairs
    . . . . Lindheimer's Milkwort
    . . . . (*Rhinotropis lindheimeri*, synonym *Polygala lindheimeri*)

SUE CARNAHAN

CATHERINE GALLEY

VELVET-SEED MILKWORT
(*Hebecarpa obscura*)

BLUE MILKWORT
(*Hebecarpa barbeyana*)

Flowers in spike-like racemes which are 1 to 4 inches long and many-flowered; leaves mostly oblong or linear and about 1 inch long; plant with fine, mostly appressed hairs 5

5   Appendages at base of seed veil-like, covering a third to more than half of the seed . . . . ❧ Velvet-Seed Milkwort
. . . . (*Hebecarpa obscura*, synonym *Polygala obscura*)
Appendages of seed hat-like, with hairy, rounded crown and narrow, papery margin . . . . ❧ Blue Milkwort
. . . . (*Hebecarpa barbeyana*, synonym *Polygala barbeyana*)

BUCKWHEAT FAMILY (POLYGONACEAE)

This is a large family containing trees, shrubs, and herbs, but only herbs are represented in the Park. The flowers, for the most part, are small and inconspicuous, and the family contains relatively few ornamental plants. It contains some pernicious weeds; the cultivated buckwheat is a valuable food plant. Three genera are keyed below; several species of *Polygonum* are also reported.

1 Flowers subtended by an involucre . . . . **WILD BUCKWHEAT**
. . . . (*Eriogonum*, p. 240)
   Flowers not subtended by an involucre **2**
2 Sepals 6; 3 turned back and 3 erect in fruit **DOCK** (*Rumex*, p. 241)
   Sepals 5; all erect in fruit. . . . . **KNOTWEED** (*Persicaria*, p. 240)

■ **Wild Buckwheat** (*Eriogonum*)—The plants of this genus have flowers with a 9-parted perianth (calyx and corolla combined), nine stamens, and one pistil with three styles. The leaves are entire. Eight species are reported from the Park, occurring mostly in dry places, seven are listed in the following key:

1 Fruit winged above the middle . . . . **Hawkweed Wild Buckwheat**
. . . . (*Eriogonum hieraciifolium*)
   Fruit angled but not winged **2**
2 Perennials **3**
   Annuals **5**
3 Calyx densely long-hairy . . . . ❧ **James' Wild Buckwheat**
. . . . (*Eriogonum jamesii*)
   Calyx not hairy **4**
4 Stems leafy; involucres sessile **Bastard-Sage** (*Eriogonum wrightii*)
   Stems not leafy, the leaves usually all basal; involucres stalked . . .
. . . . **Tall Wild Buckwheat** (*Eriogonum tenellum*)
5 Involucres sessile; stems leafy . . . . **Sorrel Wild Buckwheat**
. . . . (*Eriogonum polycladon*)
   Involucres stalked **6**
6 Stems leafy ❧ **Abert's Wild Buckwheat** (*Eriogonum abertianum*)
   Stems naked, the leaves all basal. . . **Round-Leaf Wild Buckwheat**
. . . . (*Eriogonum rotundifolium*)

■ **Knotweed** (*Persicaria*)—The knotweeds are herbaceous plants with alternate, entire leaves and with the swollen nodes of the stems encased in sheaths, which are often more or less fringed or lobed. The flowers are borne in terminal spikes with dry bracts. The calyx is usually 5-parted and more or less petallike. The stamens vary from four to nine and the pistils or stigmas from 2 to 3. There are no petals.

Lady's-Thumb (*Persicaria maculosa*) is an annual, nearly smooth plant (or with the sheaths and bracts somewhat bristly-hairy) with lance-shaped leaves often have a dark, triangular or moon-shaped spot near the center. The flowers are white or rose-color and have six stamens. They are arranged in spikes. ❧ **Pinkweed** (*Persicaria pensylvanica*) is

THOMAS HERMAN

DOMINIC GENTILCORE

JAMES' WILD BUCKWHEAT
(*Eriogonum jamesii*)

ALBERT'S WILD BUCKWHEAT
(*Eriogonum abertianum*)

similar, but the upper branches and especially the flower stalks are beset with stalked glands and the flowers are larger and often bright rose-color, and they usually have eight stamens. **Swamp Smartweed** (*Persicaria hydropiperoides*) is similar, but the leaves do not have the peculiar dark spot in the center and the flowers have seven or eight stamens.

■ **Dock** (*Rumex*)—The docks are coarse herbs with small, mostly greenish flowers, which are crowded and usually whorled in panicled racemes. The calyx has six sepals, the three outer of which are green and usually turned back while the three inner are larger, often colored, and converge over the 3-angled, 1-seeded fruit.

Five species have been found in the Park, three are described here. **Curly Dock** (*Rumex crispus*) is a smooth herb with lance-shaped leaves with strongly wavy-curled margins. The whorls of flowers are crowded in long, wandlike racemes. This is an exotic plant, naturalized from Europe, and is widely distributed in the United States, but is uncommon in wooded canyons in the Chisos Mountains. ⤳ **Mexican Dock** (*Rumex triangulivalvis*) has narrowly lance-shaped or oblong leaves which are pale green and sometimes have a waxy covering. The flowers are in a very dense panicle. Found along the Rio Grande. **Violet Dock**

SANDY WOLKENBERG

CALEB CATTO

PINKWEED
(*Persicaria pensylvanica*)

MEXICAN DOCK
(*Rumex triangulivalvis*)

(*Rumex violascens*) is an annual plant with basal leaves three to six times as long as wide. The stems are erect and the leaves are oblanceolate or obovate in shape.

PURSLANE FAMILY (PORTULACACEAE)

The plants of this family have simple, entire leaves and are more or less fleshy. The family contains some rather pernicious weeds but also some very beautiful flowers. The flowers open only in sunlight or on very bright days. They are characterized by having only two sepals, usually five petals, five to 20 stamens, and one pistil with two to eight styles.

■ Purslane (*Portulaca*)—Annuals or perennials with cylindrical or flattened, fleshy leaves. The two sepals are united to form a 2-cleft calyx, and the ovary is partly below the other parts of the flower so that the calyx appears to be growing from its middle. The fruit is a short 1-celled pod, which opens at maturity by the upper part separating as a lid. The three species found in the Park may be distinguished as follows:

1   Leaves cylindrical, hairy in the axils. 2
    Leaves flat, not hairy in the axils. . . . . Common Purslane
    . . . . (*Portulaca oleracea*)

KISS-ME-QUICK
(*Portulaca pilosa*)

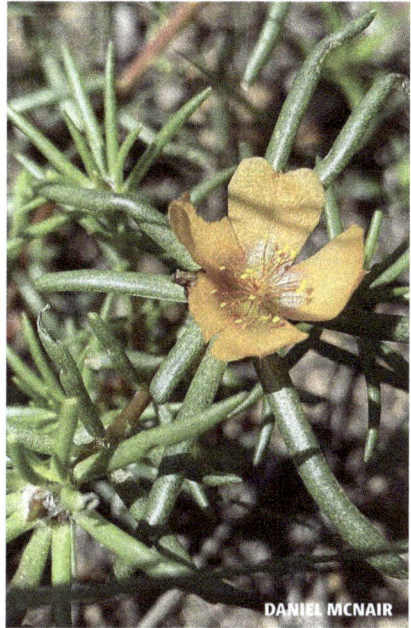

SHRUBBY PURSLANE
(*Portulaca suffrutescens*)

2   Petals carmine to purple ... ❧ Kiss-Me-Quick (*Portulaca pilosa*)
    Petals yellow...... ❧ Shrubby Purslane (*Portulaca suffrutescens*)

PRIMROSE FAMILY (PRIMULACEAE)

A family of herbs with simple leaves and many members with very beautiful flowers. The flowers have a numerical plan of five. The sepals are united to form a 5-lobed calyx, and the petals are likewise united to form a tubular, 5-lobed corolla. The five stamens are attached to the tube of the corolla, and there is a single pistil. The fruit is a capsule.

❧ **Western Rock-Jasmine** (*Androsace occidentalis*) is a tiny annual herb growing to about 3 inches tall. Plants form from a basal rosette of oblong hairy leaves less than 1 inch long. Flowers are in an umbel and of white or pinkish petals above reddish sepals.

■ **Brookweed** (*Samolus*)—Smooth herbs with alternate, entire leaves and small, white flowers in terminal clusters. The leaves are more or less spatula-shaped or oval. ❧ **Limewater Brookweed** (*Samolus ebracteatus*) has leaves 1 to 3 inches long, that are somewhat fleshy, and have winged petioles with the wings extending down on the stems. The

SUE CARNAHAN

WESTERN ROCK-JASMINE
(*Androsace occidentalis*)

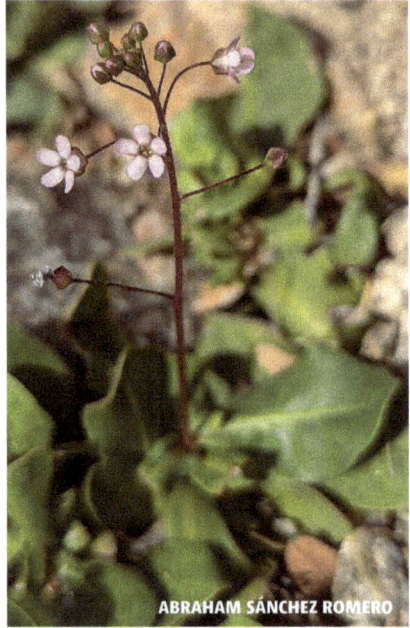

ABRAHAM SÁNCHEZ ROMERO

LIMEWATER BROOKWEED
(*Samolus ebracteatus*)

flowers are about three-sixteenth of an inch across. Seaside Brookweed (*Samolus valerandi*) is similar, but the leaves are only about half as large, the flowers smaller and more numerous, and none of the leaves with clasping bases.

BUTTERCUP FAMILY (RANUNCULACEAE)

The Buttercup Family is a large family of plants with varying character-istics. None of them is of great economic importance except as orna-mental plants, but many have beautiful and interesting flowers; a few are poisonous when eaten by animals. They all agree in having all parts of the flower distinct, however much they may differ in other ways. Only eight species representing six genera have been found in the Park; four species are described below.

➷ Long-Spur Columbine (*Aquilegia longissima*)—Easily recognized by its five-spurred, regular flowers, the columbine has 5 sepals and 5 petals colored alike; the petals are prolonged backward into spurs, often 4 or 5 inches long. This is a Mexican species not known to occur in the United States other than in Brewster and Jeff Davis Counties in Texas

LONG-SPUR COLUMBINE
(*Aquilegia longissima*)

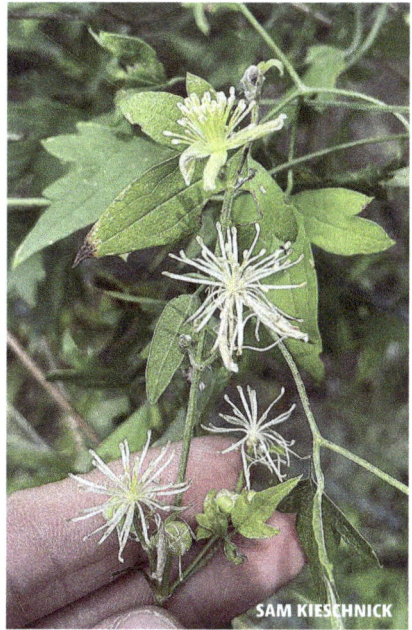

TEXAS VIRGIN'S-BOWER
(*Clematis drummondii*)

and in southern Arizona. It has been found in several canyons in the Chisos Mountains.

⌇ Texas Virgin's-Bower (*Clematis drummondii*)—This is a common vine that climbs by the twisting of its leaf-stalks and spreads profusely over shrubs, fences, or anything else that it finds handy. The small, white flowers are produced abundantly and are imperfect, some plants producing flowers with stamens and other plants flowers with pistils. There are no petals, but the sepals are thin and white. The 1-seeded fruits have long, hairy tails and are borne in clusters fully as conspicuous as the flowers.

⌇ Leatherflower (*Clematis pitcheri*)—This is another vine that climbs by the twisting of the leaf-stalks, but it differs from the Virgin's-Bower in having larger, perfect flowers borne singly instead of in clusters and having very thick, purplish sepals with the tips turned back. It is found in several canyons in the Chisos Mountains.

⌇ Organ Mountain Larkspur (*Delphinium wootonii*)—The larkspur is readily recognized by the blue flowers, which are irregular. The sepals and petals are similar, but there are five irregular sepals, the upper one

NATHAN AARON

BOB NIEMAN

LEATHERFLOWER
(*Clematis pitcheri*)

ORGAN MOLUNTAIN LARKSPUR
(*Delphinium wootonii*)

of which is prolonged into a spur, and only four irregular petals, two of which have spurs included within the calyx spur. Uncommon.

MIGNONETTE FAMILY (RESEDACEAE)

The only member of this family in the Big Bend flora is ➤ **Line-Leaf Whitepuff** (*Oligomeris linifolia*) but which is frequently found on the desert north of the Chisos Mountains and on eroded places along creeks and along the Rio Grande. It is a low, branching herb, somewhat fleshy, with numerous linear, entire leaves, and small, inconspicuous flowers in terminal spikes. The flowers have four sepals, two petals, three to eight stamens, and one pistil, which develops into a small, four-beaked pod.

BUCKTHORN FAMILY (RHAMNACEAE)

A family of shrubs or small trees with simple, unlobed leaves and small flowers, which are regular and have five calyx lobes, five petals, and five stamens, except that in some cases the petals are lacking. The single pistil has a 2- or 3-lobed style and a 2- to 4-celled ovary.

JASON SCHOCK

LINE-LEAF WHITEPUFF
(*Oligomeris linifolia*)

ALEXIS LÓPEZ HERNÁNDEZ

TEXAS ADOLPHIA, JUNCO
(*Adolphia infesta*)

1 Fruit fleshy with a single hard nut **2**
   Fruit fleshy or dry with 2 to 4 separate nutlets **4**
2 Seeds in each nutlet 2 . . . . **COYOTILLO**
   . . . . (*Karwinskia humboldtiana*, p. 249)
   Seeds in each nutlet 1 . . . . **3**
3 Flowers in umbellike clusters . . . . **LOTEBUSH**
   . . . . (*Sarcomphalus obtusifolius*, p. 249)
   Flowers solitary **JAVELINA-BUSH** . . . . . (*Condalia ericoides*, p. 248)
4 Fruit fleshy. . . . . **BUCKTHORN** (*Frangula, Rhamnus*, p. 248)
   Fruit dry or nearly so **5**
5 Stems leafy . **DESERT CEANOTHUS** (*Ceanothus pauciflorus*, p. 248)
   Stems green and nearly leafless . . . . **TEXAS ADOLPHIA**
   . . . . (*Adolphia infesta*, p. 247)

🪶 Texas Adolphia, Junco (*Adolphia infesta*)—A very spiny, nearly leafless shrub with opposite, green branches which end in spines. Usually there are a few very small leaves and the small flowers are borne in scattered, loose clusters in the leaf axils.

STEVE MATSON

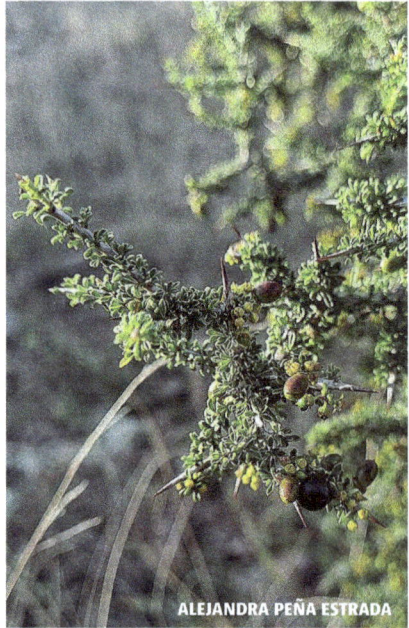

ALEJANDRA PEÑA ESTRADA

DESERT CEANOTHUS
(*Ceanothus pauciflorus*)

JAVELINA-BUSH
(*Condalia ericoides*)

➤ **Desert Ceanothus** (*Ceanothus pauciflorus*)—A shrub with oppo-site, rather thick and leathery leaves, which are entire or with very few teeth. The white or bluish flowers are borne in loose clusters in the leaf axils, and the fruits have three hornlike or wartlike prominences just below the tip.

➤ **Javelina-Bush, Little Buckthorn** (*Condalia ericoides*, synonym *Microrhamnus ericoides*)—A spiny shrub with clustered leaves and small, solitary flowers. The leaves are very small and have strongly inrolled margins and the enclosed grooves are densely short-hairy. The fruits are oblong and about ¼ inch long.

■ **Buckthorn** (*Frangula, Rhamnus*)—Unarmed shrubs with rather large alternate leaves and flowers in small, axillary clusters. ➤ **Birch-Leaf Buckthorn** (*Frangula betulifolia*, synonym *Rhamnus betulifolia*) has rather numerous flowers, and the leaves are more than 1½ inches long and green on both sides. **Saw-Leaf Buckthorn** (*Rhamnus serrata*, synonym *Endotropis serrata*) has only two or three flowers in each axil, the leaves usually less than 1¼ inches long and yellowish on the lower surface.

RODOLFO GUTIÉRREZ-SÁNCHEZ

JO ROBERTS

BIRCH-LEAF BUCKTHORN
(*Frangula betulifolia*)

COYOTILLO
(*Karwinskia humboldtiana*)

➤ **Coyotillo** (*Karwinskia humboldtiana*)—An unarmed shrub with opposite, pinnately veined leaves and small flowers in short-stalked, few-flowered, axillary clusters. The leaves are 1 to 3 inches long and slender-petioled. The brownish-black fruits are said to be very poisonous.

➤ **Lotebush** (*Sarcomphalus obtusifolius*)—Spiny shrub with more or less 3-nerved leaves and small flowers in umbellike clusters. Leaves pale green to bright green that vary from ½ to 1 inch long.

ROSE FAMILY (ROSACEAE)

This is a large and important family containing herbs, shrubs, and trees, with alternate leaves and regular, perfect flowers. Besides the innumerable kinds of roses the family contains many other ornamental plants and many popular fruits, including strawberries, raspberries, blackberries, apples, pears, peaches, plums, and cherries. The members of the family found in the Park may be distinguished as follows:

RICH SOMMER

LOTEBUSH
(*Sarcomphalus obtusifolius*)

SUE CARNAHAN

HAIRY MOUNTAIN-MAHOGANY
(*Cercocarpus breviflorus*)

1 Pistil 1 2
   Pistils more than 1 3
2 Fruit fleshy, a drupe .... PLUM, CHERRY (*Prunus*, p. 252)
   Fruit dry, an achene with a long feathery tail ....
   .... MOUNTAIN-MAHOGANY (*Cercocarpus*, p. 250)
3 Ovary inferior; fruits fleshy.......... BIG BEND SERVICEBERRY
   .... (*Malacomeles denticulata*, p. 251)
   Ovary superior; fruits not fleshy 4
4 Leaves pinnately divided; fruits with long feathery tails ....
   .... APACHE-PLUME (*Fallugia paradoxa*, p. 251)
   Leaves simple; fruits without feathery tails.................... 5
5 Leaves long, narrow, evergreen .... SLIM-LEAF ROSEWOOD
   .... (*Vauquelinia corymbosa*, p. 252)
   Leaves short, ovate, not evergreen .... OCEANSPRAY
   .... (*Holodiscus dumosus*, p. 251)

Mountain-Mahogany (*Cercocarpus*)—Shrubs 3 to 12 feet high with simple leaves and inconspicuous flowers which lack petals but have numerous stamens. The fruit consists of a hairy achene with a long, hairy

APACHE-PLUME
(*Fallugia paradoxa*)

tail often 2 inches or more in length. Much relished by deer as a browse plant. One species occurs in the Park: ⤷ **Hairy Mountain-Mahogany** (*Cercocarpus breviflorus*) has leaves 1/2 to 1½ inches long, these entire or toothed from the middle to the tip.

⤷ **Apache-Plume** (*Fallugia paradoxa*)—A very ornamental shrub growing 3 to 6 or more feet tall with small leaves pinnately divided into narrow lobes. The flowers are white and almost as large as apple blossoms and the numerous, long-tailed fruits, which may become reddish tinged and remain on the plant for some time, are as attractive as the flowers.

⤷ **Oceanspray** (*Holodiscus dumosus*)—This is another very ornamental shrub growing 3 to 8 or 9 feet high, usually with few main stems and numerous spreading branches, bearing simple, toothed leaves, and terminated by large, compound clusters of small, white or pinkish flowers. The leaves are oval with a wedge-shaped base and are about ½ inch long.

⤷ **Southern False-Serviceberry** (*Malacomeles denticulata*, synonym *Amelanchier denticulata*)—A large shrub or small tree with rounded or oval leaves usually less than a half inch long. The flowers are white; the

GARTH HARWOOD

RICARDO SÁNCHEZ

OCEANSPRAY
(*Holodiscus dumosus*)

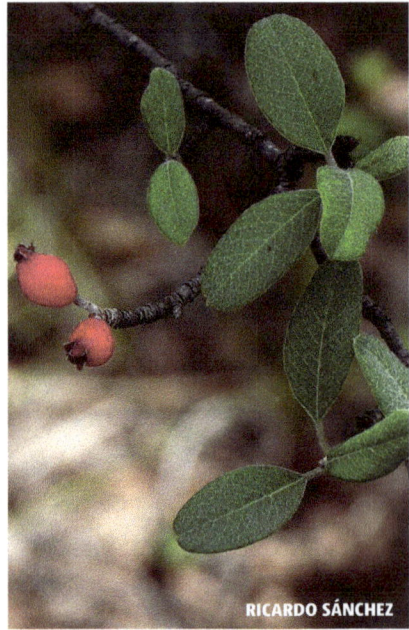

SOUTHERN FALSE-SERVICEBERRY
(*Malacomeles denticulata*)

fruits are purple or purplish black, berrylike, and edible. A Mexican species not known in the United States outside of the Big Bend region.

■ **Plum, Cherry** (*Prunus*)—Shrubs or small trees with alternate, simple leaves, perfect, regular, white flowers, and sweet or bitter fruit. Four species occur in the Park, two are described below. ➢ **Havard's Plum** (*Prunus havardii*) has wedge-shaped oblanceolate leaves that are usually less than ½ inch long and toothed at the rounded tip. **Black Cherry** (*Prunus serotina*) has oval leaves that are 1 to 2 inches long and have very small teeth along the entire margins. The small flowers are borne in racemes. The fruits are conspicuous and colorful, red or reddish black.

➢ **Slim-Leaf Rosewood** (*Vauquelinia corymbosa*)—A rather uncommon shrub or small tree with narrow, toothed, evergreen leaves 4 to 6 inches long. The fruit a woody capsule with five cells and two seeds in each cell. Present in eastern Mexico, but in the United States only known from Brewster and Presidio counties of Texas.

HAVARD'S PLUM
(*Prunus havardii*)

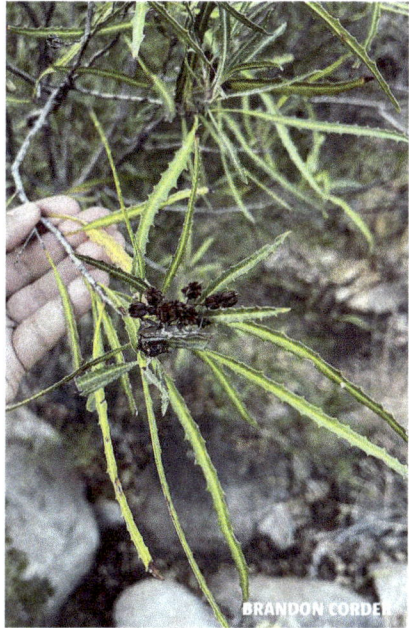

SLIM-LEAF ROSEWOOD
(*Vauquelinia corymbosa*)

MADDER FAMILY (RUBIACEAE)

Trees, shrubs, or herbs with opposite or whorled leaves and flowers mostly in clusters. The ovary is below the other parts of the flower, the petals are united to form a tubular corolla, and the stamens are of the same number as the lobes of the corolla and are attached to its tube. In the Tropics there are numerous shrubs that belong to the madder family, some of them with peculiar nodules on their leaves that are inhabited by nitrogen-fixing bacteria closely related to those found in the roots of members of the bean family. The coffee plant is the most important economic member of the family.

➷ **Firecracker-Bush** (*Bouvardia ternifolia*)—A somewhat shrubby plant, usually growing four or less feet high, with slender branches, leaves in threes, and clusters of conspicuous red or scarlet flowers. The leaves are lance-shaped or nearly linear and ½ to 1½ inches long. The flowers have slender corolla tubes about an inch long.

➷ **Buttonbush** (*Cephalanthus occidentalis*)—A large or medium-sized shrub growing in moist places; it has lance-shaped or oblong leaves, opposite or in threes, and white or yellowish flowers in conspic-

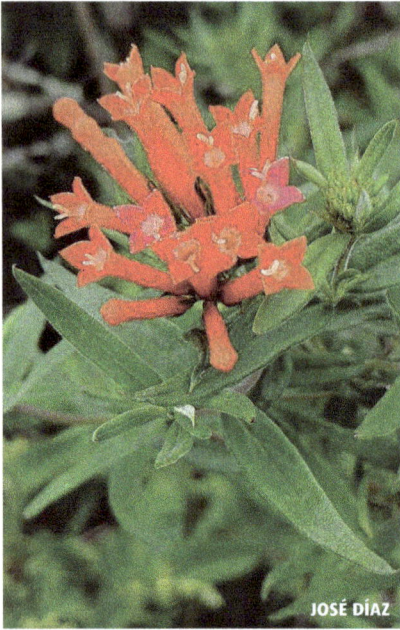

JOSÉ DÍAZ

FIRECRACKER-BUSH
(*Bouvardia ternifolia*)

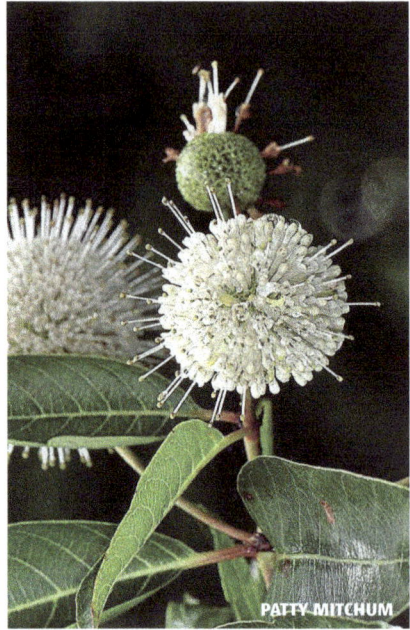

PATTY MITCHUM

BUTTONBUSH
(*Cephalanthus occidentalis*)

uous, spherical heads about 1 inch in diameter with the stamens protruding in such a way as to make it look like a little pincushion.

■ **Bedstraw** (*Galium*)—Weak herbs with slender, square stems, leaves in four's, small, white, purple-brown, or red flowers, and globular, twin fruits that separate when ripe into two seedlike, one seeded parts. Six species occur in the Park; three are described below. ⤳ **Desert Bedstraw** (*Galium proliferum*) has stems 4 to 8 inches long, roughened on the edges by very short, stiff prickles. The leaves are lance-shape and one-fifth to one-third of an inch long. The flowers are nearly sessile in the axils of two leafy bracts on a stalk, which, in turn, is in the axil of a stem leaf. The fruits are covered with prickles. **Southwestern Bedstraw** (*Galium virgatum*) has broadly oval leaves about ¼ inch long; the small, white flowers are borne on leafy-bracted stalks in the axils of leaves. The stems are rough, the fruits bristly, and the leaves somewhat hairy, with very short, whitish hairs. **Wright's Bedstraw** (*Galium wrightii*) has very numerous smooth slender stems, and linear or narrowly oblong leaves. The flowers are short-stalked and purple-brown. The bristles on the small fruit are about as long as its diameter.

DESERT BEDSTRAW
(*Galium proliferum*)

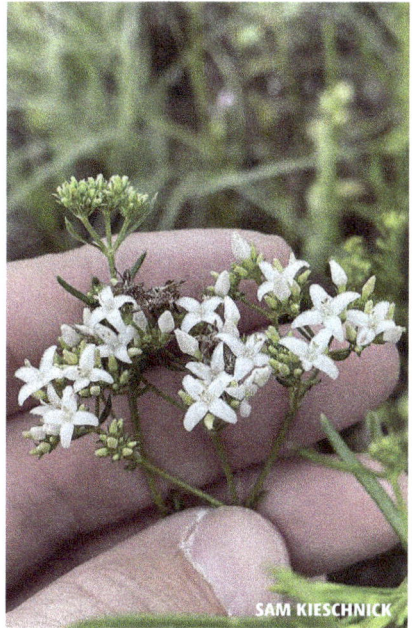

DIAMOND-FLOWERS
(*Stenaria nigricans*)

■ **Bluets** (*Houstonia*, others)—Herbs or somewhat woody perennials with opposite or clustered leaves and flowers of two forms, some having short stamens and long pistils and others long stamens and short pistils. Fruit a thin pod containing a few saucer-shaped or thimble-shaped seeds. ⇥ **Diamond-Flowers** (*Stenaria nigricans*, synonym *Houstonia angustifolia*) has numerous square stems arising from a woody base and growing from a few inches to a foot or more high. The leaves are opposite and very narrowly linear. The numerous dainty, little, white or lavender flowers have the four lobes of the corolla densely bearded on the inside. ⇥ **False Cluster-Bluet** (*Arcytophyllum fasciculatum*, synonym *Houstonia fasciculata*) is decidedly shrubby and grows 3 inches to a foot or more high. The linear leaves are less than a half inch long and are borne in opposite clusters. ⇥ **Needle-Leaf Bluet** (*Houstonia acerosa*) grows only about 2 to 4 inches high but produces a dense cluster of somewhat shrubby stems with linear, rigid leaves, which are opposite, sharp-pointed, and less than ½ inch long.

ERIC KNIGHT

FALSE CLUSTER-BLUET
(*Arcytophyllum fasciculatum*)

CATHERINE GALLEY

NEEDLE-LEAF BLUET
(*Houstonia acerosa*)

RUE FAMILY (RUTACEAE)

A family of trees or shrubs, or sometimes partly herbaceous shrubs, usually aromatic from an abundance of a pungent, volatile oil. The leaves, in our representatives of the family, are alternate and the flowers are regular but not always perfect. This is a large family in the Old World and in the Southern Hemisphere, but it is represented in the Park's flora by only two species.

❧ **Common Hoptree** (*Ptelea trifoliata*)—A large shrub or small tree with aromatic bark and foliage, alternate, compound leaves with three leaflets, and small, greenish flowers, which are partly perfect and partly imperfect. Perfect, staminate, and pistillate flowers often occur together in the same cluster. The fruit is a samara, a dry, 2- or 3-seeded fruit with a broad wing all around. Readily recognized by its trifoliate leaves and its winged fruits.

❧ **Desert-Rue** (*Thamnosma texana*)—A low, partly herbaceous shrub growing 4 to 20 inches high. The leaves are alternate, very small, narrow, and entire. Small, yellow, partly closed flowers are scattered over the plant and are followed by little 2-lobed pods with two or three

COMMON HOPTREE
(*Ptelea trifoliata*)

DESERT-RUE
(*Thamnosma texana*)

seeds in each lobe (the pods resembling 'Dutchman's-Britches', another common name). Found in several places in the desert scrub, not in the mountains.

WILLOW FAMILY (SALICACEAE)

Trees or shrubs having alternate, deciduous leaves with stipules. The wood is soft and light. The flowers are imperfect, and the staminate and pistillate flowers are usually on separate plants. Both kinds of flowers are borne in pendulous, taillike clusters called catkins, each flower in the axil of a scalelike bract. There are no sepals and no petals. The fruit is a capsule or pod bearing numerous seeds with long, silky down.

⚘ **Eastern Cottonwood** (*Populus deltoides*)—A tree with broadly ovate, thin leaves, the blades finely toothed with incurved teeth, the petioles slender and about 2 inches long. In the Park it occurs only along the Rio Grande, in the vicinity of springs, and along some of the more moist arroyos.

⚘ **Quaking Aspen** (*Populus tremuloides*)—A tree with ovate leaves, the blades closely toothed with glandular teeth and rather abruptly

EASTERN COTONWOOD
(*Populus deltoides*)

QUAKING ASPEN
(*Populus tremuloides*)

short-pointed, the petiole slender and flattened laterally causing the leaf to tremble with the slightest breeze. This is a very widely distributed tree, the species or its varieties occurring in mountainous regions nearly throughout North America. In the Park it is found only on a limited area on the upper slope of Mount Emory.

■ **Willow** (*Salix*)—Usually it is easy to recognize a willow on sight. One distinguishing characteristic is that each winter bud is covered by a single scale. The recognition of different species of willow, however, is sometimes difficult unless one has both flowers and fruits. Only six species occur in the Park (four are described below), and these are most readily distinguished by their leaves.

Black Willow (*Salix nigra*) has leaves that are 3 to 6 inches long and one-eight to three-fourths of an inch wide and are finely toothed along the margins. The twigs are usually reddish purple.

➤ **Sandbar Willow** (*Salix exigua*) has leaves that are about the length of those of *Salix nigra*, but they are never more than one-third of an inch wide and the teeth are glandular and relatively far apart.

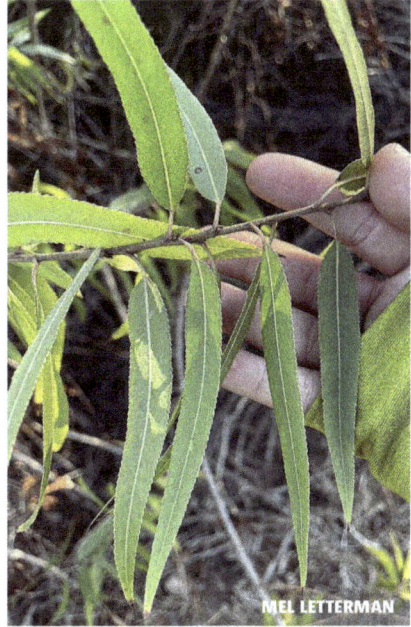

SAM KIESCHNICK

MEL LETTERMAN

SANDBAR WILLOW
(*Salix exigua*)

GOODDING'S BLACK WILLOW
(*Salix gooddingii*)

↗ **Goodding's Black Willow** (*Salix gooddingii*) has leaves that are usually 1½ to 3 inches long and ¼ to ½ inch wide, though they may be larger on young, vigorous shoots. The twigs are usually yellowish gray.

Yew-Leaf Willow (*Salix exifolia*) has the smallest leaves of the four species. They vary from one-third of an inch to 1¼ inches long and from one-twelfth to one-eighth of an inch wide. They are usually entire but sometimes are obscurely toothed above the middle.

All willow species occur along the Rio Grande, and one, Goodding's Willow, is also found in Fisk Canyon in the Pinnacle Mountains, along Tornillo Creek, and along several creeks and draws in the vicinity of the Rio Grande.

SANDALWOOD FAMILY (SANTALACEAE)

In Big Bend, includes members of the family which are green shrubs growing as parasites on the branches of other woody plants. The leaves are opposite, entire, and somewhat fleshy. The flowers are small and imperfect, and the fruits are small, usually white berries.

BARBARA BANFIELD

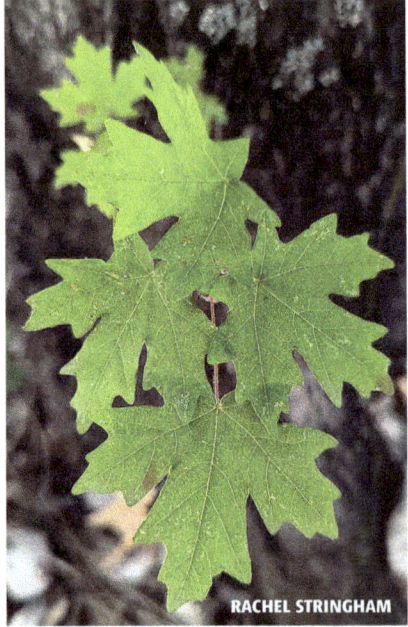

RACHEL STRINGHAM

BIG-LEAF MISTLETOE
(*Phoradendron macrophyllum*)

BIGTOOTH MAPLE
(*Acer grandidentatum*)

■ **Mistletoe** (*Phoradendron*)—The main characters are those given above for the family. Seven species occur in the Park and they can be distinguished, in part, by the plants on which they grow. For example: **Rough Mistletoe** (*Phoradendron bolleanum*) has small, linear leaves and grows only on juniper. Two species have broad, usually oval leaves: ➽ **Big-Leaf Mistletoe** (*Phoradendron macrophyllum*) grows on acacias and mesquite. **Cory's Mistletoe** (*Phoradendron coryae*) grows on oak and hackberry.

SOAPBERRY FAMILY (SAPINDACEAE)

Trees or shrubs with mostly alternate, pinnately compound leaves (opposite and simple in Maple, *Acer*). The flowers and fruits are variable. A large family but chiefly tropical and represented in the Park's flora by only three species.

➽ **Bigtooth Maple** (*Acer grandidentatum*)—A small or medium-sized tree with 3-lobed, coarsely-toothed leaves that occurs in several canyons in the Chisos Mountains. The small, yellowish flowers appear at the same time as the leaves, and the fruits, which are double samaras

WINGLEAF SOAPBERRY
(*Sapindus saponaria*)

MEXICAN BUCKEYE
(*Ungnadia speciosa*)

(two small nuts, each with a wing), are often rose-colored in midsummer but green at maturity.

❧ **Wingleaf Soapberry** (*Sapindus saponaria*)—A shrub or small tree with pinnately compound leaves with four to nine pairs of entire leaflets each 2 to 4 inches long. The greenish-white flowers are small but are borne in large, much-branched, terminal clusters. Each flower has 4 or 5 very small petals and 8 or 10 stamens. The fruits are orange-colored berries about the size of cherries. The berries were formerly used as soap by soaking several hours and then rubbing until suds were produced.

❧ **Mexican-Buckeye** (*Ungnadia speciosa*)—A shrub or small tree with pinnately compound leaves with three to seven rather large, saw-toothed leaflets The clusters of deep pink or rose-colored flowers are scattered along the branches. The flower has 4 petals, each with a tuft of white or yellow, fringed scales at its base, and 7 to 10 stamens usually with pink filaments and red anthers. The fruits are 3-lobed, leathery pods containing three large, shiny, dark brown or black, almost round seeds.

MATT BERGER

STAN SHEBS

PINK ALUMROOT
(*Heuchera rubescens*)

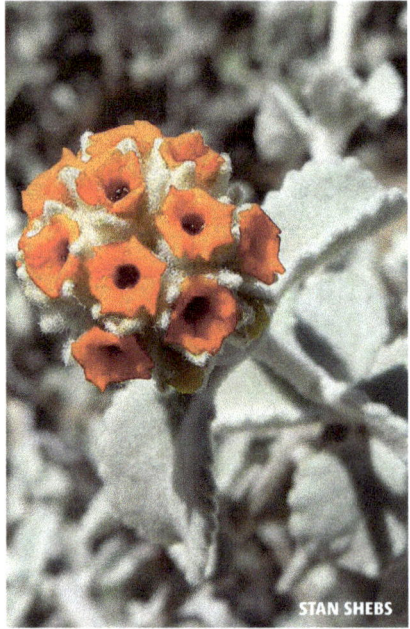

WOOLLY BUTTERFLYBUSH
(*Buddleja marrubiifolia*)

SAXIFRAGE FAMILY (SAXIFRAGACEAE)

This is a rather large and variable family but is represented in the Park only by the ➷ Pink Alumroot (*Heuchera rubescens*), which is a perennial herb with a basal cluster of round, heart-shaped, slightly lobed and toothed leaves and a naked stalk, 6 to 10 inches tall, bearing several reddish-purple or greenish purple flowers with a bell-shaped calyx, five distinct and very narrow petals, five stamens, and one pistil, which develops into a one-celled, two-beaked capsule.

FIGWORT FAMILY (SCROPHULARIACEAE)

Formerly a large family containing many plants with ornamental flowers but no important food or other economic plants other than *Digitalis* (now in Plantaginaceae), which supplies a drug. Recent changes, however, have assigned most former members of the family to Orobanchaceae, Phrymaceae, and Plantaginaceae. Typically, the sepals are united to form a toothed or lobed calyx, and the petals are also united to form a more or less irregular, often distinctly 2-lipped corolla.

BIG BEND SILVERLEAF
(*Leucophyllum minus*)

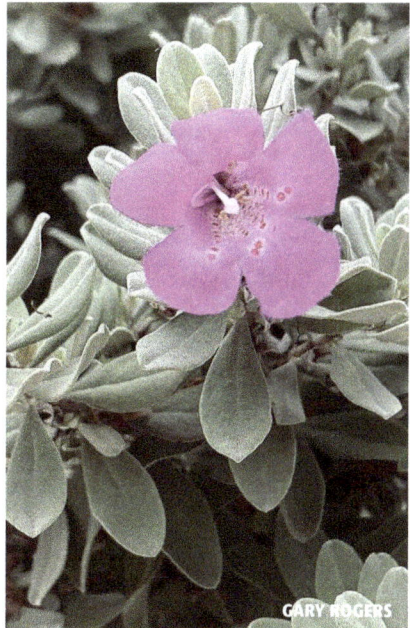

CENIZO
(*Leucophyllum frutescens*)

Woolly Butterflybush (*Buddleja marrubiifolia*)—A velvety-hairy shrub with ovate or oval, short-petioled leaves about ½ inch long. The creamy-yellow or yellow-orange flowers are borne in axillary headlike clusters near the ends of branches. The calyx and corolla are 4-toothed or lobed, and the four very short stamens are attached to the middle of the corolla tube. Found in several places along or near the Rio Grande. *Buddleja scordioides*, which has narrower leaves, has been found on shrub-inhabited slopes and hills near the Park. It is usually a larger plant than *B. marrubiifolia*, ranging in height to about 4 feet.

Silverleaf (*Leucophyllum*)—Shrubs with relatively small, oval, whitish leaves and showy, pinkish, violet-purple, or blue flowers. Three species are found in the Park. **Cenizo** (*Leucophyllum frutescens*) has leaves 3/4 to 1 inch long and violet-purple or pinkish flowers about an inch across. This species does well under cultivation. **Big Bend Silverleaf** (*Leucophyllum minus*) has leaves ½ inch or less in length and somewhat smaller flowers, which are nearly blue in color. **Brewster County Silverleaf** (*Leucophyllum candidum*) appears much like *L. minus* in habit but is readily recognized by the violet-colored flowers.

NIGHTSHADE FAMILY (SOLANACEAE)

This is an extremely important family because it contains such important economic plants as the potato, tomato, and tobacco, as well as a number of ornamental plants and some weeds. The flowers are regular and perfect with a 5-lobed calyx, a more or less 5-lobed corolla, 5 stamens, and 1 pistil with a single style and stigma. Most members of the family found in the Park may be distinguished as follows:

1   Fruit a capsule 2
    Fruit a berry 4
2   Fruit spiny; seeds flattened. . . . . . . THORN-APPLE (*Datura*, p. 265)
    Fruit not spiny; seeds not flattened 3
3   Flowers white or yellow, in racemes TOBACCO (*Nicotiana*, p. 266)
    Flowers purplish red, in leaf axils . . . . SEASIDE-PETUNIA
    . . . . (*Calibrachoa parviflora*, p. 264)
4   Shrubs . . . . DESERT-THORN (*Lycium*, p. 265)
    Herbs 5
5   Calyx, in fruit, bladdery-inflated 6
    Calyx, in fruit, not bladdery-inflated 8
6   Corolla wheel-shaped, violet or purple . . . . . . CHINESE-LANTERN
    . . . . (*Quincula lobata*, p. 267)
    Corolla funnel-shaped, bell-shaped, or urn-shaped, yellowish or
    greenish 7
7   Corolla minutely toothed, urn-shaped . . NETTED GLOBE-CHERRY
    . . . . (*Margaranthus solanaceus*, p. 266)
    Corolla not toothed, bell-shaped or funnelform . . . .
    . . . . GROUND-CHERRY (*Physalis*, p. 267)
8   Calyx not enclosing the fruit, or if so the calyx prickly . . . .
    . . . . NIGHTSHADE (*Solanum*, p. 267)
    Calyx enclosing the fruit; calyx never prickly . . . . FIVE-EYES
    . . . . (*Chamaesaracha*, p. 265)

Seaside-Petunia (*Calibrachoa parviflora*, synonym *Petunia parviflora*)—This plant belongs to the same genus as the petunias of our flower gardens, but in general appearance it does not closely resemble them. It is a prostrate or spreading, much-branched plant with numerous, almost linear leaves and flowers that are less than ½ inch long. The corolla is purple, with a pale or yellowish tube.

■ Five-Eyes (*Chamaesaracha*)—Low, perennial, much-branched

ELLIOTT GORDON

IULIA COTY

GRAY FIVE-EYES
(*Chamaesaracha conioides*)

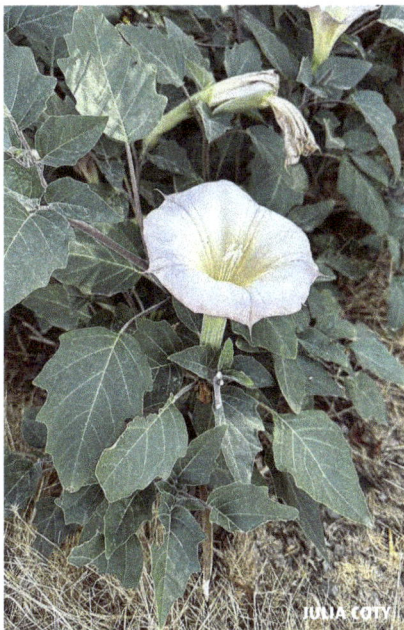

SACRED DATURA
(*Datura wrightii*)

herbs with entire or pinnately lobed leaves and flowers in few-flowered axillary clusters. Fruit a pulpy berry. ➷ Gray Five-Eyes (*Chamaesaracha conioides*) is quite sticky and has leaves that are entire or only slightly lobed. Green-Leaf Five-Eyes (*Chamaesaracha arida*) is scarcely at all sticky and has leaves that are narrower and pinnately lobed.

■ Thorn-Apple (*Datura*)—Rank herbs with ovate leaves and large, showy flowers in the forks of the branching stem. The plants contain a narcotic poison. Two species occur in the Park: ➷ Sacred Datura (*Datura wrightii*) has nearly entire leaves and white or violet-tinged, fragrant flowers that are about 7 inches long. Oak-Leaf Thorn-Apple (*Datura quercifolia*) has deeply lobed leaves and pale violet flowers that are about 3 inches long.

■ Desert-Thorn (*Lycium*)—Spiny shrubs with small, alternate, entire leaves, small, axillary flowers, and red berries. Silver Desert-Thorn (*Lycium berlandieri*) has nearly linear leaves to one inch long and white or cream-colored flowers sometimes tinged with violet. ➷ Pale Desert-Thorn (*Lycium pallidum*) has pale, spatula-shaped or inverted lance-shaped leaves 1 to 2 inches long and greenish flowers tinged with purple.

PALE DESERT-THORN
(*Lycium pallidum*)

DESERT TOBACCO
(*Nicotiana obtusifolia*)

Netted Globe-Cherry (*Margaranthus solanaceus,* synonym *Physalis solanacea*)—This resembles a small groundcherry except that the calyx and corolla are both globular. It is a smooth, branched herb with ovate leaves, which are entire or nearly so and 1 to 2 inches long. The small flowers are nearly white or violet-tinged, and the small, rather dry, 20- to 30-seeded berry is completely enclosed within the globular calyx.

■ **Tobacco** (*Nicotiana*)—Rank, acrid-narcotic plants with fairly large leaves and flowers with tubular corollas. In ours the corolla is greenish white or yellowish. The fruit is a dry pod with numerous minute seeds. Two species occur in the Park. ⚘ **Desert Tobacco** (*Nicotiana obtusifolia*) is a herb and is somewhat sticky-hairy. **Tree-Tobacco** (*Nicotiana glauca*) is a large shrub and is smooth throughout. This shrub is a native of South America but is now found in suitable habitats from Texas to California.

■ **Ground-Cherry** (*Physalis*)—Herbs with entire or toothed leaves and usually solitary flowers borne in the leaf axils. The corolla is yellowish, often with a dark center, and the calyx becomes much inflated and completely covers the fruit, which is a globose, pulpy berry with

IVY-LEAF GROUND-CHERRY
(*Physalis hederifolia*)

CHINESE-LANTERN
(*Quincula lobata*)

numerous seeds. Species found in the Park are most readily distinguished by the presence or absence and the general character of hairs on stems and leaves. Mexican Ground-Cherry (*Physalis philadelphica*, introduced) is entirely without hairs, or nearly so, throughout. Ivy-Leaf Ground-Cherry (*Physalis hederifolia*) is covered with fine, dense hairs, and is also very sticky.

Chinese-Lantern (*Quincula lobata*)—This plant looks very much like a ground-cherry, but the corolla is violet instead of yellowish and wheel-shaped instead of bell-shaped or funnelform.

Nightshade (*Solanum*)—Herbs with white, blue, purple, or yellow flowers usually in few-flowered clusters. The corollas are wheel-shaped and 5-lobed, and the stamens have short filaments. The five anthers are close together, forming a cone or cylinder in the center of the flower. The fruit is a several-seeded berry.

Black Nightshade (*Solanum americanum*) is a smooth or nearly smooth herb with ovate leaves, which are usually entire but sometimes have a few coarse teeth, white flowers, and black berries. Silverleaf Nightshade (*Solanum elaeagnifolium*) has narrowly oblong or lance-

BLACK NIGHTSHADE
(*Solanum americanum*)

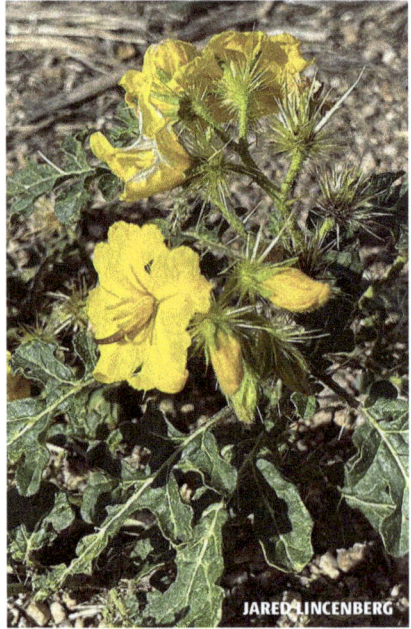

BUFFALOBUR NIGHTSHADE
(*Solanum rostratum*)

shaped leaves, and both stems and leaves are pale or whitish from a covering of whitish hairs. The flowers are violet or blue and the berries are yellow. Some plants of this species are well supplied with small, slender prickles, while other plants are not prickly at all. ➤ Buffalobur Nightshade (*Solanum rostratum*), is a very prickly plant, both stems and leaves being supplied with stout, pointed prickles. The flowers are yellow and the berries are closely enclosed within the very prickly calyx. The introduced Sticky Nightshade (*Solanum sisymbriifolium*) is also very prickly, with bright yellow, flattened prickles, and also quite sticky. The flowers are whitish and the berries are red and only partly enclosed within the prickly calyx.

FAMEFLOWER FAMILY (TALINACEAE)

■ Fameflower (*Talinum*)—Formerly placed in the Purslane Family, these genera differs from Purslane (*Portulaca*) in having the sepals distinct and the ovary entirely above the place of attachment of the sepals. Most of the species have very attractive flowers. Several of the Park's species may be distinguished as follows:

SUE CARNAHAN

ANDERS HASTINGS

ORANGE FLAMEFLOWER
(*Talinum aurantiacum*)

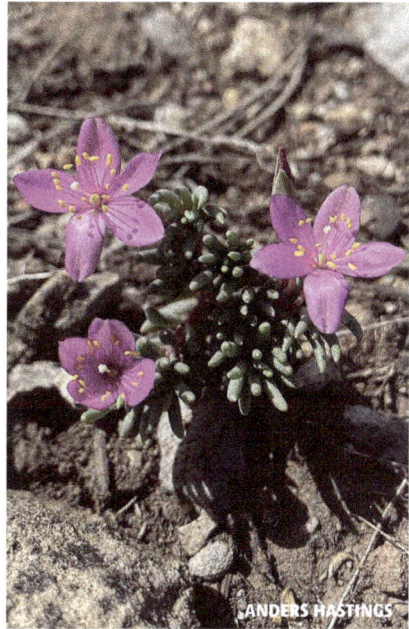

DWARF FALSE FLAMEFLOWER
(*Talinum brevicaule*)

1   Flowers in the axils of leaves. 2
Flowers in terminal clusters; flowers pink or red. . . . .
. . . . **Prairie False Flameflower**
. . . . (*Talinum parviflorum*, synonym *Phemeranthus parviflorus*)
2   Leaves flat; flowers orange . . . . ⤨ **Orange Flameflower**
. . . . (*Talinum aurantiacum*)
Leaves cylindrical; flowers pink or red ⤨ **Dwarf False Flameflower**
. . . . (*Talinum brevicaule*, synonym *Phemeranthus brevicaulis*)

TAMARISK FAMILY (TAMARICACEAE)

⤨ **French Tamarisk, Salt-Cedar** (*Tamarix gallica*)—Shrub or small tree 10 to 15 feet or more in height, with slender upright or spreading branches and narrow or rounded crown, resembling a juniper though not evergreen. Leaves deciduous, many, crowded, scalelike, about 1/16 inch long. Flowers numerous, crowded in many narrow clusters 1 to 2 inches long at ends of twigs, 1/16 inch long, pink. Seed capsule reddish brown, with many tiny hairy seeds. This is one of several tamarisk species (all introduced into the USA from the Mediterranean region) that can be invasive along waterways such as the Rio Grande and irrigation canals. It spreads by seeds, grows rapidly, and is alkali-tolerant and drought-resistant. Once established, plants can form large thickets, and transpire large quantities of water. Three additional species of tamarisk are reported from the Park, all introduced and all similar in appearance.

CAT-TAIL FAMILY (TYPHACEAE)

A small family represented in the Park by the Southern Cat-Tail (*Typha domingensis*), which is widely distributed in marshy places throughout the southern United States. It produces a basal cluster of leaves, which are an inch or less in width but several feet long and stand nearly vertical. The upright, unbranched stem bears a long, dense spike of inconspicuous flowers at the upper end. The upper part of this spike is covered with stamens intermixed with long hairs, each stamen constituting a flower, while the lower part of the spike supports the pistillate flowers, each consisting simply of an ovary bearing an abundance of dark hairs at the base. The abundant down of the very small fruits was formerly used for stuffing pillows. Southern Cat-Tail occurs at several places along the Rio Grande, especially near Boquillas.

NETTLE FAMILY (URTICACEAE)

In the Tropics some members of the nettle family are trees or shrubs, but in the United States they are all herbs. The flowers are small, greenish, mostly imperfect, and inconspicuous. The fruits are small and one-seeded. Some members of the family are armed with stinging hairs, which are very potent, but none of these occur in our flora. The only member of the family found in the Park is ⇥ Pennsylvania Pellitory (*Parietaria pensylvanica*), which has been found in Oak Creek Canyon in the Chisos Mountains. It is an annual plant with rather weak, often reclining stems, lance-shaped or elliptic leaves with thin and flimsy, entire blades, and small clusters of flowers in all but the lowest leaf axils. The flowers are partly imperfect and partly perfect in the same cluster.

IAN WRIGHT

FREANCH TAMARISK, SALT-CEDAR
(*Tamarix gallica*)

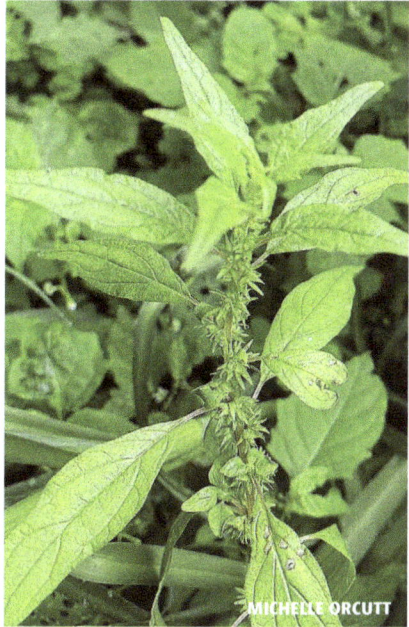

MICHELLE ORCUTT

PENNSYLVANIA PELLITORY
(*Parietaria pensylvanica*)

VERBENA FAMILY (VERBENACEAE)

Herbs or shrubs with opposite, simple leaves, flowers with 2-lipped or irregular corollas, and stamens in two pairs of unequal length. The fruit consists of two or four 1-seeded nutlets, formed from the splitting of the unlobed ovary.

1   Nutlets, in fruit, 4 2
    Nutlets, in fruit, 2 3
2   Flowers borne in terminal spikes or headlike spikes . . . VERBENA
    . . . . (*Glandularia, Verbena*, p. 273)
    Flowers borne in axillary, 3-flowered clusters . . . .
    . . . . (see *Tetraclea coulteri*, Lamiaceae, p. 199)
3   Herbs . . . . FROGFUIT (*Phyla nodiflora*, p. 274)
    Shrubs 4
4   Leaves broadest near the base; corolla much less than ½ inch long
    5
    Leaves broadest near the apex; corolla more than ½ inch long. . . .
    . . . . SPOONLEAF (*Bouchea spathulata*, p. 272)

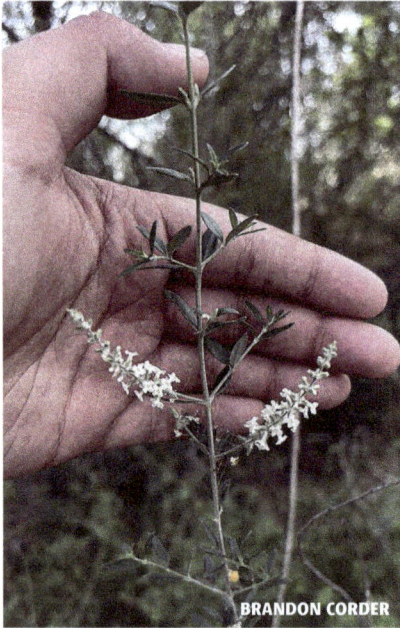

BRANDON CORDER

WHITEBRUSH
(*Aloysia gratissima*)

DAWN NELSON

WRIGHT'S BEEBRUSH
(*Aloysia wrightii*)

5   Fruits fleshy at maturity . . . . **BRUSHLAND SHRUB-VERBENA**
. . . . (*Lantana achyranthifolia*, p. 274)
Fruits dry . . . . **LIPPIA** (*Aloysia, Lippia*, p. 272)

■ **Lippia** (*Aloysia, Lippia*)—Shrubs with spikes of small flowers with 2-lipped corolla and 2- or 4-toothed or 2-lipped calyx enclosing the dry fruit, which separates into two nutlets. The leaves are usually ovate or oval or oblong and may be either toothed or entire. **Mexican Oregano** (*Lippia origanoides*) has yellowish-white flowers in short, headlike spikes and is not especially fragrant. ⭜ **Whitebrush** (*Aloysia gratissima*, synonym *Lippia ligustrina*) has white or violet-tinged flowers in long, slender spikes and with the fragrance of vanilla. It is considered an excellent honey plant. ⭜ **Wright's Beebrush** (*Aloysia wrightii*, synonym *Lippia wrightii*) has white flowers in long, slender spikes and with the odor of sage.

Spoonleaf (*Bouchea spathulata*)—A densely branching, low shrub, occurring in dry canyons and on dry, rocky ridges and mountainsides. In the United States, known only from areas east of the Chisos Mountains in Big Bend National Park.

DAVIS MOUNTAIN MOCK VERVAIN
(*Glandularia wrightii*)

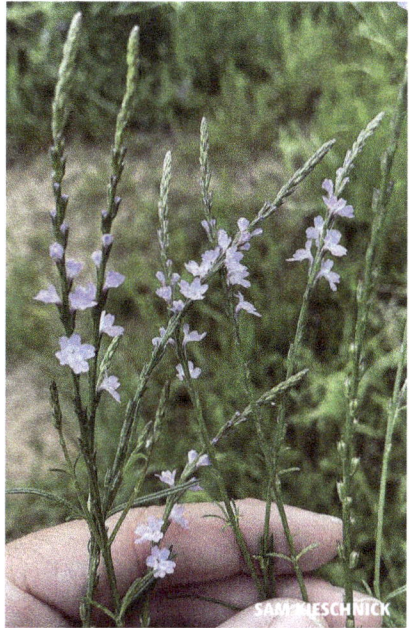

TEXAS VERVAIN
(*Verbena halei*)

■ **Mock Vervain, Vervain** (*Glandularia, Verbena*)—Erect or prostrate herbs with simple, often pinnately lobed leaves and terminal, bracted spikes of flowers, which are usually blue or purple but sometimes white. The calyx is 5-toothed, the corolla has five unequal lobes, the stigma is 2-lobed, and the fruit at maturity consists of four nutlets.

About a dozen species occur in the Park; four are described here: ⌇ **Davis Mountain Mock Vervain** (*Glandularia wrightii*, synonym *Verbena bipinnatifida*) is a low, hairy plant with leaves 1 to 4 inches long and two or three times cleft into sharply cut and toothed lobes. The bluish-purple or lilac flowers are about one-third of an inch across and are borne in spikes that become quite long as they mature. Frequent in the Chisos Mountains. **Pale Mock Verbena** (*Glandularia racemosa*, synonym *Verbena racemosa*) is also similar to the above species and is sometimes difficult to distinguish from it in the field, but usually its flowers are white. All three species resemble the common cultivated verbenas of flower gardens. ⌇ **Texas Verbena** (*Verbena halei*) is a slender, nearly smooth herb 8 inches to nearly 3 feet tall, usually branching only near the top, with variously toothed or lobed leaves and slender, open spikes with small, bluish flowers. **Hillside Verbena** (*Verbena*

RICARDO SÁNCHEZ

SPACEGECKO

BRUSHLAND VERBENA
(*Lantana achyranthifolia*)

FROGFRUIT
(*Phyla nodiflora*)

hirtella, synonym *Verbena neomexicana* var. *hirtella*) is a short-hairy plant with stems branched from the base, the branches 4 to 14 inches long, with coarsely toothed or lobed, rather narrow leaves which are usually less than 2 inches long, and slender, open spikes of purple flowers.

❧ Brushland Verbena (*Lantana achyranthifolia*)—A small shrub with ovate or oblong leaves and clusters of white or purple flowers borne on stalks two or three times the length of the leaves. The bracts are nearly as long as the corolla and the fruit is a thin-fleshed or nearly dry drupe.

❧ Frogfruit (*Phyla nodiflora*)—Herb with leaves oblanceolate and toothed only near the tip and short, dense, cylindrical spikes of small flowers. The corolla is 2-lipped, the upper lip notched and the lower lip much larger and 3-lobed.

ARROW-WOOD FAMILY (VIBURNACEAE)

❧ Black Elderberry (*Sambucus nigra*)—A large shrub or small tree having pinnate leaves with 5 or 7 leaflets narrowly oblong and toothed along the margin with rather fine teeth except along the rather long tip. The small, white flowers are produced in large, flat-topped clusters 2 to 6 inches across. The berries are blue and edible.

GRAPE FAMILY (VITACEAE)

Woody vines that climb by means of tendrils opposite the leaves. The flowers are variable and are produced in clusters in the axils of leaves; they may be perfect or imperfect, and, when imperfect, the staminate and pistillate flowers may be on the same plant or on separate plants. The fruit is a 1- or 2-seeded berry.

➵ Sorrelvine (*Cissus trifoliata*)—A vine with fleshy leaves, which may be merely 3-lobed or palmately compound with three coarsely toothed leaflets. the fruit has very little pulp and is not edible.

Grape (*Vitis*)—Woody vines with simple, toothed, more or less heart-shaped leaves. The fruit is pulpy and usually edible. A single species occurs in the Park: Canyon Grape (*Vitis arizonica*) has leaves that are closely toothed but not much lobed. They are white-cottony on the underside when young but may become smooth later. The fruit is small or middle-sized.

CREOSOTEBUSH FAMILY (ZYGOPHYLLACEAE)

Trees, shrubs, or perennial herbs with pinnately compound leaves and perfect flowers, which are regular or nearly so. There are usually five, but occasionally four or six, sepals, with the same number of petals and twice as many stamens. There is usually one pistil made up of two to five parts united into one. Some members of the family have extremely hard and heavy wood; others are strong-scented and yield a bitter and acid gum-resin. The family is largely tropical and subtropical. Four genera are found in the Park's flora:

1 Shrubs or trees 2
  Herbs 3
2 Leaves with 2 leaflets, shrubs . . . . CREOSOTEBUSH
  . . . . (*Larrea tridentata*, p. 276)
  Leaves with 8 to 12 leaflets, shrubs or small trees . . . .
  . . . . TEXAS LIGNUM-VITAE (*Guaiacum angustifolium*, p. 276)
3 Ovary 5-celled; fruit spiny . . . . PUNCTUREVINE
  . . . . (*Tribulus terrestris*, p. 278)

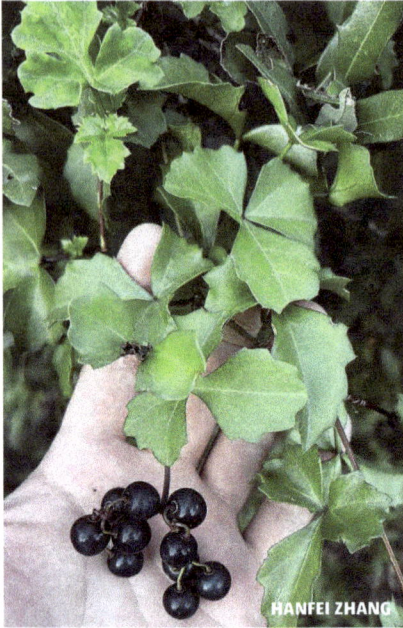

HANFEI ZHANG

SORRELVINE
(*Cissus trifoliata*)

NORMAN KURING

TEXAS LIGNUM-VITAE
(*Guaiacum angustifolium*)

Ovary 10- or 12-celled; fruit not spiny . . . . **CALTROP**
. . . . (*Kallstroemia*, p. 277)

➷ Texas Lignum-Vitae (*Guaiacum angustifolium*, synonym *Porlieria angustifolia*)—Sometimes a small tree but more often a compact, scrubby, evergreen shrub, which is very leafy and produces beautiful purple or violet flowers followed by small, heart-shaped pods that at maturity burst open and expose two orange or red, shiny seeds. The dark green, opposite leaves are pinnately compound with four to eight pairs of small, entire, leathery leaflets.

➷ Creosotebush (*Larrea tridentata*)—A strongly scented, sticky-leaved, evergreen shrub with bright yellow, 5-petaled flowers and small, rounded capsules that are densely hairy. Abundant in the Park's desert flats. The stems are very leafy, but the leaves, which often have a yellowish-green hue, are small with only two leaflets. The plant is considered something of a weed on the desert range because animals do not eat it and it increases with overgrazing. Formerly the plant was much used for making an antiseptic lotion by steeping the twigs and leaves in hot water. This lotion was used for treating cuts and bruises on both

CREOSOTEBUSH
(*Larrea tridentata*)

humans and animals. It was considered especially good for the treatment of saddle sores on horses.

■ Caltrop (*Kallstroemia*)—Perennial herbs with opposite or alternate, pinnately compound leaves. The flowers have 5 or 6 sepals, 5 or 6 petals, and 10 or 12 stamens. The stamens are in two series. Those in the outer series are attached to the bases of the petals, while each of those of the inner series has a small gland at the base. The fruit is a 10- or 12-angled capsule, which separates at maturity into 10 or 12 cells with 1 seed in each cell. Three species are found in the Park: **Hairy Caltrop** (*Kallstroemia hirsutissima*) has small flowers with petals only about ¼ inch long, while ⚘ **Orange Caltrop** (*Kallstroemia grandiflora*) has larger flowers with petals about 1 inch long. The flowers of both species are yellow to deep orange (also called **Arizona Poppy**). **Warty Caltrop** (*Kallstroemia parviflora*) is also reported.

⚘ **Puncturevine** (*Tribulus terrestris*)—This is a perennial herb resembling a caltrop, but the fruits are armed with stiff spines, whence the common name, puncturevine. Since this plant often grows in alleys and backyards, the burs are a source of annoyance to bare feet. In some

ORANGE CALTROP
(*Kallstroemia grandiflora*)

PUNCTUREVINE
(*Tribulus terrestris*)

places also they are a menace to bicycle and automobile tires. The plant is a native of southern Europe and was probably introduced into this country years ago by burs embedded in the wool of imported sheep. The leaves have 10 to 14 entire leaflets, and the orange-yellow flowers are ½ inch or less across.

FERNS

Ferns reproduce by spores borne in spore cases (sporangia) clustered in little dots (sori), and often covered by a scale (indusium), on the lower surface or the margins of the leaf (frond). Most ferns require a rather moist habitat, but in spite of the dry climate of the Big Bend region a considerable variety of ferns have been collected. The stem (rhizome or rootstalk) of a fern is underground, and the plants as we commonly see them consist of the leaves only. The leaf has a flat or expanded portion (blade), which is more or less pinnate, and a leaf-stalk (stipe). Most ferns found in the Park may be distinguished as follows. Note that botanists do not agree on which genus many of the Park's ferns should be placed; alternate names and synonyms are included in the keys and descriptions that follow.

1   Mature sori round or little elongated, appearing as separate small dots on the back of the leaf 2
    Mature sori elongated, oblong or narrower, mostly running into each other 4

2   Leaves mostly twice pinnate or pinnately cut, with very small leaflets . . . . NEW MEXICO CLIFF FERN (*Woodsia mexicana*, p. 287)
    Leaves once pinnate or pinnately cut, having few large leaflets . . 3

3   Sori with indusia; leaf margins spiny . . . . VEIN FERN
    . . . . (*Phanerophlebia umbonata*, p. 280)
    Sori without indusia; leaf margins not spiny . . . .
    . RIO GRANDE SCALY-POLYPODY (*Pleopeltis riograndensis*, p. 280)

4   Sori without indusia 5
    Sori with indusia 6

5   Sori scattered on the back of the leaf, following the course of the veins . . . . COPPER FERN (*Bommeria hispida*, p. 282)
    Sori marginal near the ends of the veins . . . . CLOAK FERN
    . . . . (former *Notholaena*, p. 282)

6   Sori on the back of the leaf, not marginal . . . .
    . . . . BLACK-STEM SPLEENWORT (*Asplenium resiliens*, p. 279)
    Sori marginal and covered by the inrolled margins of the leaflets 7

7   Inrolled margin of leaflet discontinuous, appearing as separate large indusia . . . . SOUTHERN MAIDENHAIR FERN
    . . . . (*Adiantum capillus-veneris*, p. 281)
    Inrolled margin more or less continuous around each leaflet . . . . .
    . . . . . . LIP FERN (*Myriopteris, Gaga*, synonym *Cheilanthes*, p. 283)

SPLEENWORT FAMILY (ASPLENIACEAE)

⌖ **Black-Stem Spleenwort** (*Asplenium resiliens*)—The spleenwort occurs in several places in the Chisos Mountains, usually where it is protected by rocks. It bears a tuft of once-pinnate leaves that vary from 4 to about 12 inches long, with dark brown or black leaf-stalks and midribs and mostly opposite, oblong, nearly entire leaflets, each with a conspicuous hump on the upper edge of the base. The oblong sori are on the backs of the leaflets, usually about halfway between the margin and the midrib.

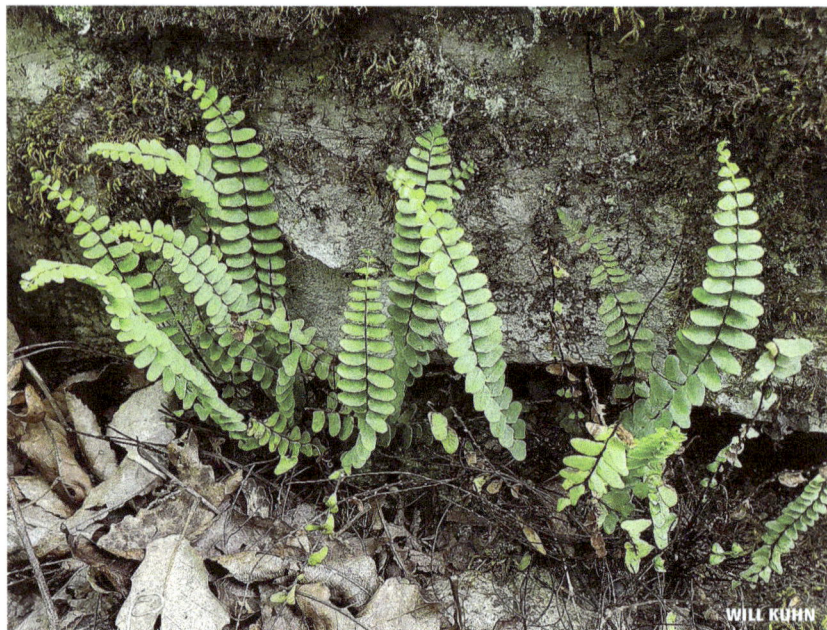

BLACK-STEM SPLEENWORT
(*Asplenium resiliens*)

WOOD FERN FAMILY (DRYOPTERIDACEAE)

➤ **Belly-Button Vein Fern** (*Phanerophlebia umbonata*)—This fern has been found in the Chisos Mountains. It is our largest fern, with leaves sometimes 2 feet long and leaflets up to 4 inches long. The leaves are once pinnate, and the leaflets are toothed along the margins with fine, slender teeth. The sori appear as small, round dots, mostly arranged in four rows on the backs of the leaflets; the upper surface is dimpled due to the underside sori ('belly-buttons'). Each sorus is covered by a little indusium shaped like an umbrella.

POLYPODY FERN FAMILY (POLYPODIACEAE)

➤ **Rio Grande Scaly-Polypody** (*Pleopeltis riograndensis*, synonym *Polypodium thyssanolepis*)—Some species of polypody ferns grow as epiphytes upon other plants, but this one grows on moist soil in shady places in the Chisos Mountains. It is not common. It is a very small fern; the entire leaf is only 2 to 4 inches long. The leaf is not truly pinnate but is pinnately lobed nearly to the midrib, which divides it into

BELLY-BUTTON VEIN FERN
(*Phanerophlebia umbonata*)

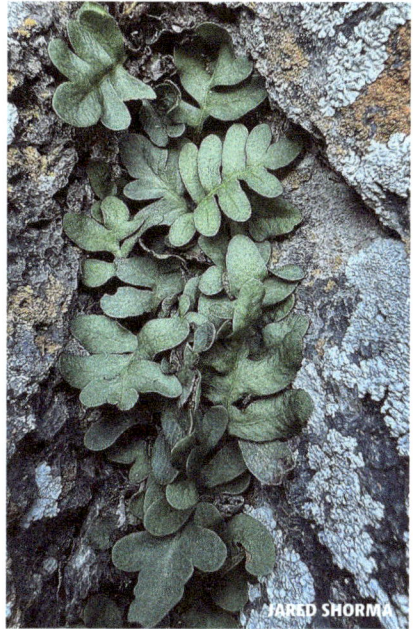

RIO GRANDE SCALY-POLYPODY
(*Pleopeltis riograndensis*)

from half a dozen to a dozen lobes. The sori are round and are borne in two rows on the backs of the lobes of the leaf; each row is about halfway between the margin and the midrib.

MAIDENHAIR FERN FAMILY (PTERIDACEAE)

⚘ **Southern Maidenhair Fern** (*Adiantum capillus-veneris*)—This fern has been found in lower Oak Creek and other moist canyons in the Chisos Mountains. It grows from 4 to 20 inches high and is readily recognized by its wedge-shaped leaflets, which are deeply and irregularly cut. The leaves are twice, or sometimes three times, pinnate at the base, while the upper third or more is usually only once-pinnate. The sori are marginal and roundish in shape, and the margin of a lobe of the leaf is inrolled to form an indusium for each sorus. The leaf-stalks are slender and dark, giving rise to the common name, maidenhair.

⚘ **Copper Fern** (*Bommeria hispida*)—This fern is a typically southwestern plant. It occurs from Texas to Arizona and adjacent parts of Mexico. It has been collected in the Chisos Mountains, mostly on dry slopes in pinyon pine-juniper-oak woodlands. It is a small fern with the

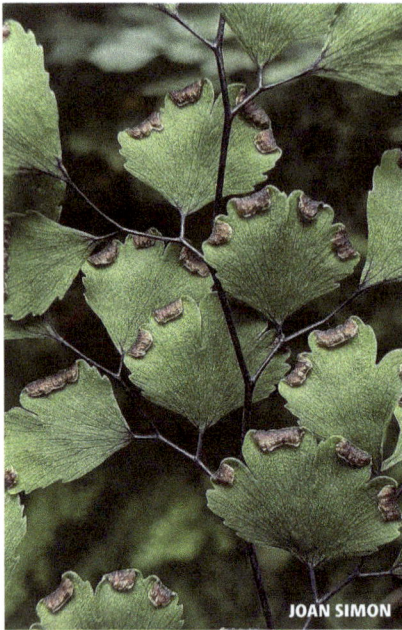

SOUTHERN MAIDENHAIR FERN
(*Adiantum capillus-veneris*)

COPPER FERN
(*Bommeria hispida*)

slender leaf-stalks 4 to 6 inches long and the pinnate and somewhat hairy leaf blades only about 2 inches long. The sori are elongated and scattered on the backs of the leaves. They follow the course of the veins, sometimes branching to do so.

■ Cloak Fern (former *Notholaena*)—The cloak ferns are characterized by marginal sori, often continuous and without an indusium. At first, however, they may be partly covered by the inrolled margin of the leaflet. Five members of this group have been found in the Park:

1   Leaf blades once-pinnate 2
    Leaf blades palmately parted or twice-pinnate, not hairy or scaly, but with a white or yellow waxy covering 4
2   Leaflets densely covered beneath with large scales 3
    Leaflets densely hairy beneath, not scaly. . ➷ Golden Cloak Fern
    . . . . (*Myriopteris aurea*, synonym *Notholaena aurea*)
3   Leaflets coarsely lobed. . . . . ➷ Wavy Cloak Fern
    . . . . (*Astrolepis sinuata*, synonym *Notholaena sinuata*)
    Leaflets nearly entire . . . . Scaly Cloak Fern
    (*Astrolepis cochisensis*, synonym *Notholaena sinuata* var. *cochisensis*)

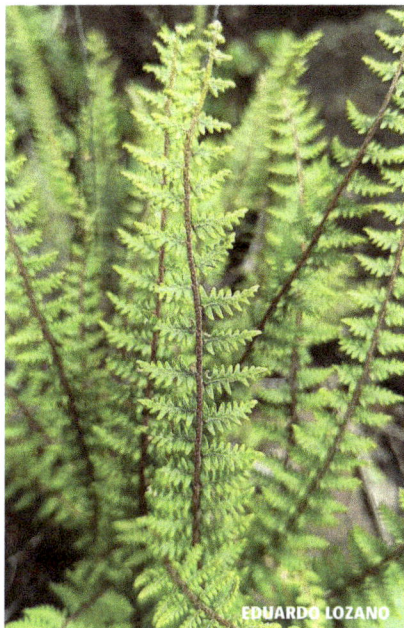

GOLDEN CLOAK FERN
(*Myriopteris aurea*)

WAVY CLOAK FERN
(*Astrolepis sinuata*)

4   Leaf blades palmately parted, the midrib winged almost through-
    out .... ⚑ Star Cloak Fern (*Notholaena standleyi*)
    Leaf blades 2- to 4-pinnate, the midrib not winged, the leaf branches
    and leaflets stalked .... Southwestern Cloak Fern
    .... (*Argyrochosma limitanea*, synonym *Notholaena limitanea*)

■ Lip Fern (*Myriopteris, Gaga*, synonym *Cheilanthes*)—The lip ferns
are small or medium-sized ferns with the leaves once or twice pinnate,
usually very small leaflets, and the indusium of the sori formed by the
inrolled margin of the leaflet, but the sori are so close together that practically the entire leaflet margin is involved in any case. Eight species of
lip ferns have been found within the Park. These may be distinguished
as follows:

1   Leaf blades lacking scales 2
    Leaf blades bearing scales.................................... 5
2   Leaves not hairy, the leaflets quite long 3
    Leaves hairy, the leaflets very small 4

RACHEL STRINGHAM

JEFF CLARK

STAR CLOAK FERN
(*Notholaena standleyi*)

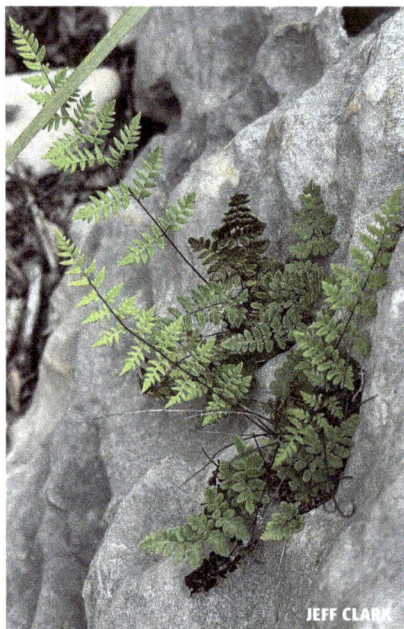

ALABAMA LIP FERN
(*Myriopteris alabamensis*)

3   Leaf stalk and midribs black, cylindrical, shining . . . .
. . . . ⟩ Alabama Lip Fern
. . . . . (*Myriopteris alabamensis*, synonym *Cheilanthes alabamensis*)
Leaf stalk and midribs light brown, with a broad, deep groove on
the lower side, not shining . . . . ⟩ Wright's Lip Fern
. . . . (*Myriopteris wrightii*, synonym *Cheilanthes wrightii*)
4   Leaves red-hairy beneath, not glandular . . . Nit-Bearing Lip Fern
. . . . (*Myriopteris lendigera*, synonym *Cheilanthes lendigera*)
Leaves glandular-hairy . . . . Kaulfuss Lip Fern
. . . . (*Gaga kaulfussii*, synonym *Cheilanthes kaulfussii*)
5   Underground stems slender, creeping . . . . Fairyswords
. . . . (*Myriopteris lindheimeri*, synonym *Cheilanthes lindheimeri*)
Underground stems large, scarcely creeping. 6
6   Leaflets whitish on the upper surface from the numerous, whitish,
densely tangled hairs . . . . Eaton's Lip Fern
. . . . (*Myriopteris rufa*, synonym *Cheilanthes eatonii*)
Leaflets greenish above and delicately hairy with very short hairs,
which are not tangled 7

WRIGHT'S LIP FERN
(*Myriopteris wrightii*)

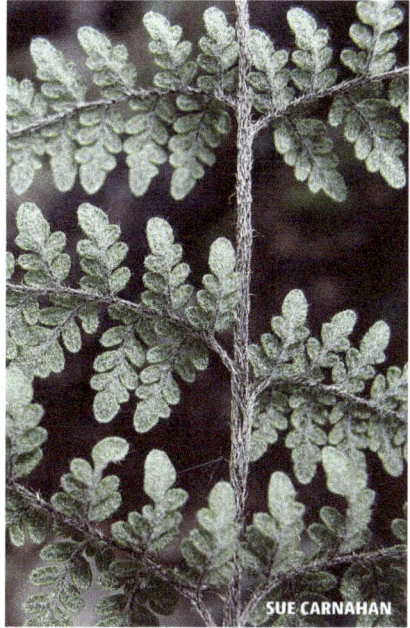

WOOLLY LIP FERN
(*Myriopteris tomentosa*)

7   Scales of the midrib very narrow . . . . ➤ **Woolly Lip Fern**
. . . . (*Myriopteris tomentosa*, synonym *Cheilanthes tomentosa*)
Scales of the midrib abundant and narrowly lance-shaped . . . .
. . . . **Eaton's Lip Fern**
. . . . (*Myriopteris rufa*, synonym *Cheilanthes castanea*)

■ **Cliffbrake Fern** (*Pellaea*)—The cliffbrake ferns are characterized by having marginal sori covered by an indusium formed by the inrolled margin on the leaflet, like those of the lip ferns, but the leaflets are leathery and are not lobed or toothed. These ferns grow in dry, rocky places in the Chisos Mountains. Six species are found in the Park:

1   Leaf four times pinnate, the leaflets round and minute . . . .
. . . . **Small-Leaf Cliffbrake**
. . . . (*Pellaea microphylla*, synonym *Argyrochosma microphylla*)
Leaf once or twice pinnate **2**
2   Underground stems slender, creeping ➤ **Intermediate Cliffbrake**
. . . . (*Pellaea intermedia*)
Underground stems thick, not creeping **3**

INTERMEDIATE CLIFFBRAKE
(*Pellaea intermedia*)

PURPLE-STEM CLIFFBRAKE
(*Pellaea atropurpurea*)

3   Scales of underground stems of same color throughout 4
   Scales of underground stem each having a blackish middle stripe 5
4   Fertile leaflets narrow . . . . ⤴ **Purple-Stem Cliffbrake**
   . . . . (*Pellaea atropurpurea*)
   Fertile leaflets broad . . . **Heart-Leaf Cliffbrake** (*Pellaea cordifolia*)
5   Leaf-stalk and midrib chestnut colored; leaflets with 2 or 3 pairs of
   segments or, if divided into 3 parts, the terminal part stalked . . . . .
   . . . . **Wright's Cliffbrake** (*Pellaea wrightiana*)
   Leaf-stalk and midrib dark purple; leaflets cleft or divided into 3
   parts, rarely divided clear to the midrib, the 3 parts nearly equal in
   size, the terminal one usually not stalked **Trans-Pecos Cliffbrake**
   . . . . (*Pellaea ternifolia*)

CLIFF FERN FAMILY (WOODSIACEAE)

New Mexico Cliff Fern (*Woodsia neomexicana*)—This little fern is
rather rare in the Park but has been found in moist places along streams
in the Chisos Mountains. The leaves vary from 3 to 7 inches long and

SUE CARNAHAN

ALINA MARTIN

WRIGHT'S CLIFFBRAKE
(*Pellaea wrightiana*)

NEW MEXICO CLIFF FERN
(*Woodsia neomexicana*)

are twice pinnate or pinnately cut, making many small leaflets. The sori are round, but they are so thickly placed that, after the indusia have split, they appear like masses nearly covering the under surfaces of the leaflets.

FERN RELATIVES

SPIKEMOSS FAMILY (SELAGINELLACEAE)

The members of the Selaginella Family are called spikemoss or sometimes "little clubmosses." Some species are called "resurrection plants" because they produce a dense cluster of stems that roll up into a nestlike ball when dry, but when placed in water they rapidly freshen up and seem to "come to life." These plants are related to ferns and reproduce by spores, but the spore cases are borne in the axils of the leaves, those toward the end of a branch being small and producing large numbers of minute male spores and those near the base of a branch being larger and each producing four female spores. The leaves are small but are placed so close together that they overlap like the shingles of a roof, completely covering the stem. *Selaginella* is the only genus in the family, and eight species are reported in the Park:

1   Leaves in 4 rows, those in the 2 lateral rows larger than those in the two middle rows **2**
     Leaves in more than 4 rows and all alike **3**

2   Leaves blunt, not ending in awns . . . .   **Flower-of-Stone**
     . . . . (*Selaginella lepidophylla*)
     Leaves ending in long, hairlike awns . . . . . .   **Resurrection Plant**
     . . . . (*Selaginella pilifera*, see p. 290)

3   Stems erect or partly so **4**
     Stems all prostrate; leaves with a bristle at the tip **5**

4   Leaves without a terminal bristle . . . . **Green Spikemoss**
     . . . . (*Selaginella viridissima*)
     Leaves with a terminal bristle . . . .   **Rock-Loving Spikemoss**
     . . . . (*Selaginella rupincola*)

5   Leaves blunt at tip, the terminal bristle short, white, fragile . . . . . .
     . . . .   **Blunt-Leaf Spikemoss** (*Selaginella mutica*)
     Leaves pointed at tip, tapering into the bristle **6**

6   Terminal bristle yellow, stout . . . .   **Wright's Spikemoss**
     . . . . (*Selaginella wrightii*)
     Terminal bristle white, fragile **7**

7   Bristle absent on leaves of the lower side of the stem . . . .
     . . . . **Arizona Spikemoss** (*Selaginella arizonica*)
     Bristle present on all leaves . . . .   **Blunt-Leaf Spikemoss**
     . . . . (*Selaginella mutica*)

FLOWER-OF-STONE
(*Selaginella lepidophylla*)

ROCK-LOVING SPIKEMOSS
(*Selaginella rupincola*)

BLUNT-LEAF SPIKEMOSS
(*Selaginella mutica*)

WRIGHT'S SPIKEMOSS
(*Selaginella wrightii*)

RESURRECTION PLANT
(*Selaginella pilifera*)
(UPPER dry plants; LOWER after receivng water)

GLOSSARY,

Achene—A small, dry, 1-seeded, indehiscent fruit.

Alpine—Above timberline on mountains.

Alternate—One leaf at each node or joint of the stem.

Annual—Living during one season only.

Anther—That part of a stamen that contains the pollen.

Awn—A bristlelike appendage.

Axil—The upper angle between the leaf and the stem.

Axillary—Occurring in an axil.

Berry.—A fruit that is pulpy or juicy throughout.

Biennial—Living for two seasons only.

Bladdery—Thin and inflated.

Bract—Reduced leaves among or subtending flowers.

Bulb—A fleshy bud such as an onion.

Bulblet—A small bulb.

Calyx—The outermost set of organs of a flower, usually green.

Capsule—A dry fruit that opens at maturity.

Chaff—Small bracts on the receptacle of flowers of the Aster family.

Corolla—The set of floral organs next within the calyx, usually not green.

Disk—The central region of a head of flowers, such as the sunflower, as opposed to the rays or margin.

Dissected—Cut deeply into many lobes or divisions.

Divided—Cut deeply into a few lobes or divisions.

Downy—Clothed with a coat of soft, short hairs.

Drupe—A stone fruit, such as a cherry.

Elliptical—Oval or oblong with the ends regularly rounded.

Entire—The margin not at all toothed, notched, or divided.

Fertile—Capable of producing seeds or pollen.

Free—Not united with any other parts of the plant.

Fruit—The seed-bearing portion of a plant.

Gland—A secreting surface or structure.

Herb—A plant with no woody parts above ground.

Herbaceous—Of the texture, color, or appearance of an ordinary foliage leaf.

Imperfect flower—One that lacks either stamens or pistils.

Involucre—A set of bracts around a flower or cluster of flowers.

Lanceolate—Lance-shaped.

Legume—The fruit of a member of the Pea family.

Linear—Narrow and flat like a grass leaf.

Membranous—With the texture of a membrane; thin and more or less translucent.

Midrib—The middle or main rib of a leaf.

Nerve—A name applied to the veins or ribs of a leaf.

Node—A place on a stem where a leaf is borne.

Oblanceolate—Lance-shaped with the tapering end downward.

Oblong—Two to four times as long as broad and more or less elliptical in shape.

Obovate—Inversely ovate, the broad end upward.

Opposite—Two leaves at each node or joint of the stem.

Oval—Broadly elliptical.

Ovate—Shaped like the longitudinal section through an egg with the broad end downward.

Ovule—One of the bodies in the ovary that may develop into a seed.

Palmate—The leaflets of a compound leaf all arising from the end of the petiole, like the fingers of the hand.

Panicle—An open cluster of flowers like a raceme but more or less compound.

Pappus—The hairs, awns, or scales at the base of the corolla or the tip of the fruit in a member of the composite family.

Pedicel—The stalk of a flower in a cluster.

Peduncle—The stalk of a solitary flower or of a cluster of flowers.

Perfect flower—Having both stamens and pistils.

Perennial—Living from year to year.

Perianth—Calyx and corolla together, especially when they cannot be distinguished.

Petal—One of the parts of the corolla.

Petiole—The stalk part of a leaf.

Pinnate—Leaflets arranged along the main axis of a leaf.

Pistil—The seed-bearing organ of a flower.

Puberulent—Covered with fine and short, almost imperceptible down.

Pubescence—Fine and soft hairs.

Pubescent—With pubescence.

Raceme—A flower cluster with one-flowered pedicels along the axis of the cluster.

Ray—One of the marginal flowers in a head in the composite family.

Receptacle—The end of a pedicel or peduncle to which the flowers or flower parts are attached.

Regular—The parts of each set of organs of a flower the same size and shape.

Rhizome—An underground stem.

Runner—A slender and prostrate stem rooting at the end or at the joints.

Sepal—One of the parts of the calyx.

Sessile—Without any petiole or stalk.

Shrub—A small woody plant.

Simple—Not compound.

Sinus—The notch between two lobes.

Smooth—Without hairs or other roughness.

Spike—A flower cluster like a raceme but with the flowers sessile.

Stamen—A pollen-bearing organ.

Sterile—Not capable of producing fruit or pollen.

Stigma—The upper end of the pistil which receives the pollen.

Stipules—Appendages at the base of the petiole of some leaves.

Style—That part of a pistil between the ovary and the stigma.

Taproot—A stout, vertical root.

Ternate—In threes.

Umbel—An umbrella-shaped flower cluster with a flat top.

Veins—The conducting strands in a leaf or other organ.

Vine—A trailing or climbing plant.

Woolly—Clothed with long, matted, soft hairs.

REFERENCES

The Big Bend of the Rio Grande: A Guide to the Rocks, Geologic History, and Settlers of the Area of Big Bend National Park. Ross A. Maxwell. Texas Bureau of Economic Geology, 1968.

Cacti of Texas and Neighboring States. Del Weniger. University of Texas Press, 1984.

Cactuses of Big Bend National Park. Douglas B. Evans. University of Texas Press, 1998.

A Check List of the Ferns, Gymnosperms, and Flowering Plants of the Proposed Big Bend National Park. Omer E. Sperry. Volume 19, No. 4. Sul Ross State Teachers College Bulletin, Alpine, Texas, 1938.

Grasses of the Trans-Pecos and Adjacent Areas. A. Michael Powell. University of Texas Press, 1994.

Little Big Bend: Common, Uncommon, and Rare Plants of Big Bend National Park. Roy Morey. Texas Tech University Press, 2008.

Manual of the Vascular Plants of Texas. D. S. Correll and M. C. Johnston. Texas Research Foundation, 1970.

Plants of Brewster County, Texas. Omer E. Sperry and Barton H. Warnock. Volume 22, No. 1. Sul Ross State Teachers College Bulletin, 1941.

Trees and Shrubs of Trans-Pecos Texas. A. Michael Powell. Big Bend Natural History Association, Inc., 1988.

Wildflowers of the Big Bend Country, Texas. B. H. Warnock. Sul Ross State University Press, 1970.

Wildflowers of the Davis Mountains and Marathon Basin, Texas. B. H. Warnock. Sul Ross State University Press, 1977.

ABOUT THE AUTHORS

Walter B. McDougall (1883–1980) attended the University of Michigan where he received his Ph.D. in botany in 1913. In 1914 he began his career as instructor in botany at the University of Illinois where he remained until 1928. Just before he left the University of Illinois his textbook, Plant Ecology, was published. From 1935 until 1953 Dr. McDougall was associated with the National Park Service and U.S. Fish and Wildlife Service. During this period he authored classic plant guides for Yellowstone, and Grand Canyon national parks in addition to this work on Big Bend. In 1936 he published a Field Book of Illinois Wildflowers. At age 72, Dr. McDougall began his final career at the Museum of Northern Arizona, Flagstaff.

Omer E. Sperry (1902–1975) received his Ph.D. in botany from the University of Nebraska. He moved to Alpine, Texas, during the Great Depression, where he founded the biology department at the new Sul Ross State Teachers College. He continued his botanical research in the Chisos and Davis Mountains of West Texas. Later, he moved to College Station, where he co-founded the range and forestry department at Texas A&M. For the next 30 years, Sperry worked as a range ecologist and weed control specialist for Texas A&M.

Steve W. Chadde (1955–) is a botanist and plant ecologist who has degrees in Range Management and Plant Ecology from the University of Wyoming and Montana State University. In addition to his professional work as a botanist and ecologist for the U.S. Forest Service, the Montana Natural Heritage Program, and various consulting firms, he has published numerous books on plants, including state floras for Minnesota, Wisconsin, and for the Upper Peninsula of Michigan. After a decade in the Philippines, he now resides in the Ozark Mountain region of Arkansas.

ACKNOWLEDGMENTS

I would like to give my sincere thanks to the many people who have made their photographs available under the appropriate Creative Commons license allowing for commercial use. Nearly all photographs were obtained from the *inaturalist.org* website, the leading community-driven site for sharing ecological data. Photographer names (as provided on inaturalist) are listed on each image. This book would not have been possible without their efforts to document our diverse flora.

Acknowledgment is also given to the **Biota of North America Program** (BONAP) for use of their data to confirm species presence within the Big Bend region (see *www.bonap.org*). Current taxonomic names largely follow those of BONAP and of the *Plants of the World Online* database maintained by the Royal Botanic Gardens, Kew (see *powo.science.kew.org*).

—STEVE CHADDE

FROM THE ORIGINAL 1951 EDITION:
The authors are greatly indebted to C. V. Morton, United States National Museum, Smithsonian Institution, for the identification of many specimens over a period of several years, for special help with the Polypodiaceae, and for reading the entire manuscript and making many corrections and helpful suggestions; to the late Dr. William R. Maxon, United States National Museum, for splendid cooperation in the identification of many specimens and for special aid with the Polypodiaceae; to Charles Livingston, Alpine, Tex., for freely giving assistance to the junior author both in field work and in photography; and to Barton H. Warnock for much assistance in field work and for the collection of many specimens. They are also grateful to the following workers for assistance with special groups of plants, as noted: Dr. Harold N. Moldenke, New York Botanical Garden, the Verbenaceae; Dr. Robert T. Clauson, Cornell University, the Gentianaceae and Crassulaceae; Dr. Louis C. Wheeler; University of Southern California, the Euphorbiaceae; the late Dr. Lincoln Constance, University of California, the Umbelliferae and Hydrophyllaceae; Dr. C. H. Muller, Santa Barbara College, University of California, the Fagaceae and the genus *Agave*, es-

pecially the determination and publication of *Agave chisosensis* as a new species; Dr. Ivan M. Johnston, Arnold Arboretum, the Boraginaceae and Aristolochiaceae; Dr. Francis W. Pennell, Academy of Natural Sciences of Philadelphia, the Scrophulariaceae; Dr. S. F. Blake, United States Department of Agriculture, the Compositae and Polygalaceae; Jason R. Swallen, United States National Museum, the Gramineae; Dr. Frederick J. Hermann, United States Department of Agriculture, the Cyperaceae; Dr. Lyman Benson, Pomona College, California, the Cactaceae; Mrs. Susan Delano McKelvey, Boston, Mass., the genus *Yucca*; Dr. Carl C. Epling, University of California at Los Angeles, the Labiatae; and Dr. Robert E. Woodson, Jr., Missouri Botanical Garden, the Asclepiadaceae.

Finally, to Paul H. Oehser, Chief, Editorial Division, United States National Museum, Smithsonian Institution, who gave freely of his personal time to edit the manuscript, and to all others who have aided in any manner in the preparation or publication of the book, the authors extend sincere and grateful thanks.

www.ingramcontent.com/pod-product-compliance
Lightning Source LLC
Chambersburg PA
CBHW052108030426

42335CB00025B/2896